PELICAN LATIN AMERICAN LIBRARY

Editor: Richard Gott

Guatemala – Another Vietnam?

S0-BYA-660

Thomas and Marjorie Melville were once Roman
Catholic missionaries. He was a priest and she a nun.
Through their ministry with the Guatemalan Indians
they became identified with the cause of
revolutionary land reform. They were dismissed as
missionaries and incurred the still greater displeasure
of the Church by their marriage. Chased out of
Guatemala, they narrowly escaped assassination in
Mexico by the Guatemalan Secret Police, and are now
serving prison sentences for their part in the draft
card destruction campaign in the United States.

Guatemala– Another Vietnam?

Thomas and Marjorie Melville

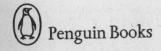 Penguin Books

Penguin Books Ltd, Harmondsworth,
Middlesex, England
Penguin Books Australia Ltd, Ringwood,
Victoria, Australia

Copyright © Thomas and Marjorie Melville, 1971
Published by Penguin Books Ltd, 1971

Made and printed in Great Britain
by Hazell Watson & Viney Ltd,
Aylesbury, Bucks
Set in Linotype Juliana

Contents

Maps and Charts

Editorial Foreword

In August 1968 I flew into Guatemala City on the day the guerrillas shot the American ambassador. It was a week of violence, the same week that Mayor Daley broke up the Chicago Democratic Convention. But in Guatemala itself the death of the ambassador caused hardly a ripple. The Guatemalan civil war had begun long since, and amid the daily violence and the shootings the loss of an ambassador was scarcely remarked.

The international press descended briefly – as it did when the West German ambassador was shot eighteen months later – but basically the war in Guatemala has remained unreported and unknown. The principal news agencies keep no full-time correspondents there.

Only the Guatemalan newspapers reported the US ambassador's speech the previous year when he presented the Armed Forces with a vast quantity of American weaponry for use in what we have grown to describe euphemistically as 'counter-insurgency' operations. 'These articles,' he said, 'especially the helicopters, are not easy to obtain at this time since they are being utilized by our forces in defence of the cause of liberty in other parts of the world.'

The American ambassador was not alone in rallying to the defence of 'liberty' in Guatemala. Earlier in 1967, the Archbishop of Guatemala gave his blessing to fifty-four new radio police cars. 'Take good care of them,' the cleric told an assembled group of policemen, 'they were purchased with money of the people.'

A week after the American ambassador was shot, when most of the journalists had gone home, a French girl called Michele Firk shot herself in Guatemala City as the police came to her room to make 'inquiries'. In her notebook Michele had written:

It is hard to find the words to express the state of putrefaction that exists in Guatemala, and the permanent terror in which the inhabitants live. Every day bodies are pulled out of the Motagua River, riddled with bullets and partially eaten by fish. Every day men are kidnapped right in the street by unidentified people in cars, armed to the teeth, with no intervention by the police patrols.

Throughout the 1960s revolutionary guerrillas existed in Guatemala, struggling to remedy this state of affairs. In December 1967 the authors of this book, together with two other priests of the Maryknoll Order, were expelled from the country. Their crime had been to attend a meeting organized by one of the guerrilla movements.

In a letter to Senator William Fulbright, early in 1968, Thomas Melville wrote as follows:

I have been working in Guatemala for over ten years. I personally started three credit unions, two agricultural cooperatives, one industrial cooperative, two land distribution programmes, the country's only cooperative league, aided in the formation of nearly a dozen other cooperatives, and worked as hard as anybody in Guatemala to improve the miserable lot of the peasant. I didn't accomplish much because we forever ran into government indifference at best, and government interference at worst. If any programme showed signs of success, the Alliance for Progress men were right there to offer money in exchange for the right to hang their publicity signs.

I don't write this letter as a complaint. I write it as a warning. The masses of Latin America are becoming more and more restless.

Their governments do not want any real progress, because it would have to come at the expense of the landed oligarchy, which in turn controls these governments. There is only one solution: Revolution.

I would like to think that these revolutions could be peaceful, but I know from personal experience that the two per cent that are bleeding the masses white will not give up their power peacefully. It must be taken from them. It is they then who are provoking the violence, not the poor.

Father Melville returned to the United States to face the monumental apathy that exists in the developed world when confronted with the detail of the oppression of underdevelopment. In this book he remedies the lack of information that exists about the real nature of the problem.

For most people the only date in Guatemalan history that sticks out is 1954, when the CIA threw out President Jacobo Arbenz for expropriating the unfarmed estates of the United Fruit Company. That's a simplification, but the subsequent course of Guatemalan history was determined by the simple fact that the Arbenz land reform, which so annoyed the Guatemalan oligarchy and its American backers, was put into reverse by succeeding governments.

This is the story told by the Melvilles. It is of the first importance, not just for Guatemala, but also for all Latin America – where land reform remains the key to breaking the power of the continent's oligarchic social structure. And of course the Melvilles' story has a familiar ring, as the title suggests. In South Vietnam, in the areas liberated before 1954, the Viet Minh put through a land reform that expropriated the landlords. After 1954, when the Viet Minh withdrew, the government of Ngo Dinh Diem returned the land to the landlords. In this fertile soil, revolts grow. So too, in Guatemala, the land reform of Arbenz, once put into reverse, created conditions for rebellion.

This book is written by two people who love Guatemala in

a way that perhaps only a foreigner can love a country – observing and acknowledging its faults, but actually more conscious and aware of its virtues than the inhabitants themselves, lost in the rituals of daily life.

Here, spelt out, are the details of a contemporary system of slavery. Sometimes looking through a microscope, sometimes painting with a broad brush, the Melvilles observe and describe a society which is nothing less than horrifying – a society whose integrity the 'West' is pledged to maintain intact, and which on occasion it has not hesitated to prop up by military force.

From the very first days of the revolution in 1944 of Juan Jose Arevalo, the word 'communism' was on the lips of the Guatemalan aristocracy – a fear that was soon to be echoed and amplified in Washington. Even to this day, the authors explain from bitter experience, founding cooperatives or credit unions is an activity tantamount to 'communism'.

For more than ten years after 1954 the oligarchy and their military presidents had everything their way. But in 1960 a guerrilla movement began. By 1966 it had made formidable gains. The situation was becoming desperate for the country's controlling interests. As the Melvilles explain :

> The military support of the oligarchic structure supplied by the Guatemalan Air Force, Army and police is, by itself, insufficient to oppose and control the rising cries for justice that shatter the calm rural atmosphere.

Faced with this new situation, in which the social and political structure of Guatemala was actually crumbling, the Americans intervened, throwing their military weight behind the new civilian president elected in 1966, Julio Cesar Mendez Montenegro. With the help of American advisers, the Guatemalan army created a new brand of counter-guerrilla terrorist. In her notebook, Michele Firk wrote :

> The urgent problem is to begin to alert world public opinion to

the fact that in Guatemala, a country in which a 'democratically elected' civil government is in power, 'civilian' terrorist groups of the extreme right (which are part of the army when you look more closely) are creating a reign of terror, and threaten, denounce, and assassinate to an extent never reached *by any military dictatorship*.

In 1970 the most successful counter-guerrilla colonel, Carlos Osorio Arana, was elected president of Guatemala. In the last three months of the year, according to figures of the World Confederation of Labour, more than 600 people were killed by the security forces.

The Melvilles' conclusion, after ten years in Guatemala, and three years' research producing this book, is that the destruction of the 'system' at its oppressive centre – in the United States itself – is the only course of action that will bring liberation closer for the Guatemalan and Latin American peasant.

In 1967, when Thomas Melville was thrown out of Guatemala, the Father Superior of the Maryknoll Order rebuked him for an action that, he said, constituted 'a personal intervention on the part of American citizens in the internal affairs of the country in which they were guests'. Late in 1970 the Melvilles went to prison in their own country, the United States, sentenced for entering a draft induction centre and burning the files of the young men scheduled to go to kill the peasants of Vietnam. And of Guatemala?

RICHARD GOTT

Acknowledgements

The authors wish to acknowledge the invaluable suggestions and encouragement given them by Dr Harold E. Davis and Dr John J. Finan of the School of International Service of the American University, and Dr James Bodine of the Anthropology Department; also by Mr Gerrit Huizer of the International Labor Organization, Dr James Petras of Pennsylvania State College and Dr Mario Rodríguez of George Washington University. The extensive typing assistance given by Miss Roberta Harrison is deeply appreciated. The opinions herein expressed are the full responsibility of the authors.

CHAPTER 1

The Right to Alter
or Abolish

We hold these truths to be self-evident, that all men are created
equal, that they are endowed by their Creator with certain inalienable rights, that among these are life, liberty and the pursuit of
happiness. That to secure these rights, governments are instituted
among men, deriving their just powers from the consent of the
governed. That whenever any form of government becomes destructive of these ends, it is the right of the people to alter or abolish it,
and to institute new governments, most likely to effect their safety
and happiness.

THOMAS JEFFERSON
The American Declaration of Independence

The title of this book, *Guatemala – Another Vietnam*, is in
no way prophetic. It is an observation, a simple statement
of fact. The war in Guatemala has already begun, sides have
been chosen, and to date thousands of Guatemalans have
been killed as well as several North Americans, among them
the US Ambassador and two US military attachés. The war
will continue until a new social system evolves, a new
type of government is established, a new economy and life
for the people is brought into existence; or until a more effective programme for the extermination of peasant lives is con-
ceived. This war is a civil war, between the 'haves' and the
'have-nots', and the commodity being disputed in Guatemalan
lands.

We have made the comparison between Vietnam and

Guatemala for two basic reasons. First, the cause of both wars, that is to say, the reason most people are fighting in both countries – for their lands – is essentially the same. Second, the United States' view of both wars is equally misconceived, misinformed and mistaken, with the resulting interference in both countries serving only to exacerbate the original problems and points of conflict.

Let us elaborate on the first point: that the struggles are basically over land ownership and control. The book as a whole will demonstrate this as far as Guatemala is concerned. For those who may doubt that such a simple notion applies to the conflict in Vietnam, we quote here from a report released by the Committee on Government Operations of the Ninetieth Congress of the United States, dated 5 March 1968. The conclusion reads as follows:

The importance of an effective program of land reform, one that would meet the just aspirations of the masses of farmers who work the land, has been emphasized on numerous occasions by a wide variety of authorities on Vietnamese affairs. Perhaps more than any other single program, land reform offers the opportunity to the Government of Vietnam to secure the allegiance of the Vietnamese people, which is the ultimate objective of the entire range of activities known as the pacification program. One of the leading candidates in the recent Vietnamese presidential elections is quoted as saying that 'Land Reform is the issue of the Vietnam war, not communism. ... Land Reform is the most crucial problem. .... If a good land reform program were set up, the tide of the war would change very quickly.'[1]

There are few serious and knowledgeable academicians who would quarrel with the above views. Dr Roy L. Posterman, Professor of Law at the University of Washington, a promi-

1. Committee on Government Operations, *Land Reform in Vietnam*, Twentieth Report, Washington, DC: US Government Printing Office, 1968, p. 14.

nent and well-known consultant to the US mission in Vietnam, in reference to the Tet offensive, said:

It is wholly unlikely that they [the attacks] could have occurred
without multiple specific advance intelligence warnings except in
a setting in which the wills of the population ranged from
apathetic to hostile toward their government. My research in
Vietnam convinces me that until massive land reform is undertaken, there will be no winning the loyalty of the people and
there will be no way to discourage through fear of advance intelligence even such incredibly audacious attacks as those today.[2]

These concepts are not new to the men who formulate our
Government's policies. Indeed, since 1954, beginning with
the Diem Government, the US has given more than $20 mil-
lion in support of land reform in Vietnam.[3] But such a
contribution represents a pittance compared with the real
needs, and, more to the point, neither President Diem nor
his successors have been interested in land reform. The Johnson Government finally commissioned Stanford University
to do a study on the subject and in December 1968 they
published their findings:

There is evidence that a substantial part of South Vietnam
was under the control of the Viet Minh just before the Geneva
Accords, but little is known of the amount or location of land
that was redistributed by the Viet Minh. Of the absentee landlords interviewed in the SRI Landlord survey, 65 per cent indicated that at least some of their land was under Viet Minh control
in 1954. By 1956, there had been a slight improvement (15–20
per cent) in the security status of their land, and it may be
reasonably assumed that during this period and for the next
few years these and smaller landlords took advantage of security
conditions to reclaim their land and to evict Viet Minh appointed
occupants. The number of landlords and area affected by such
evictions cannot be estimated, but for Viet Minh land reform to

2. ibid., p. 21.   3. ibid., p. v.

have been effective, it must have been significant. The return of the landlords is still used as a basic propaganda theme by the Viet Cong and as a basis for expropriation and redistribution of land. Thus, the way was prepared for the second cycle of Communist land reform in Vietnam – this time under the Viet Cong.[4]

The cynicism that is attributed to the Viet Minh and Viet Cong in this study is matched only by the cynicism of those who would repeat the land-reform programme of the communists for similar purposes – to gain the people's allegiance – or by the lack of understanding of those who would oppose it. As a result of this study the Saigon Government promised to institute a more modest programme of land reform that would put $100 million in the pockets of absentee landlords. One half this amount was to be paid by the United States, the other half by Saigon.[5]

By the end of 1969 the programme looked as if it was a failure for several reasons. But the basic difficulty is the very same mentality that has been the essential cause of the war in the first place: the unwillingness of Vietnam's wealthy minorities to share the resources of their country with the poverty-stricken masses. As late as October and November 1969 President Thieu was in serious political trouble because he was attempting to implement a new set of import taxes that would affect only the wealthy.[6]

Perhaps part of the failure of the programme can be attributed to a Rand Corporation study financed by the Defense Department which must have influenced the Pentagon's policies. The thesis of this study is: 'From the point of view of government control, the ideal province in South Vietnam would be one in which few peasants operate their own land, the distributions of landholdings are unequal, no land redis-

4. Stanford Research Institute, *Land Reform in Vietnam*. Menlo Park, California: SRI, Contract No. AID/VN-8, 1968, pp. 27–8.

5. *New York Times*, 15 February 1969.

6. *Washington Post*, 28 October 1969.

tribution has taken place.'[7] The Senate Committee was harsh in its judgement of such a policy, as well it might be:

We strongly believe it is morally wrong to deliberately keep people of any nation weak and dependent in order to control them – whatever the end. Such a Machiavellian policy, if adopted, could only serve as a device to delay and dilute necessary reforms. If our aim is to build the foundations of a free society in South Vietnam, we cannot do it by keeping the peasants in economic serfdom, nor by failing to act on the pervasive corruption in the South Vietnamese government at all levels.[8]

This brings us to our second point: the misconceived, misinformed and mistaken interference of the United States in Vietnam. It is beyond the scope of this book to deal with the sundry and diverse reasons offered by American politicians for the presence of US troops in Vietnam. Nor would it be advisable to do so since many such reasons are only meant to be political palliatives to encourage the uninformed to maintain the level of sacrifices necessary until the conflict is 'honourably' terminated. Nevertheless, in order to deal with the American military involvement in Southeast Asia, we have to acknowledge some *raison d'être* offered by the politicians. The mortal fight against 'communism' seems to be the most likely reason, for it is the one most often hoisted up the flag pole and it is the one most ardently and faithfully saluted by the majority of Americans.

We cannot discuss here the nature of communism and why the United States regards this philosophy as such a threat to itself, to its system of government, to its economy. It is enough to acknowledge that it is seen as a threat and this in itself is a begrudging compliment that may or may not be merited. However, the facility with which the United States reduces so many internal conflicts of rights and values

7. Committee on Government Operations, op. cit., p. 22.
8. ibid.

to a struggle between freedom and tyranny, democracy and totalitarianism, is absurd. These terms are very difficult to define and they participate in cultural and philosophical value systems that may actually render them crossculturally indefinable. Democracy has been called 'the dictatorship of the majority' and Catholicism 'the totalitarianism of the spirit'. Much depends upon where you stand.

As a Western industrialized nation we can barely begin to understand the dynamics of Eastern, or African, or Mediterranean, or Latin peasant cultures. To peasant societies, agricultural societies, the nations of the underdeveloped world, the most important possession that a person, a group or a nation has, is the land. Land means food and food means life. The peasant's mystical identification with the land is perhaps only translatable by what the Guatemalan peasant calls *la santa tierra*, the holy land.

Now that we have with us the so-called 'population explosion' and we are told that two thirds of the world is going to bed hungry every night, most of them peasants in agricultural societies, the problem can only be rectified (and then only temporarily) by giving these peasants the lands they need. Peasants are farmers and they are perfectly capable of growing enough food to fulfil their wants, besides raising a surplus. The problem is that they do not have the use of lands to do this.

The same process of history that gives one man a white skin and a name like Rockefeller, gives another man a black skin and a name like Washington; so, too, in peasant societies throughout the world, the lands needed for the many to live have been concentrated, by a similar historical process, in the hands of the few. Now, the peasants must rectify the imbalance or starve.

The problem for the United States, since it has taken upon itself the responsibility of being the non-communist world's policeman, is that it has not figured out a way to get the unexploited lands of the underdeveloped nations out of the hands of the few wealthy landlords and into the multiplying peasants' hands, and this in a manner consistent with the Western concept of private property. 'Possession is nine tenths of the law,' we say. Such a concept may work in an industrialized society where food production has been mechanized and even supplemented with synthetic foods, but it will not work for long in a peasant society where human life is equated to the use of the land. It positively cannot work in a peasant society undergoing the throes of the population explosion. The superfluous lands of the few must be taken from them and made available to the many.

Only the Marxists seem to have come up with a way of doing this, and, whether we like it or not, their way is consonant with the historical process that gave the few the lands of the many, and their tenure pattern is most often compatible wih peasant values. Anyone acquainted with peasant societies recognizes that their value system is somewhat communistic and totalitarian if viewed from our ethnocentric vantage-point, which, ultimately, is a relative judgement. Yet nothing is more absolutely totalitarian than is hunger, and to talk to a hungry people of freedom and democracy that in no way alleviates their hunger, but often increases it, is the most absurd of inanities.

This is demonstrated in the account we present here of Guatemalan society and Guatemalan history. It has also been demonstrated time and again by social studies of peasant peoples around the globe made by competent scientists of every political persuasion.

The rule that a person must work lands recently acquired from the public domain in order to retain title is a general and basic one among the primitive gardeners the world over. It effectively guards against one of man's besetting social evils – land hoarding by a wealthy few and the closing of the doors of opportunity to the land hungry.... On the whole, primitive people overwhelmingly treat their land resources as a communal asset. In this sense they are preponderantly communistic.[9]

This is why the United States is so threatened today by the peasant unrest in the underdeveloped world. It is not prepared to allow others to be 'communistic' even if the 'communism' pre-dates Marx by milleniums, since this would be a supposed admission of the inadequacy of the American system. It is better to let them starve, seems to be the answer. But it will be difficult to convince the peasants themselves that it is better to be 'free' and hungry than to be 'communist' and fed.

Marxism may be the only social system consistent with peasant values and capable of satisfying peasant needs. This may be the lesson of Vietnam that the United States' foreign-policy experts seem incapable of learning. It may also be the lesson that peasants in varying degrees of unrest, rebelliousness and revolution in Malaysia, the Philippines, Guatemala, Peru, Brazil, Colombia and numerous other countries are trying to give the world. It should have been the lesson learned both from China and Cuba. As Mr Chester Bowles, the former US Ambassador to India, has stated :

Many years of observation in the developing nations of Asia, Africa and Latin America have convinced me that in these vital areas the most important economic and political question is: Who owns the land? Where the land is owned by the few, millions of landless laborers are inevitably left with a deep sense of insecurity which makes them an easy target for determined Communist agitators.[10]

As long as the United States' response to these values and needs is the response of Vietnam, the response envisioned by the Rockefeller report, we are in for decades of bloody con-

9. Hoebel, E. Adamson, *Anthropology: The Study of Man*. New York: McGraw Hill, 1966, p. 419.

10. *New York Times*, 22 July 1967.

flict, destruction and death, especially here in the Western hemisphere.

All the American nations are a tempting target for communist subversion. In fact, it is plainly evident that such subversion is a reality today with alarming potential ... of growing intensity.[11]

The Rockefeller report goes on to recommend to the Nixon administration vast increases in military hardware and aid so that the 'haves' of Latin America will be able to hang on to their 'private property' while they give to the 'have-nots' the choice of starvation or execution. Nixon came close to giving the plan his official support when he stated: 'We must deal realistically with governments in the inter-American system as they are. We have of course a preference for democratic procedures ...'[12]

The leaders of all the military establishments of Latin America met at Fort Bragg, North Carolina, from 28 September to 4 October 1969, in 'closed-door' meetings to discuss 'internal security and the military defence of the Americas'.[13] At these meetings General William Westmoreland shared with his guests the lessons he has learned in Vietnam. Judging from the book that he and Admiral Sharp wrote on the subject, which is considered to be the official rationale of the Johnson administration's involvement in the war, land reform was not one of the lessons learned in Vietnam. Not once in the 350-page double-columned book is the subject even mentioned.

If we think the price that the Vietnamese and the North Americans have paid in Vietnam is high, we should stop for a moment before ruffled passions preclude all rational discussion, and think of the implications of what Latin America holds in store for us all. Because here, too, the 'Domino

11. *Washington Post*, 14 November 1969.
12. ibid., 1 November 1969.
13. *Prensa Libre*, 4 October 1969.

Theory' is certainly valid and even necessary, so that when Guatemala goes, Salvador, Honduras, Colombia will also go and we might find out that going to the moon before Russia is not the answer to the world's problems, nor for that matter is our war against 'communism' in Vietnam.

CHAPTER 2

A World
Cut in Two

This world divided into compartments, this world cut in two is inhabited by two different species. The originality of the colonial context is that economic reality, inequality, and the immense difference in ways of life never come to mask the human realities.

FRANTZ FANON

The Mayan People of Guatemala, more than half the population of that country, constitute an autochthonous nation within a nation. They participate in national life on a secondary plane and at the same time they are the work force that makes possible the economic existence of that country. After 445 years of Spanish and *ladino*[1] domination, they continue to hold on to their own culture and largely refuse to be assimilated into the pattern of the Western world.

Many cultural elements, different from their own, have been thrust at them: language, dress, religion, land tenure. Some have been adopted, others rejected; some of these new cultural elements have replaced old ways. But Mayan culture persists. The concept of private property has been imposed by physical and/or legal force with persistence – often ignorant, sometimes malicious – by the full succession of governments. A Western concept of private property in relation to land is presupposed to be within the cultural experi-

1. The term *ladino* is used in Guatemala to refer to mestizos or Indians who have adopted Western costume and culture.

ence of the indigenous population, a people with their own highly developed concept of ownership. It is presumed that the Indians understand land property in the same terms as do the governing élites who possess a Western cultural heritage.

The concept of 'property' is a cultural universal. For a group to utilize the natural resources at its disposal with some degree of security and continuity, it must have adequate definitions as to right of ownership and use.[2] Land can be held privately or collectively, and both terms can be modified by any number of variations in the rules that limit the use of that land. The ownership of land, or natural resources such as water or forest areas, is a fundamental aspect of economic organization. Where property is held collectively, the title may be vested in the group, which in turn determines the mode of use.

In the Western mind 'private property' has come to be such a basic concept of civilization that it is seldom understood that other cultures can have different but equally valid patterns for the organization of land tenure.

Yet this individualistic and complex system of Western countries is a comparatively recent development. It did not take form until the sixteenth century, when the 'enclosure movement' and peasant rebellions, together with the growth of an increasingly large landless class, indicated the transformation of feudalism and collectivism into private ownership in the modern sense.

Land-holding is an important element of culture since its significance involves many factors besides the economic ones. It affects political, religious and sentimental elements, particularly when it has been a prime concern of a people for a long period of time.

2. Keesing, Felix, *Cultural Anthropology*. New York: Holt, Rinehart & Winston, 1958, p. 233.

Land tenure deals with the conditions under which people own or occupy land. The nature of its subject matter is the behaviour of people with respect to land as property, as a source of income, as a place of residence and family life. Tenure conditions must be judged according to how well they meet the needs of the people. Clearly, all people visualize certain goals towards which they strive, and want the tenure system to help them and their society obtain these.

The question of how the present-day Maya of Guatemala understand land tenure is a problem of history and of actuality. We know relatively little of ancient Mayan customs and way of life. However, an understanding of the complex problem of somewhat evasive Mayan attitudes towards land tenure, and their psychological dependence on the *milpa*,[3] are basic to any projected land-reform or agricultural reorganization. Guatemala's social and economic progress depends on this. As the indigenous population is awakened to national and international realities through the use of transistor radios and through increased mobility, the traditional fatalism that characterizes them is being transformed into new determination. Their cultural heritage is still rich enough to provide them with an ethnic identity and unity that will make them demand justice in no uncertain terms, regardless of the consequences.

The Maya inhabit the area of Middle America that today constitutes the Yucatán Peninsula in Mexico and some of the Southern states of that country, as well as Belice (British Honduras), Guatemala, Northern Honduras and Western Salvador. Beginning approximately one millenium before the birth of Christ, they set out on a road of societal development and civilization that carried them to heights of greatness that

3. *Milpa* is a cornfield.

went far beyond those of contemporary Europe within a few hundred years of Christ's death. Their organization enabled them to build monuments that are still the marvel of the Western hemisphere. Their mathematics and astronomy facilitated the plotting of the movements of the planets and the stars to a degree of accuracy that was not attained by so-called Western Man until more than a thousand years later. The Mayan calendar made the Gregorian calendar seem juvenile in its calculations. Their writing, art forms and architecture still intrigue our social scientists today. They accomplished all this as a theocracy, their social organization being more religious than civil, under the leadership and rule of priests and with a minimum of internal conflict. This development reached its peak in the ninth century AD and then took a sudden downward turn. There is no exact explanation for this decline but it is variously attributed to the influx of warlike ideas from the Toltec nation of Mexico that converted the priest class to warriors in order to maintain control over the people, as well as to invasions of the Toltec themselves. The modern Maya-Quiché of Guatemala are the descendants of these Toltec, and by AD 1054 they had established a composite civilization, and possessed a flourishing dynasty.

In the *Popol Vuh*, sacred book of the Quiché, it is related how the conquered tribes were made vassals and were forced to pay tribute to the conquerors. Quicab was the king of the Quiché, who succeeded in dominating the surrounding tribes:

He made war on them and certainly conquered and destroyed the fields and the towns of the people of Rabinal, the Cakchiquel, and the people of Zaculeu; he came and conquered all the towns, and the soldiers of Quicab carried his arms to distant parts. One or two tribes did not bring tribute, and then he fell upon all the towns and they were forced to bring tribute to Quicab and Cavizimah. They were made slaves, they were wounded and they were killed, and for them there was no longer any glory, and they no longer had any power.[4]

The population must have grown considerably because when the Spanish came they are reported to have annihilated large hosts of other Maya such as the Mam, Pocomam and the Zutuhil. And in the battle against the Cakchiquel they claimed that thousands had been killed. It is calculated that the Spaniards reduced the indigenous population of Middle America from fourteen million to two million within 130 years of their arrival, owing largely to newly imported diseases and to Spanish brutality.[5]

One source of Mayan history is the land titles that were written between 1554 and 1580 in which the Indians related the basis for their land-holdings. Title to lands was acquired not only through conquest but through the rights of the legend of the origins of lineage. In fact, the principal source of their rights to an area was the lineal descent from their ancient kings.

The individual farmers held their lands communally and used them according to their needs and their possibilities. They considered the land to belong to the tribal community much as does air or water. They used plots assigned to them or picked out by them. The right to work the land and to enjoy the fruits thereof might be inherited by immediate descendants in an unbroken line of succession, but the concept of private ownership of land *per se* was apparently alien

4. Recinos, Adrian, *Popol Vuh*, *The Sacred Book of the Ancient Quiché Maya*. Norman: University of Oklahoma Press, 1950, p. 221.

5. The 'Black Legend', according to some historians, is an exaggerated report by colonial chroniclers of the loss of Indian lives during the conquest and colonialization periods. Recent studies, however, confirm the original estimates of 'the most careful of all bureaucratic observers'. See Wolf, Eric, *Sons of the Shaking Earth*. Chicago: University of Chicago Press, 1959, pp. 31 and 195; Dobyns, Henry F., 'Estimating Aboriginal American Populations', *Current Anthropology*, vol. 7, October 1966, pp. 395–416.

to indigenous thought.[6] Private property had to be personal property, the fruit of one's own labours, to agree with their beliefs about life. Only society as a whole can 'own' what nature has produced.

Another feature of Mayan culture which helped them to develop a sense of duty to neighbour and community besides the use of communal lands was group labour for clearing forest land, for building homes, for clearing and planting fields. A man will help a team of other men in exchange for labour on his own project. This extended the concept of communal lands even to the idea of the communal labour[7] which is so prevalent throughout Guatemala today.

The Maya share a highly mystical explanation of nature with other ancient civilizations. Although syncretism has occurred from the mixture of Catholicism with the Mayan religion, they still retain many of their basic concepts about the nature of the world. Most of their agricultural techniques centre about the cultivation of 'maize' and these are all indigenous and pre-Columbian. In varying degrees they still maintain the custom of elaborate prayers, fasting and continence before beginning any new stage in the cultivation of their crops, as well as consulting a shaman (a priest or medicine man), in order to determine the best day to initiate the work.

The Maya apologizes to the gods or saints of the earth when he cuts the trees to clear the land, when he burns the underbrush and disfigures the landscape. His prayer indicates that he feels that he owns his work and the fruit his work will produce, but that the land is there for his use, lent to him by God.

6. Naylor, Robert A., 'Guatemala: Indian Attitudes Toward Land Tenure', *Journal of Inter-American Studies*, October 1967, p. 622.

7. Thompson, J. Eric, *The Rise and Fall of Maya Civilization*. Norman: University of Oklahoma Press, 1954, p. 136.

O God, my Mother, my Father, Lord of the hills and valleys, Spirit of the forests, be patient with me for I am about to do as I have always done. Now I make my offerings to you that you may know that I am troubling your good will, but suffer it, I pray. I am going to destroy your beauty, I am going to work you that I may live.[8]

A great upheaval for the Mayan people came with the conquest by the Spanish in the early 1500s. Battle, conquest, slavery and tribute were hardships that they had known, but never to the genocidal proportions effected by the white man. In addition to these the Spanish also brought their own conflicting elements of culture which they both consciously and unconsciously imposed on the Maya.

Land to the early Spanish *conquistadores* meant power and prestige, in much the same way a large bank-account or a famous name is regarded by North Americans today. As a result land was coveted for itself, as well as for economic considerations. This meant owning not a sufficient plot where the owner could do his own work, but rather large tracts of land where he could have slaves, peons, tenants or share-croppers to do the work for him. The social prestige that comes from land ownership was obtained as well from the 'ownership' of the peons who worked these lands, and this was also independent of economic factors. Thus it was not all-important if one had an excessive number of labourers on a huge plantation since often it cost the owner only the use of a small piece of his otherwise unused land in payment for the inefficient labour supplied by these tenants. The reliance of the early Spanish settlers on the exploitation of cheap labour prevented them from introducing new and more productive methods of agriculture. This practice is one of the chief causes for the present-day backwardness of agriculture in Guatemala.

To the *conquistadors* God, as Creator, was the supreme

8. ibid., p. 132.

owner, and the Pope, as His representative, could dispose of lands. It was thus that the Pope ceded these new lands to the King of Spain, whose subjects had discovered them. And so the *conquistadores* took possession of the Mayan lands. King Ferdinand V dictated in 1513 a law that stated: 'It is our will that houses, lots, lands, *caballerías* and *peonías* be or may be distributed to all those who go to colonize new lands according to the will of the Governor.'[9]

The land-ownership pattern, begun as early as 1524, only five years after the arrival of the Spanish in Guatemala, is enforced even to the present day. It has been the subject of dispute; it has caused the overthrow of governments and it demands reform. Lands were distributed among the infantry in lots called *peonías*, and among the cavalry, *caballerías*, so that they could support themselves. Those in higher positions in the governing force of colonial society received *encomiendas* as well. The latter constituted a certain number of indigenous villages whose inhabitants could be taxed and could also be used as a work force in the town and in the fields. Their village lands were not taken from them as such, but they were required to pay such exorbitant taxes, and to render so much labour, that they slowly lost possession of their lands, and some became actual slaves.[10] On the other hand the Spanish came to see the tribute not as exchange for protection and for teaching them Catholic doctrine, but as due rent for land they began to consider as their property.

A common usage that exists in modern-day Guatemala and is the direct result of this practice is to include the *colonos* (tenants) or *peones* in the enumeration of the goods of a given plantation when it is offered for sale, enhancing

9. Comité Interamericano de Desarrollo Agrícola, *Tenencia de la Tierra y Desarrollo Socio-Económico del Sector Agrícola: Guatemala*. Washington, DC: Pan American Union, 1965, p. 31.

10. ibid., p. 32.

the selling price. They are thus sold along with the rest of the farm.

Not all the land was confiscated from the Indians. The *ejido* was established, by which villages were assigned communal lands to be used in very much the same way as that to which the Indians were accustomed. The *ejidos* were inalienable and administered by the local Indian functionaries. They also had forest and pasture lands and the surrounding uncultivated areas. The Indians in the *altiplano* were able to conserve their lands because the Spanish found communications so difficult in that mountainous area and because much of that land was not worth taking.[11]

As more land was given out to the Spanish conquerors, the need for a work force was provided by *mandamientos*, which were squads recruited forcibly to work for miserable salaries. Many Indians were moved from their highland villages to large land-holdings on the coastal plain to cultivate *añil* and *cochinilla*, dyes which constituted the first agricultural export crops.

There is no question that a strong economic factor existed in the exploitation of these lands and their workers. It was not only a prestige factor. The wealth and power produced by ownership was and is a very important consideration. Coffee and cotton are the principal exports of Guatemala and they constitute seventy per cent of its foreign exchange.[12] They come largely from the great landed *fincas*. To produce these crops, the individual land-holdings themselves need not be large, but the care of the plants and the harvesting of the coffee bean must be done by hand labour. If a *finquero* is going to dedicate his land to coffee production, he must have a large number of hired labourers to do the work for him.

11. Higbee, Edward, 'Agricultural Regions of Guatemala', *Geographical Revue*, vol. 37, 1947, p. 180.

12. Guatemala: Dirección General de Estadística, *Anuario de Comercio Exterior*, 1962, p. iii.

Although the harvesting of cotton could be mechanized, the quality is greatly enhanced by hand labour. It is in the best interest of the Government, whose economy depends on these crops, to see that hired labour is available.

Coffee is a crop whose production apparently cannot be mechanized and which therefore requires great quantities of labor and strong initial capital. . . . In the past, the Governments that were dependent on the coffee fincas for their national income, did nothing to urge diversification and thus the low standard of living in Guatemala was perpetuated as the finqueros continued to exploit their colonos and jornaleros.[13]

How better can the Government guarantee the *finca*-owner a cheap source of plentiful labour and thus insure that many people will be obliged to work for him, than to see that they do not have enough land of their own? Without these seasonal labourers, known as *cuadrilleros*, the present commercial agricultural economy of the country would collapse.

Although there are laws against child labour, a migrant worker is usually accompanied to the fields by his wife and children and the whole family shares the work. In Guatemala in 1965–6 the number of migrant labourers was estimated as between 200,000 and 250,000 families, which means about one million persons.[14] These figures do not represent the tenant farmers living on the plantations, and even the National Cotton Council estimates that from 300 to 400 thousand workers are needed to pick the cotton crop alone.

This work force has been obtained since colonial days chiefly by the *habilitación* system. Money was lent or goods were given on credit in exchange for work. In this way many were virtually enslaved. It is this method that persists to the

13. Suslow, Leo A., *Aspects of Social Reform in Guatemala*. Hamilton, NY: Colgate University, 1949, p. 70.
14. Schmid, Lester, 'El Papel de la mano de obra migratoria en el desarrollo económico de Guatemala', *Economía*, No. 15, 1968, p. 56.

present day although Governor Alvaro de Quiñónez y Osorio (1634–42) 'officially' outlawed it. Most of the money lending today is done immediately before a local *fiesta* for the purchase of new clothes and enough alcohol for a celebration that lasts several days, then the contract is called up at the time of harvest when the workers are needed. Since this does not always work, it is not unknown for *finca*-owners to go to the Government and request aid from the Army or some other security force to find the necessary but unwilling hands to do the job. This last happened in 1965. Most often it is not necessary since the amount of drinking that occurs during the days of *fiesta* will usually guarantee a sufficient supply of money borrowers and therefore contracted migrant workers. It is a system aimed at providing cheap seasonal labour at those times when the plantation owners need it. It is doubtful that the Government could go very far in eradicating it, even if it wished to, without causing a profound social upheaval.

In 1821, with Independence, the dominion of the lands passed directly from the authority of the King to that of the newly established independent government with little change for the individual owners or for the Indian population.

The Catholic Church had accumulated large estates during the colonial period and some religious orders had exploited their holdings to provide for their maintenance. In 1829 the Government expropriated their lands and reduced the number of Indian *ejidos* and Government idle lands. This caused such an uproar that it became a political question and finally brought the conservative Carrera to the presidency. He restored the lands to the Church and ruled with a strong hand for thirty years.

President Justo Rufino Barrios (1871–85) was a liberal in the great tradition of the nineteenth century. He came to power in 1871 as the result of a revolutionary movement, and his reforms were sweeping and serious. However, he destroyed one *latifundio* to construct another. His confiscation of Church lands was definite. He distributed these lands among some peasants, but mostly among his supporters. His attempts to integrate the Indians into Western culture brought about the strong resurgence of the forced-labour practices of colonial times. Though he made some attempts to protect the Indians, his desire to develop the economy led him to support the landowners in the institution of a brutal system of debt-peonage that spelled virtual enslavement.

President Manuel Lisandro Barillas (1885–92) was in office long enough to demand once again that all lands be recognized officially by a title of private property, a good way to dispossess the Indians of their communal lands. During his term in office the Government took great tracts of land from the Indians, declaring them to be uncultivated, not taking into consideration that *milpa* lands are left to lie fallow for some time so that they can regain their strength. These lands were given to *ladinos*. From Nahualá hundreds of Indians came to see the President:

'You have ordered us to leave our lands so that coffee can be grown', the leader said when he was finally permitted to see the President. 'In exchange you have offered us 600 caballerías on the coast. We know how to grow coffee – we do this for the landowners on their fincas – but we want our fathers' lands for corn. They have always been ours. We have paid for them three times. We came to President Carrera and said, here are the titles. Then we came to President Cerna and paid for them again and we got new titles. Here they are. Then President Barrios again demanded the same thing. Here are the titles we got from him. We have the money now. How much do you want for our own lands this time?' [15]

This concept of private property seems to have become the

15. Osborne, Lilly de Jongh, *Four Keys to Guatemala*. New York: Funk & Wagnalls, 1952, p. 58.

prime concern of the *ladinos* and their government. For them, prestige and wealth lay in the possession of land. No other form of wealth provides the same sense of stability and assurance as does land. For the Indians, land also meant stability and well-being; but not to be possessed as private property, rather to be used as the communal wealth of a village. The *ladinos* continued to accumulate lands at the expense of the Indians, whose labour as well as their lands were needed so that these expanding *fincas* could be made to produce. The Indians were taken from their lands on two counts : to make their lands available to *ladinos* and to make the Indians available as a source of cheap labour.

During his long tenure of office, Manuel Estrada Cabrera (1898–1920) welcomed foreign investors. Principal among these was the United Fruit Company, which, in 1906, in the name of Mr Minor Keith, was granted the right to finish the construction of the cross-Guatemalan railroad, which was still lacking one third of its tracks. Upon completing the railroad, the United Fruit Company received from Estrada Cabrera the ownership of the complete line and, with this, 170,000 acres of the best agricultural land, which was to be chosen by Mr Keith himself.

Jorge Ubico (1931–44) was Guatemala's last strong-man President of the order of Cabrera, Batista, Trujillo and Somoza.

In 1934 he promulgated his 'Vagrancy Laws', a new method to obtain labourers for the *fincas*, since he had already abolished 'debt peonage' or inherited debts and the plantation owners were feeling its effects. Those men who owned from ten to sixty-four *cuerdas* of land (1–6·5 acres) had to give 100 days of work a year for wages. Those who owned less than ten *cuerdas* were obliged to give 150 days a year. The work need not be done consecutively or for the same employer. A record of each man's labour was kept in an official *libreto* that he must always carry with him. If at the end of the year a man had not completed the allotted work-days, he must either be imprisoned as a vagrant or else he had to work out the incomplete time on the construction and repair of the roads.[16] The number of peasants who owned more land than the designated minimum was small enough to ensure that needed labour for the plantations was easily available.

An agrarian law was passed in 1935 reiterating the sup-pression of inherited debts that agricultural workers owed the *finqueros*. However, the *finqueros* were given the right to kill any peasant who would enter a plantation or demand his rights by force. The *boletos de vialidad* were issued in addition to the *libretos*. The former were designed to pro-vide labour for the construction of roads. Every man had to give thirty days of free work. *Ladinos*, or at least those who had money, could pay instead, but this left a great majority of peasants with the obligation to work thirty days more without wages. In addition the *fincas de mozos* were re-established. The *finqueros* on the coast had Indian families living in the highlands on broken and poor lands who would work on their plantations in exchange for the use of these small plots. These were obtained 'mainly by invasion of community holdings. ... In consequence, the Indian, al-though he has secured a considerable degree of emancipation, is still frequently drafted for forced labour on the *fincas*. The problem of the Indian community's relation to the white man's labour needs has not yet been solved satisfactorily.'[17]

We can now see the direct relationship between small land-holdings and large land-holdings, poverty and riches, weak-ness and power, humility and prestige. The one depends upon the other, the first feeds on the second and vice versa. The

16. Suslow, op. cit., p. 85.

17. McBride, George, 'Highland Guatemala and Its Maya Com-munities', *Geographical Revue*, vol. 32, 1942, p. 264.

two cultural patterns lend themselves to such a society, such an economy: an economy that spells backwardness and injustice at the same time.

Two-thirds of the total Guatemalan population or nine out of every ten rural families are engaged in subsistence agriculture, chiefly corn for tortillas grown on small plots.... The primitive farming methods in use consist mainly of the machete, the hoe and the pointed stick. The life of the subsistence farm family is one of poverty, malnutrition, sickness, superstition and illiteracy.[18]

The mass of the population is forced up the hill-sides on to slopes and soils that can only be destroyed by the methods of subsistence agriculture that are used. It not only does not matter that 'the finest lands are generally held in large coffee *fincas* and ranches, or by foreign corporations'[19] but it is necessary that there be no alternative but to live on the plantations as migrant workers because the peasants are either entirely landless or lack enough land for even a subsistence agriculture.

The complexity of the situation has been further aggravated by the lack of understanding on both sides for the cultural values of the other. The Maya generally goes his way, suffering, patient, hardworking, living from day to day, believing that God or the gods have made him inferior and doomed him to his lot for some past sin; all the while hating the white man who perpetuates this system against him. The white man goes his way, believing the native's capacity for suffering to be infinite, that he is not conscious of his misery,

18. Hildebrand, John R., 'Latin American Economic Development, Land Reform and U.S. Aid with Special Reference to Guatemala', *Journal of Inter-American Studies*, vol. 4, 1962, p. 356.

19. Vogt, Evon Z. and Alberto Ruz, ed., *Desarrollo Cultural de los Mayas*. Mexico: Editorial de la Universidad Autónoma de México, 1964, p. 486.

that he would not have things any different even if he could change them.

There have been sufficient signs, however, for those who read them, that such a judgement is superficial. Since the death of the great Quiché king, Tecún Umán, at the hands of the Spanish *conquistador* Pedro de Alvarado, there have been other uncoordinated and spasmodic shudders of Indian ethnic life directed against the white man.

In 1817, Anastasio Tzul declared himself king of the Quiché (he was of royal lineage) and led an unsuccessful Indian uprising in Totonicapán against the Spaniards. In 1898 an uprising of the K'anjobal in San Juan Ixcoy resulted in the death of all *ladinos* in the area with the exception of a deaf mute. His uncommon powers of perception enabled him to anticipate the danger and escape to warn federal troops. When the rebellion was put down, even the few lands the Indians possessed before their uprising were confiscated and many of them have not been returned to this day.

In 1943 a revolt aimed at recovering stolen lands began in Patzicia, but Ubico was able to suppress it before it spread.

The struggle continues even today in the form of the guerrilla movements in which so far apparently only the Kekchí Indians have participated.[20] The outside observer (US social scientists and Embassy personnel) who might question the extent and depth of indigenous hostility to the white man, need only assist at any religious *fiesta* anywhere in the country. Loosened by alcohol, the Indian peasant's tongue, almost always restrained by a natural stoicism and a prudent fear, breaks forth into anguished cries of despair: 'Soy indio; soy hijo del pueblo; soy de esta tierra' (I am an Indian [the white man's term of opprobrium]; I am a son of my people; I am of this land).

There are white men who do recognize the problem, but

20. *Prensa Libre*, 18 October 1969.

it is seldom that they have the power to do anything about it. Individuals who would buck the system tend to disappear. The *finquero* who would provide better facilities or more wages to his labourers than do his neighbours is socially ostracized and is economically obliged to recant or sell up. The Indian who would publicly dare to protest would die from lack of work or an untimely 'accident'.

It should not be thought, though, that all the non-indigenous population is partisan to the exploitation and suppression of the Maya. There are many peasants who share, not his cultural heritage, but certainly his lot. There are the poverty-stricken *ladinos*, those whose ancestors were both European and Mayan, who were excluded from sharing the fruits of the enslavement of the Maya. These people for the most part are products of Western cultural heritage but they have not been left unaffected by their close contact with the Indians. They share the Indian's poverty, but not his sense of community, which springs from a common past. They are more individualistic, more ambitious and much more willing to take advantage of their neighbour than the Maya ever could be. These poor *ladinos* constitute about twenty-eight per cent of the total population and many of them live in urban centres, while others make up a large part of the *colono* population. It has been this difference in cultural values among the peasant class, and the corresponding distrust that it generates, which has kept the poor from a greater organization: one which would pose more of a threat to the landed class.

CHAPTER 3

Tinsel Property

... they call you dangerous
    because it's they
who cannot love
    or who
if they can love
fear for their
    tinsel property
more than they love
    who if they can love
cannot connect love
with struggle
    of earth's peoples
to make life
    liveable for
    their children.

D. GALLATIN

A new day began for Guatemala with the fall of Jorge Ubico, the dictator who had reigned with an iron fist for almost fourteen years. A growing middle class with awakening aspirations of freedom, democracy and social development overthrew him, and with the Revolution of October 1944 launched the country in a new direction.

Juan José Arévalo, teacher by vocation, philosopher by avocation, won the presidency by an overwhelming majority, after a hard-fought electoral campaign during which his life was constantly in danger, in what has been termed the freest election Guatemala has ever seen.[1] He was the idol of the intellectuals, especially teachers and university students, who insisted that he return from his voluntary exile in Argentina to participate in the elections. His thought as well as his social awareness were well known to literate Guatemalans because of the diverse books he had written, principally on education. This thought and awareness made him feared and hated by the powerful few to the degree that he was loved and revered by so many others.

Juan José Arévalo was an anomaly in the political life of Guatemala. He burst upon the political scene in much the way Justo Rufino Barrios had done seventy-five years before him, breaking with all political precedent. He was an idealist who believed in the federation of the Central American countries, combining this with a nationalism that put Guatemala first in all his interests.

If any of his compatriots had any doubts about the orientation of his Government, these were removed by his first speech as President-Elect when he stated :

There has been in the past a fundamental lack of sympathy for the working man, and the faintest cry for justice was avoided and punished as if one were trying to eradicate the beginnings of a frightful epidemic. Now we are going to begin a period of sympathy for the man who works in the fields, in the shops, on the military bases, in small businesses. We are going to make men equal to men. We are going to divest ourselves of the guilty fear of generous ideas. We are going to add justice and happiness to order, because order based on injustice and humiliation is good for nothing. We are going to give civic and legal value to all men who live in this Republic.[2]

Such ideas may seem to be vague generalities, but to the quasi-feudalistic mentality that was the birthright of Guate-

1. Suslow, op. cit., p. 12.
2. Dion, Marie-Berthe, *Las Ideas Sociales y Políticas de Arévalo.* Chile : Prensa Latinoamericana, S.A. 1958, p. 116.

mala's ruling class, such ideas were positively terrifying. It wasn't long before the epithet 'communist' was being linked to his Government and to his person. He responded on 1 May 1946 in no uncertain terms:

You have all heard the cry of our common enemy. You have heard and have seen the untiring campaigns of your enemies who are also my enemies. You already know that for those politicians of the traditional line, that is to say, the dictatorial line, the President of Guatemala is a communist because he loves his people, because he is on the side of the humble people, because he aids the workers, because he refuses to be an accomplice in the bastard interests of the powerful, because he refuses to make pacts with the perpetual corruptors of people in public life.[3]

In case his message wasn't getting through, he repeated it in September 1947 in even clearer terms:

So far in Guatemala, there are only individual communists that believe in the Communist doctrine. Fortunately, up to this moment there are no more than a dozen communists living in Guatemala, and this includes Guatemalans, Salvadorans, and Hondurans.... But at no time have they been permitted to organize into a political party, openly or covertly, nor have they been authorized to exercise within the country a political creed at the service of Communist ideology.[4]

Still, it was a mystery to many influential and land-owning people in Guatemala how their President could speak of the obligation of 'exploring the geographical reality of our country, grade the human factor, examine new possibilities of exportation, liberate Guatemalan soil, dignify the working man, give push to capital'[5] without at least being manipulated by the Communists.

Arévalo himself knew the implications of the social up-

3. Alvarez Elizandro, Pedro, *Retorno a Bolívar*. Mexico: Ediciones Rex, 1947, p. 219.

4. ibid., p. 171.   5. ibid, p. 151.

heaval his ideas would cause if he could ever implement them. He called himself a 'spiritual socialist' and told his people: 'Spiritual socialism is on the move. In this historic moment, all of us are turning towards everyman, turning around the egoistic liberalism towards the great social entity in which every man is immersed.'[6] And in case some of his more wealthy countrymen felt that such talk was a menace to their privileged position, he attempted to placate them by comparing himself to the very much admired but deceased President of the United States, Franklin Delano Roosevelt, and implied that he too had been a spiritual socialist: 'He [FDR] taught us that there is no need to cancel the concept of freedom in the democratic system in order to breathe into it a socialist spirit.'[7]

Thus it was that Juan José Arévalo embarked on the most daring experiment in Guatemalan socio-political history. He called it 'scientific politics' as well as 'spiritual socialism'. He had two fundamental aims, two fields where he intended to enact and implement legislation, the lack of which he felt was at the base of the social backwardness of Guatemala: 'Agriculture and popular education are the two fields that have been orphans of official interest in Guatemala.'[8] A programme that would improve conditions in these two fields (education being his first love) was enough to strike fear into the hearts of Guatemala's oligarchy. They listened and they fretted and they plotted against this man who talked about changing 'the very social fabric' of Guatemalan life. And the peasant, living in his humble hut in the mountains, had yet to realize that at last a man sat in the President's chair who spoke as a friend.

The new Constitution that had been drawn up and ratified by the national Congress a few days before Arévalo took over the presidency in March 1945 gave the new President the basis he needed to begin the social reforms that were close to

6. Dion, op. cit., p. 113.   7. ibid., p. 107.   8. Alvarez, op. cit., p. 151.

his heart. Two articles contained the seed of the long awaited and sorely needed land reform :

Article 91 : The State recognizes the existence of private property and guarantees it in its social function without more limitations than those determined by law, by reason of necessity, public utility or national interest.

Article 92 : Private property can be expropriated with prior indemnity to satisfy a public necessity, utility or social interest which has been legally verified.[9]

The concept that the right of private property is not absolute, but rather that it has a social function, was designed to break down the quasi-feudalistic structures that had so long prevented any type of capitalist development in Guatemala. Its implications were unsettling for the wealthy landowners, but no real outcry came from that quarter. The country was in no mood for such a protest, and besides laws had been written before in her history that had significance only in their enactment, since they had never been enforced. An attitude of 'wait and see' was the order of the day.

The process was begun by minor but still very important legislation. Decree 70, the *Ley de Titulación Supletoria*, was published before Arévalo was in office one month and ordered the registration of all lands according to ownership, category and use, and was intended to make legal all quasi-ownership, titles of the poor, especially Indians. A few months later, in July, another decree recuperated the lots of from five to ten *caballerías* (546 to 1,098 acres) which Ubico had given in 1942, 1943, and 1944 to some of his more faithful generals, returning them to the patrimony of the nation. This was the first act of expropriation, but rather a safe one in view of the class of people that were affected, as well as the shortness of their tenure. But, for some, it was a disquieting precedent.

In October of that same year, a colonization programme

9. Suslow, op. cit., p. 65.

was started at Poptún in the Petén. This was an attempt by the President to begin opening up the vast northern jungle regions as well as to quiet the voices of those who maintained that colonization of the Petén region was the answer to all of Guatemala's land problems. Poptún was a favourite project of President Arévalo but it proved to be a very expensive one. The lack of communications made the effort most difficult. All labour and equipment was dedicated almost exclusively to the building of roads, at the expense of other social needs of the colonists. Malaria proved to be a big problem. By 1948 the Government had spent several million *quetzales*[10] on the Poptún project, and its advisability was being questioned in some quarters. But no one could accuse the President of ignoring colonization as a solution to the land problem.

Two months before this project had been started, Arévalo had met in Escuintla with representatives of the different social and economic interests of the country to see what were their most pressing problems and the approach that should be made to correct them. Government, Capital and Labour were all free to speak their mind, and the meetings took on the name of the 'Triángulo de Escuintla'.[11]

In simple language a peasant explains that he has only four *cuerdas* (·4 acre) on which to grow the food he needs for his wife and family, and that he is paid thirty centavos a day for working on the plantations when there is work. He pleads that he has not enough to live on and that changes must be made.

A plantation owner urges the establishment of a 'law of workers' to avoid the class war that may arise as the discontent of the workers grows He feels that the greatest need of governmental aid to agriculture is in granting credits and

10. The *Quetzal* is pegged to and equivalent to the dollar.

11. Díaz Rozzotto, Jaime, *El Ocaso de la Revolución Democrático-Burguesa en Guatemala*. Mexico: Universidad Nacional Autónoma de México, 1957, p. 105.

in the organization of the world market. He ends by be-moaning the extensive use of alcohol that incapacitates so many workers.

Mr Bradshaw, Manager of IRCA (International Railways of Central America, subsidiary of the United Fruit Company) presents his views. He maintains that a projected high-way from the capital to the Atlantic seacoast, paralleling his rail lines, is not needed and is wasteful; that the money should be used on roads in the interior where there are no rail facilities, and where buses and trucks owned by his Company are utilizing poor roads, with consequent delay and deterioration of equipment.

It is not difficult to imagine what the President thought of some of these attitudes. He was never considered a great admirer of the United Fruit Company, and Mr Bradshaw's discourse was not of the type to change his opinion. But here, too, we can consider the move to hold such meetings as the attempt of a clever politician to bring competing interests face to face, so that each would know where the others stood. The presence and voice of the peasant was unprecedented in Guatemalan history. Everyone who had ears to hear knew where the Government stood, even as it responded that after taking all these aspects into consideration, overdue legislation would follow. And it did.

LABOUR AND SOCIAL REFORMS

The colonization at Poptún was one response. It was followed soon after with the publication of detailed instructions for the 'Dirección General de Colonizaciones y Tierras' (Department of Colonizations and Lands). The Ministry of Economy became the Ministry of Economy and Labour and it began to work in earnest on a study of changes to be made in these fields, especially the drawing-up of a labour code. The first

Institute of Social Security was founded, and INFOP (National Institute for the Development of Production) was established. All these measures affected the state of agriculture and the agricultural workers.

But before any broad and basic reforms could be instituted in this field, a comprehensive study of national resources and conditions had to be undertaken. Statistical information was incomplete and unreliable. In 1947 Congress established a Commission of Agrarian Studies presided over by Mario Monteforte Toledo, who had been President of Congress. They undertook to investigate and provide the answers by a general register of rural property according to municipalities, based on the Real Estate Registry in Quezaltenango, the internal migration of agricultural workers, data on rural population, land-holdings, agricultural production and exports. They compiled a bibliography of works on agrarian reform and a critical summary of the agrarian reforms in Rumania, Italy, Mexico and Russia. They studied rural credits in Mexico and after establishing the bases that the Constitution of Guatemala provided for agrarian reform, they presented a projected law to be studied by Congress.[12]

A preparatory law was passed in February 1949, the Organic Law for National Fincas. This decree created a new entity for handling the almost 150 *fincas*[13] that belonged to the Government. Of these, 108 had been taken from people of German descent during the Second World War by Ubico. Some of the owners were interned in concentration camps in Texas. Ubico was pressured to do so by Nelson Rockefeller, Assistant Secretary of State for Latin American Affairs, during a visit to Guatemala in March 1944. Rockefeller's task was to line up Latin American opposition to the Axis powers. These German *fincas* were nationalized and operated for the

12. Monteforte Toledo, Mario, 'La Reforma Agraria en Guatemala', *El Trimestre Económico*. Mexico: July–September 1952, p. 433.

13. CIDA, op. cit., p. 52.

State, and the 'former owners were to be paid after the war a sum determined from the declarations of the value of the property made for the payment of taxes'.[14] These plantations, along with the others that Arévalo had taken back from Ubico and his generals, represented about one third of the total coffee production in the country and provided the Government with fifteen per cent of its gross annual income. As the years passed, due to the litigation in the Courts and the lack of an organized entity responsible for these *fincas*, their production fell. The new decree was supposed to remedy this difficulty, and at the same time give the Government another opportunity to prepare the way for the real agrarian reform to come.

There were 21,378 workers altogether on these State farms and the law provided for experimentation in order to increase their productive capacity. The experiment was to consist in the mechanization of production of crops other than coffee; to give preference to products for the benefit of the people, rather than for export; to improve the breeds of cattle on the experimental lands; and to found new agricultural colonies (co-operatives).[15]

The AGA (General Association of Agriculturalists) was very bitter about the way the farms were being handled. It maintained – correctly, so it seemed – that the managers and administrators were political appointees and knew nothing of their work. The AGA, a political organization of large landowners, wanted to see these farms sold at public auction to private individuals. This organization was a lobby that had been formed to protect the vested interests of the large landowners and was the strongest political force in the country defending the *status quo*.

Collective farms had been established in May 1948 at 'La Blanca' in San Marcos and 'Montúfar' in Jutiapa. Both experiments were largely unsuccessful, owing to the lack of

14. Suslow, op. cit., p. 65.   15. ibid., p. 68.

co-ordination between different branches of the Government responsible for the experiment.[16] When it became apparent that the experiment was not going well, the two farms were transferred from the Ministry of Economy and Labour to the new Department of National and Government-administered Fincas with the explanation that they were 'neither collectives nor co-operatives'.[17]

Such a set back was temporary but real. The idea of turning the State farms into collectives or co-operatives was of paramount importance to the Government and one that had been foreseen in the new Constitution. Article 100 declares that 'the establishment of production co-operatives is of urgent social utility and similarly the need of legislation which will organize and develop them'.[18] On 1 August 1945 the new Congress had promulgated a law which had created the Department of Co-operative Development. By 31 December 1947 there were forty-one co-operatives in the country, many of them credit unions. The co-operatives continued to develop and in 1948 more emphasis was to be put on agricultural co-operatives. It was a long, slow process, and when Arévalo gave his 'State of the Union' message in March 1949, on the preceding year's accomplishments, all he could say was:

With the prudence demanded by the smallness of fiscal possibilities, the Government has counted on its political policy of protection for the Indian farmers. Congress approved a sum of Q25,000 for the acquisition of lands in the *aldeas* of Ilón, Chel and Zotzil, in the Department of Quiché; the arrangements for acquiring a part of the plantation 'Yerbabuena' in Cuilco are proceeding; also, the papers are being passed for the acquisition of lands in the *aldea* Zunzapote, Municipality of Cabañas.[19]

16. ibid.   17. ibid.   18. ibid., p. 49.
19. Azurdia Alfaro, Roberto, y Mateo Morales Urrutia, *Recopilación de las Leyes de la República de Guatemala.* Guatemala: Tipografía Nacional, vol. 68, p. ix.

It was frustrating for Arévalo as he saw how slow the process of change actually was. This attempt to protect the Indians from losing their lands, by purchasing *fincas* for the development of agricultural co-operatives in their own high-land villages, was another aspect of the Government's interest. In the light of this orientation, the failure of the two collective farms was more bitter than it might have been. And the AGA continued its outcry : 'Heads of agricultural labor unions on the National Farms want to form collectives in order to be directors and increase their personal gain.'[20]

The labour unions that AGA referred to were another outgrowth of legislation based on the new Constitution as well as the direct result of the 'Triángulo de Escuintla'. Emphasis was placed on labour unions of agricultural workers, an unheard-of step in the history of Guatemala. To present these people with the legal weapon they needed to protect themselves against the exploitation of centuries' duration was another indication of the road along which Guatemala was heading. It was the duty of these labour unions to see that the new labour code was implemented on all the plantations. They were to enforce the minimum wage requirements (another Arévalo first) as well as demand education for their children and medical protection for their families. The custom of lending land to *colonos* in payment for work was forbidden, and a requirement was made that all work had to be paid for in cash. In 1948, fifteen of these rural syndicates were approved by Congress, and in 1949 a total of ninety-two were recognized.[21]

It was the organization of these unions, more than any other measure of the Arévalo Government, that was feared by the landowners and merited the President the epithet of 'communist'. Some of these unions came to Arévalo's aid in

20. Suslow, op. cit., p. 69.   21. Azurdia, op. cit., vols. 68 and 69.

his moment of greatest crisis in July 1949, when his conservative opponents, using the assassination of Col. Francisco
J. Arana as a banner, managed to unite enough support in
the Army to almost topple the Government. Suslow
observed:

It is admitted by most Guatemalans that the labor organizations in the capital actually saved the day. Members of the national
labor organizations located in the capital, the area where the
revolutionary attack took place, obtained arms from the government arsenal and fought in the streets against the attacking anti-
government forces. They, aided by some loyal Army members
and the Airforce, proved to be the turning point.[22]

More than a score of these attempts had been made against
Arévalo's Government, and support, such as that given by
the labour organizations, only stimulated the President's desire to see the labour movement grow.

The General Confederation of Workers of Guatemala
(CGTG) was founded on 1 October 1944, predating the Revolution by three weeks, as an association of workers, since
'labour union' was still a suspect term.[23] It was not until
August 1948 that this Confederation was legally registered,
its statutes were approved and Víctor Manuel Gutiérrez, a
Marxist schoolteacher turned labour organizer, was elected
as the General Secretary.[24] In 1950, the National Peasant
Federation of Guatemala (CNCG) was founded under the
leadership of Leonardo Castillo Flores, also an ex-school-
teacher and Marxist, and Amor Velasco de León, an agricultural worker. Two hundred delegates from four regional
federations and twenty-five peasant unions assisted at the
founding meeting.

Certain Catholic priests tried to stop the peasants from

22. Suslow, op. cit., p. 9.

23. Gutiérrez, Víctor Manuel, *Breve Historia del Movimiento Sin-
dical de Guatemala*. Mexico: 1964, p. 32.

24. ibid., p. 46.

joining by labelling the movement as 'communist'[25] but were not always successful. A State Department bulletin later noted that the CNCG had 215,000 peasants organized,[26] while a Guatemalan Government publication of 1956 stated that the totals had not exceeded 100,000 members.[27]

On 12 December 1949, Decree 712 was promulgated, the law of *Arrendamiento Forzoso*, forced rental of uncultivated lands. This was the first law to potentially affect the personal interests of the mighty landowners and was viewed as explosive. It was aimed primarily at those owners who had stopped renting land to their *colonos* within the previous four years for fear of expropriation. It stated that:

Tillers of the land that do not have lands of their own or have less than one hectare of cultivatable land can solicit lots for rental. Those interested in renting lands should solicit them in writing or verbally from the proprietor who has available lands. If he denies them or demands an excessive rent (not above 10 per cent of the crop), the solicitor should appeal to the municipal authorities, who will thereupon give the proprietor an audience within three days.[28]

Mention was made of the 'notorious resistance of some proprietors to rent lots of land, which conforms to a concept of excessive right of property that is so injurious to collective interests'.[29] This was real ammunition for the cannons of the professional anti-communists who hoped to shoot the President down.

25. Huizer, Gerrit, *On Peasant Unrest in Latin America*. CIDA: Pan American Union, 1967, p. 204.

26. U.S. Department of State, *Intervention of International Communism in the Americas*. Department of State Publication No. 5556, Washington, D.C.: 1954, p. 75.

27. Guatemala, Secretaría de Divulgación, Cultura y Turismo, *Así se Gestó la Liberación*. Guatemala: Tipografía Nacional, 1956, p. 353.

28. Azurdia, op. cit., vol. 68, p. 173.   29. ibid.

But the law never accomplished what its framers hoped it would do. It was applied mostly to those lands that were already rented, fixing for them a rent ceiling. This hit harder at smaller landowners who were in the habit of renting out their lands to supplement their incomes than it did the *latifundistas* whose rental activities usually consisted only in that land used by their *colonos*. One of the reasons for the failure of this Law was that the request for lands had to be made to the owner himself, a man who is seldom on his own farm. The landless peasant who dared approach the forbidden sanctity of the *patrono's* house usually found that the owner was in the capital and that the maid did not know when he would be back or what his address in the capital was. But even if Arévalo was not getting any closer physically to a more equitable distribution of his nation's lands, psychologically he was preparing everyone for what the country knew had to come.

Clearly, this effort was too small in itself even if successful, in view of the overall needs. Something more drastic had to be undertaken. The President ordered a general Census with this in view, having stated that 'it is imperative that we create an agrarian reform'[30] as well as to provide the needed statistical information for the programmes of health, education and social security that were being stimulated. The results of the Census demonstrated a situation that was even worse than what officials had anticipated. It analyses the problem of the migratory workers, salaries and cost of living, and there was a cadastre of all rural properties. The last registration of real state had been in 1871, since his own *Ley de Titulación Supletoria* had been inconclusive.

The results of the Census were made available too close to the end of Arévalo's presidency for any effective land reform

30. Guinea, Gerardo, *Evolución Agraria en Guatemala.* Guatemala: La Nueva Éditorial, 1958, p. 23.

to be initiated, so he concentrated on creating the most favourable agro-political climate possible. He felt the publication
of these data would accomplish much in this realm.

Arévalo was not only far ahead of most of his countrymen
in his theories of socio-economic development, but had also
outdistanced the international institutions whose speciality
was this very field. The World Bank shortly thereafter made
a study of the Guatemalan economy, and although they mentioned the need for land reform, the latter came close to the
bottom on their list of priorities, and its extent was meant
to be very limited. Whether for financial, socio-political or
philosophical reasons land reform was neither a primary nor
secondary target of the World Bank.

Although Arévalo had fulfilled his word in looking after
'the two orphans, education and agriculture', he closed his
term in office without having effected the meaningful legislation that he had hoped for in the latter field. He was the
first Guatemalan president of the twentieth century to have
retired from office of his own accord, fulfilling his legal term,
but this was not the consolation it might have been. He left
to his successor the rectification of the terrible imbalance of
land tenure that had been Guatemala's inheritance for
centuries.

CHAPTER 4

Unclimbable Mountain

There is that
mountain in me
unclimbable
I must climb
Already so high
my fingers in this granite
fissured
I reach sporewise
in lichens
via bird dung
thru mist and hard rain wind
I reach that summit –
will be spoorwise
of my track
if the sun sits there
come dawn so shall I.

WILL INMAN

The transition of power from Arévalo to Jacobo Arbenz Guzmán was not without its difficulties. The latter had been a member of the Triumvirate that had come to power in the 1944 October Revolution, and had shared the control of the Government until Arévalo took over in March 1945. He had since served Arévalo as his Minister of Defence and was one of the President's strongest backers for reform. Another member of the Triumvirate, Col. Francisco J. Arana, had been given effective control over the Army, and although he identified with the conservative elements both in the Army and in Guatemalan society, he refused to participate in any plans for overthrowing the Arévalo Government, and at least on two occasions had foiled his fellow officers' attempts.[1] As the Arévalo term drew to a close, it was evident that Arana would be Arbenz's principal opponent in the coming election, since both men were actively promoting themselves.

Then tragedy struck in the form of assassin's bullets and Arana lay dead by the side of the road in Amatitlán. The driver of the dead man's car identified one of the assassins as Mrs Arbenz's chauffeur, and it was rumoured that the killing was the work of Arbenz to guarantee himself the presidency. The mystery has never been cleared up, but it has also been conjectured that many of Arana's 'friends' felt that they would profit from his death in that he had obstructed several *coups* against Arévalo, thus casting a shadow on his 'loyalty'. His murder would at one stroke remove him and cast blame and subsequent public revulsion on Arbenz.[2]

This assessment, of course, is impossible to prove, but there is a ring to it that cannot be ignored. First, there is no question that in a fair election Arbenz would have had no trouble defeating Arana; secondly, the co-ordination with which a number of military leaders attacked the Arévalo Government in response to the assassination casts a doubt on the spontaneity of their indignation; and thirdly, the survival of Col. Arana's driver and his subsequent identification of Mrs Arbenz's chauffeur as one of the assassins was more than an oversight for a man of Arbenz's abilities.

Whatever the truth may be, blame was cast on Arbenz by the Right-wing forces, but not enough of the public fell into line to deny the young colonel an impressive victory over

1. Baker, Ross K., A *Study of Military Status and Status Derivation in Three Latin American Armies.* Washington, D.C.: American University, Center for Research of Social Systems, 1967, p. 51.
2. ibid.

conservative General Miguel Ydígoras Fuentes, ex-Minister of Communications of the dictator Ubico, and seven other 'also-rans'. Arbenz polled more than 266,000 votes, sixty-five per cent of the total cast.[3]

One last attempt to eclipse Arévalo, and with him Arbenz, was made by another young Army colonel, Carlos Castillo Armas, in the form of a military *coup*, but he failed and was sentenced to be executed. Before the sentence could be carried out, he made a daring and improbable escape by digging a huge hole in the floor of his cell and burrowing under the prison walls. Arbenz would live to regret this escape.

Jacobo Arbenz's succession to Arévalo was a logical one, and the only possible one if the work of the 1944 Revolution was to continue. Arévalo was an intellectual and an idealist while Arbenz was a practical and energetic administrator of ideas. In his inaugural address to the nation he outlined his plans for economic development, stating that his three fundamental objectives were to make the country economically independent, to bring about the change from economic feudalism to a modern and capitalistic system, and to do both in a way that would effect a rise in the standard of living.

He said that he intended to encourage private enterprise. Foreign capital would be welcome if it were willing to adjust to national conditions, to agree to be subject to national laws, to co-operate with the economic development of the country, and to abstain from interfering in the political and social life of the nation. This was a direct reference to United States capital investment in Guatemala, particularly the United Fruit Company, since it enjoyed an extraordinarily privileged tax position owing to long-standing arrangements made with the dictators Cabrera and Ubico. Arévalo had challenged the Company by beginning a highway to the Atlantic Coast

3. Johnson, Kenneth, *The Guatemalan Presidential Election of 6 March 1966*. Washington, D.C.: Institute for the Comparative Study of Political Systems, 1967, p. 3.

paralleling the company's railway lines, thus to break UFCo's transport monopoly and resulting stranglehold on the national economy. The Company had refused to bargain with the newly formed labour union and had even ignored a presidential order to arbitrate disputes with the workers.[4] In fact, UFCo. had responded to the order by resorting to tactics that had succeeded in maintaining its concessions during other difficult times. It had shut down its port facilities at Puerto Barrios, crippling local industries that depended on imported raw materials. Meanwhile, in the US Congress, Senator Henry Cabot Lodge from Massachusetts had denounced Arévalo on the floor of the Senate as 'Communistically inclined'[5] because of the latter's attempts to control the Boston-based Company. Now it was Arbenz's turn to deal with the Company, and the new President realized that the task was not going to be easy.

Arbenz also detailed some of his plans to carry out the agrarian reform whose idea Arévalo had introduced. He proposed to liquidate all *latifundios* in order to bring about a fundamental change from the primitive agricultural methods then employed. He planned to distribute all land that was not cultivated or where feudalistic customs were practised and he hoped to apply scientific and technical agricultural methods. He recommended that all *fincas* should be considered and handled by their owners as capitalistic enterprises in their methods of exploitation of natural resources as well as in their labour relations.

Arbenz announced his plans for the presidency, declaring his intentions in clear terms. He said that it was not his purpose to divide all rural property that could be considered large and to give it out to those who worked that land. This would be done only with *latifundios* or uncultivated areas,

4. Rodríguez, Mario, *Central America*. New Jersey: Prentice-Hall, 1965, p. 143.
5. ibid.

but not with large economic agricultural units of a capitalist pattern.

He considered that there were four principal hindrances to progress: first, the Mayan communities that produced only for their own subsistence; second, the feudalistic practice of usurious loans; third, the lack of labour for transformation due to an excessive labour investment in harvesting; and fourth, the large *fincas* where much of the land was not cultivated. This last one he elaborated, adding that many owners did not try to obtain the highest production possible by the use of select seeds, fertilizers, and modern machinery. They rented their land to agriculturalists in exchange for labour or a part of their harvest, then they lent money to those renting, besides buying most of their crop at miserable prices. They paid their labourers in species or with hunger salaries. He suggested that the best of national lands were not being exploited and that the use of the land should be given to the landless so that they could enlarge smallholdings in order to make them productive.

He concluded with five proposals: first, landowners should convert their properties into remunerative enterprises; second, help should be given to peasants so that the land distributed to them would be productive; third, small agriculturalists should be protected from the exploitation of usurers; fourth, enough credit should be made available at cheap interest rates and at opportune times; and fifth, technical assistance should be made available in the fields of education, equipment, seed, fertilizers, and the utilization of credit.[6]

The previous Government had named a commission to study proposals for agrarian reform. Arbenz also invited proposals from other groups. Clemente Marroquín Rojas, a

6. Estrella de Centroamérica, *Transformación Económica de Guatemala: Hacia Una Reforma Agraria.* Guatemala: Tipografía Nacional, 1951, pp. 7–15.

well-known maverick politician and sharp-tongued news-paperman, a defeated candidate in the 1950 elections, presented a law in which he advocated that uncultivated Government lands be made available and that *latifundios*, *fincas* with a land extension above a huge 5,000 hectares (12,350 acres) be subject to partial confiscation with due indemnity.[7] The Census of 1950 had yielded the following: the largest *fincas* in the country were thirty-two, whose land extension was from 4,480 hectares to 8,960 hectares (11,066 acres to 22,131 acres) and another twenty-two *fincas* whose lands exceeded 8,960 hectares. The total land held by these *fincas* was 696,251 hectares of which 637,725 hectares was not cultivated.[8] According to Marroquín's proposal the lands to be given out to the peasants were either uncleared and uncultivated Government lands or a small part of these 637,725 hectares from the privately held *fincas* that were not being cultivated.

The agricultural commission of the Congress presented their projected law in April 1951. The principal authors were Víctor Manuel Gutiérrez and I. Humberto Ortiz. The general consideration that introduced the projected law formulated the social development of Guatemala. The law itself called for the establishment and internal organization of the National Institute for Agrarian Reform (INRA).[9]

Article 19 stated that land would be given in *usufructo a perpetuidad*, which means that titles wouldn't give absolute ownership but rather the right of use, and this permanently. Article 25 said that this right was to be forfeited through incapacity or old age. Article 31 provided for such land to return to the common fund and to be given out to someone who would work it, with preference to be given to a relative

7. ibid., p. 114.

8. Monteforte Toledo, Mario, *Guatemala: Monografía Sociológica.* México: Universidad Nacional Autónoma, 1959, p. 412.

9. Estrella de Centroamérica, op. cit., p. 151.

of the previous user. Article 33 provided that the decision of the Board was to be final, with no other possible appeal.

Neither of these two projected laws was to become the final draft, but that presented by the Congressional Commission did provide a number of elements that were taken into account. Víctor Manuel Gutiérrez had positive ideas on how agricultural development was to take place. He explained that in the United States 'agricultural enterprises evolved which favoured the formation of capitalist small farmers with productive farms'.[10] He emphasized that the agrarian reform was not intended to create many new small land-holders who were to continue with a subsistence economy, but rather it was meant to establish a 'capitalist system in agriculture that would bring economic development to the whole country'[11] as it did in the United States. He went on to say that the best way to bring economic development to agriculture was to nationalize the lands. It isn't clear how he proposed to work this: nationalization as well as the development of economically viable holdings in the hands of individual farmers, unless the titles *in usufructo* were meant to make this provision. His ideas on indemnization of confiscated lands were even stronger. He said, 'No indemnization at all is more just, since landowners have already profited from the lands.'[12] 'In any case,' he said, 'the Government will have to pay with long terms because it does not have sufficient funds and because it must not favour in this way those who have tenaciously opposed the work of the Revolution.'[13]

On 28 August 1951 a special commission was named by the President to study the National Fincas and how they should be developed and utilized. Three members of the commission were representatives of private enterprise: Berger, member of the AGA and a large cattle-rancher; Keilhauser,

10. ibid., p. 171.   11. ibid.   12. ibid.   13. ibid.

who owned a vegetable-oil enterprise; and Bellamy, manager of 'El Salto', a huge sugar refinery in Escuintla.[14]

The Law of 'forced rental' that had been promulgated in 1949 had proved itself largely ineffective because the owners just refused to obey it. As the problem of the landless peasants grew without any immediate prospect of an agrarian reform law being passed, Arbenz saw need to modify Decree 712 in order to cover the situation until he could be sure that his agrarian law would be received satisfactorily. On 28 November 1951, Decree 853 was passed.

Article 1 changed the previous law (Decree 712) by saying that: 'The owner of lands who is not using them for agricultural production or cattle is obliged to make them available so that those who lack lands can use them.'[15] The previous law had limited this obligation of rental to those who had been renting those lands during the previous four years. Also, the old law had put the rental fee at no more than ten per cent of the production obtained, while the new law lowered this fee to five per cent. This had to be paid in cash and it was prohibited that anyone should be required to provide labour in exchange for rental.

The old decree had limited the obligation of rental to those who owned less than one hectare (2·47 acres) or none at all. The new law provided for anyone who wanted land and who could work it. If the rented land was left unattended for two months, the right to use it was forfeited. The old law also stated that a person wanting to rent land could present himself to the owner. The new decree modified this, giving an indication of the problems that must have been encountered. It stated that a man should present himself with two witnesses either to the owner or to his representative, since absentee owners were just not available to those requesting lands.

14. Azurdia, vol. 70, p. 347.   15. ibid., p. 102.

The law guaranteed more equitable prices for rental and meant to provide for better relations between the owners and the tenants. Its weakness, in the judgement of Mario Monteforte Toledo, lay in the fact that 'the revolutionary bourgeoisie was impotent in giving it a character of genuine progress toward capitalism, while the political and labour sectors failed to make it an instrument for social change towards socialism'.[16] It was not in accord with national reality and focused almost exclusively on the elimination of idle lands, excluding fundamental social concepts. However, it opened a way to the agrarian reform law in an even more patent manner.

The idea of a Guatemalan land reform had begun to draw the attention of governments and international agencies. The Mexican Ambassador to Guatemala praised Arbenz's efforts to plan for a good agrarian reform law. His message appeared in the *Diario de la Mañana* on 6 August 1951:

In Mexico, the agrarian reform, the expropriation of the oil, and the conquest of workers' rights which constitute the best of our Revolution, caused, nevertheless, great problems nationally and internationally. Misunderstanding was very great at the beginning, almost incredible and desperate, especially for a country that has lived in darkness for generations. Without these three capital steps, all in the best democratic traditions, my country would never have reached its present stage of development. For this reason, I am captivated by the determined and brave stand of President Arbenz.[17]

In the United Nations, the United States made recommendations for FAO's programme for raising the economic level of countries in order to obtain world stability:

Land reforms are difficult to achieve and may involve substantial investments that are hard to finance. However, in under-

16. Monteforte Toledo, op. cit., p. 436.
17. Estrella de Centroamérica, op. cit., p. 27.

privileged nations where peasants now have a deep-rooted feeling that whatever they do they cannot prosper by their own efforts, land reform may prove to be the most productive of all improvement programs.[18]

Four tenets for land reform were stated by FAO as follows: first, land reform must come largely from governments themselves, not from the outside. It requires conviction of the people who live on the land as well as that of the Government. Secondly, every country must determine its own solution to problems. Thirdly, technical assistance can be requested. Fourthly, land reform must come NOW. There is little time to ponder over the perfect or ideal schemes.[19] Perhaps it was this last recommendation that most impressed Arbenz. Nevertheless, he took all of them to heart.

The President came before Congress in March 1952 for his annual report. He stated: 'In the field of economy, the agricultural question occupies first place.'[20] He brought up several of the more outstanding features of the disparity in land tenure that the 1950 Census had verified. He promised that the law for agrarian reform would soon be ready for the consideration of Congress and that it would follow the Constitution. He indicated that he was determined to act NOW, as FAO had recommended.

Meanwhile another difficulty between the United Fruit Company and its labour union developed. A wage dispute was reported in the American Press as a purely political question. Wage increases had been asked for on the basis of the new labour code. The Company again refused to grant the demands of the workers or to submit the dispute to arbitration. In fact, it began to use the economic tactics that for decades had guaranteed its position within the country.

18. *United States Department of State Bulletin*, 17 September 1951, p. 467.
19. ibid., p. 474.
20. Azurdia, vol. 71, p. v.

It sharply curtailed ship traffic to Guatemala, thus reducing both imports and exports,[21] and Guatemala's need for foreign exchange was used as a lever by UFCo. to exert even more pressure in its favour.

Arbenz had already detailed some of the aspects of the difficulties with United Fruit in his address to Congress.[22] He stated that in answer to the wage demands of UFCo.'s workers, Mr Walter Turnbull had come from Boston representing the presidency of the Company on 22 October 1951 and had demanded that the previous work contract be renewed for three more years. He also asked that the Government promise not to increase the Company's taxes and that should there be a decrease in the rate of exchange of the Guatemalan currency, a guarantee be given that UFCo. would not be affected by it. None of these requests were aimed at endearing the Company to the Guatemalan Government.

On 10 November the Government answered that if the contract should be extended, the Company would first have to agree that the Government would be the arbitrator of all disputes between workers and management and that the Constitution and laws of Guatemala would have to be respected. It further stated that the nation's sovereignty would not permit the Government to give legislative preference to a foreign company any more than to national companies or individuals. The guarantee against a decrease in currency exchange rates was viewed as an intentional insult, since the country's currency had been stable for twenty-five years. The Guatemalan Government presented seven counter-propositions of its own.

They were the following:

1. Any contract between labour and the Company should be in accord with the Constitution.

21. *The New Republic*, 28 January 1952, p. 7.
22. Azurdia, vol. 71, pp. xi–xiv.

2. The docks owned by the Company in Puerto Barrios should be improved.

3. The Company should begin paying export duties, and all exonerations previously granted should be reviewed since they were outdated.

4. There should be Government revision and control of contracts made by the Company with individual fruit-growers.

5. Compensation should be paid to the Government for the 'exhaustion' of lands used by the Company.

6. Periodic revision of contracts must be made.

7. Railroad transportation costs should be reduced.[23]

The Company regarded these propositions as a frontal attack on its privileged position as well as a lack of gratitude on the part of the Government for the contribution made by UFCo. to the development of the country. They were all of this, but nobody could dispute the fact that the United Fruit Company had taken out of Guatemala far more in excessive profits than it ever put into that poverty-stricken nation. The International Development Bank had reported in 1951 that IRCA, the UFCo. railroad monopoly, was charging the highest rates in the world. The Company answered that they had to charge such rates since Guatemala was a mountainous country.[24]

The Company's answer to the seven Government proposals was to lay off 4,000 workers. It was then that the Court ruled that a 26,100-acre farm belonging to UFCo. in Tiquisate be confiscated as guarantee for the back-wage demands of the

23. ibid., p. xiii.

24. In March 1960 the case of twenty-seven minority stockholders of IRCA *v.* UFCo. was finally decided in the Court of Appeals in New York after eleven years of litigation. They had claimed that their Company undercharged UFCo. for banana transportation and overcharged its other patrons. The Court decided that UFCo. should pay $4,531,055 for losses to IRCA up to December 1955. Prices were stabilized after that date, adding up to millions more. No reimbursement was made to overcharged Guatemalans (*El Imparcial*, 24 March 1960).

workers. Finally, in March, the Company got what it wanted when Arcadio Chávez, representing the labour union, agreed to end the dispute by signing a renewal of the old three-year contract in exchange for the $650,000 in back wages. *Time* magazine referred to Mr Chávez as the Union's 'non-communist' leader,[25] since any anti-American Guatemalan of the day was commonly regarded as a communist. That Mr Chávez would agree to the Company's demands made him pro-American and 'non-communist'.

On 17 June 1952, Decree 900, the Agrarian Reform Law, was finally approved and promulgated. Various peasant rallies had been held during the previous months in Guatemala City to force Congress into action and to give thousands of peasants a sense of taking part in the making of legislation that was to govern them.[26] It was ultimately the work of Arbenz himself, who had proved to know much more about the national land situation than the many members of AGA who had been consulted on possible solutions to the land problem. The greatest outside influence on Arbenz and his law was thought to be a Mexican agrarian lawyer and sociologist, Licenciado Lucio Mendieta y Núñez.[27] Congress passed the law with a smaller majority than Arbenz had expected. It was criticized in the Guatemalan Press and by the landowners as anti-scientific, premature, vague and unconstitutional.[28] But the real basis for opposition came because of political considerations:

The fervent nationalism which forms the main drive of this revolutionary movement has been harnessed to a principal purpose, which appears to be the liquidation of all foreign land

25. *Time Magazine*, 17 March 1952, p. 36.

26. Huizer, op. cit., p. 205.

27. Monteforte Toledo, 'La Reforma Agraria en Guatemala', *El Trimestre Económico*, p. 393.

28. Stern, David, 'Guatemalan Agrarian Law', *The American Journal of Comparative Law*, Spring 1953, p. 235.

holdings of any size and the reduction of all native land holdings to manageable proportions.[29]

The United Fruit Company was the largest single land-owner in Guatemala, possessing more land than that owned by fifty per cent of the total population.[30] The Company had demonstrated in its recent difficulties with Guatemalan labour that it not only did not respect the rights of the Guatemalan Government over its own internal affairs, but also had the ability to put a stranglehold on the economy in pursuit of its own interests. Its monopoly on rail lines, international communications, and port facilities made it a very dangerous enemy and one whose power had to be broken. No one could deny that it provided jobs for thousands of workers, but at what price to the country? Besides the affront that the very existence of such a company rendered to the concept of national sovereignty, the taxes it paid were negligible. International Railroads of Central America, an UFCo. subsidiary, had not paid any taxes to the Government since its incorporation more than sixty years earlier.[31] The visible benefits provided to its workers in the form of living-quarters, hospitalization, and higher-than-average wages, were indirectly paid for by the Government many times over in the taxes it never received. Added to this was the fact that UFCo. kept more than ninety per cent of its lands in reserve, giving Arbenz plenty of economic reasons for going after it. Its lands seemed to be a much more likely subject for expropriation than the German *fincas*, since the owners of these latter at least had lived and worked in Guatemala, not as foreigners, but as immigrants and citizens.

United Fruit was not meant to be the only object of the new law, despite its claims to be such. Arbenz was as in-

29. ibid.

30. Beals, Carlton, 'Guatemala Takes Land from Peasants', *Christian Century*, 8 September 1954, p. 873.

31. El Imparcial, 23 June 1958.

terested in applying the weight of the law against native landowners, for two reasons: most of the labourers were working under medieval conditions, receiving little cash wages, which left them economically marginal; the 1950 Census showed that *latifundistas* with land-holdings over 900 hectares were keeping 60·7 per cent of their cultivable lands idle, while hundreds of thousands of landless peasants had no place to grow the food needed to feed their families. David Stern, an American lawyer, in a community on the new law, stated:

The law was the blending of various traditions. One was the American land-grant tradition to open new frontiers. Another was the revalidation of the civil law tradition that all arable lands and national wealth are essentially endowed with the public interest. The third tradition in the new decree was its affirmation of the validity of private property notwithstanding its socialistic overtones.[32]

He also went to the very core of the matter and indicated one of the basic motives for its enactment: 'A fair, impartial and democratic administration of this law would go very far toward destroying the political power of the minority ... who are vested property-holding interests, both native and foreign.'[33]

The first article of the new law gave its orientation: the liquidation of all feudal property. The second stated its purpose: abolition of all types of servitude in that all labour must be adequately remunerated. The succeeding article determined that the expropriated lands would be at first nationalized and subsequently given out to the landless in usufruct or rental. Other lands would be expropriated in favour of the beneficiaries and given as private property in lots not exceeding twenty-five *manzanas* (42·5 acres). All lands belonging to a single owner would be considered as a single piece of property regardless of the location, and indemnity would be made with Government bonds of twenty-

32. Stern, op. cit., p. 236.   33. ibid.

five years duration at three per cent interest. Value of the land would be determined by the declarations made for tax purposes up to 9 May 1952.

The vagueness of the wording of the articles determining what lands would be expropriated and what lands exonerated caused unnecessary doubt and subsequent opposition. No one knew what 'two-thirds cultivated' or even 'uncultivated lands' were supposed to be, nor was it certain how it was to be decided if lands were cultivated 'for' the owner. And what product was not necessary for the national economy? The generality of these elements provided for much uncertainty as to what was meant.

The biggest stumbling-block of all, if we can pin the blame on any one aspect of a law that was meant to revolutionize a society to its foundations, was the naming of persons or agencies responsible for expropriations, the manner in which these were to be made and the time given for effecting them, as well as the process of appeal from their decisions. The fact that appeals could only be made to the President himself, effectively eliminating the judiciary from participating in the machinery of expropriation, frightened many. That the declarations or denunciations were made by peasants to peasant organizations without landowner representation scared many others. What affected the *latifundistas* most was the summary nature of the expropriation procedure, which enabled the whole operation to be accomplished in six weeks. In a country accustomed to red tape and bureaucracy, where 'wait and see' is a way of life, where social legislation in the past had always been circumvented, if not in its promulgation, at least in its implementation, this was just too much.

When UFCo. officials first read the law, they were concerned, but they considered the Company exempt because its lands were 'cultivated'.[34] They should have known better. In

34. *Time* Magazine, 23 January 1952, p. 37.

other sectors, the law had been expected for some time so it came as no surprise. Yet there was immediate reaction throughout the country – either of hope or of fear. Near the Eastern frontier, peasant members of CNCG (National Confederation of Guatemalan Peasants) had even anticipated the law by publishing lists of land-holders whose lands they considered would be eligible for expropriation. When the law was promulgated, they began to measure off these lands. Small farmers with *machetes* seized police headquarters in San José Arcada, and in Camotán a union leader was killed by a group opposing land reform. An amendment was proposed to the three-day-old law: 'Landowners who oppose the agrarian reform law by violent or subversive means will be totally expropriated without regard to the limitations and indemnization provided by the law.'[35]

It was not the law itself that was now causing difficulty, but its implementation. Analysis and commentaries on the law were favourable, despite its glaring generalities and lack of preciseness on many points. Local agrarian committees were being formed in order to determine what lands were to be expropriated and to carry out that procedure. On 6 August the regulations for these committees were approved by Congress.[36] They consisted of five members: one Government representative, one municipal representative and three peasant representatives. The latter were to be members of any local union, co-operative or other peasant organization. There was no representative from among the landowners. Usually, the Government representatives would be considered on the side of the landowners, but not in this Government. For the first time in the history of Guatemala instructions such as these had been issued to Government employees: 'In any dispute

35. ibid.
36. *Revista de la Facultad de Ciencias Jurídicas y Sociales de Guatemala*, 'Cuatrocientos Cuarenta y Cuatro Años de Legislación Agraria', Epoca IV, Nos. 9–12, Enero–Diciembre de 1960, p. 772.

between a peasant and a landowner, the peasant is to be given preference; in any dispute between labour and management, labour is to be given preference.'[37]

Although AGA had been invited to send representatives and spokesmen to the planning sessions for the agrarian reform law, they refused to do so, to indicate that they were opposed to the very concept of land reform and the 'social function of property'. Now that expropriations were to begin, many felt it was fitting that they not be invited to participate or to have representatives on the committees.

It was not until six months after the law's promulgation that the expropriations began. The first decree was approved on 5 January 1953, expropriating a total of 24·2 *caballerías* (2,658 acres), which were assessed at $10,622. From this date on, the expropriations continued quickly, amid disputes and violence on both sides. Marroquín Rojas gleefully published accounts of these in his newspaper, *La Hora*, seeing in this a vindication of himself and his own rejected project for a land-reform law : 3 January – three peasants killed by landowners in San Cristóbal Verapaz and Santa Ana Huista. 9 January – twenty-three houses burned and people ousted, light and water cut off because the landowners feared expropriation. 22 January – peasants invade lands that had been refused to them in customary rental. 23 January – two hundred peasants on rented lands invaded and ousted by other peasants. 30 January – fences of small farms removed so that the cattle invaded and destroyed the crops. 4 February – small farms invaded. 14 February – agrarian committees request permit to carry arms. The agrarian committees were having as much trouble controlling the peasants who saw the immediate hope of acquiring lands as they did with the landowners who tried to impede the law's application through terrorism and deceit.

37. Authors' personal interview with labour court official, June 1965. See also Nathan Whetten, *Guatemala: The Land and the People*. New Haven: Yale, 1961, p. 166.

On 22 January, Ernesto Leal Pérez, a large landowner affected by the expropriation decree, put in an appeal to the Supreme Court. The law specifically stated that ultimate recourse was to the President and that appeals on land-reform questions were not subject to the Supreme Court. However, the judges decided to consider the appeal, and deliberations began. The country waited. On 2 February, the justices declared that 'the right of appeal could not be made vulnerable by the agrarian law',[38] and on 5 February a final vote of five to four gave approval to admit appeals on the land-reform law, suspending further expropriations until the law itself could be studied further. Congress convened that very night to discuss the constitutionality of this declaration.[39] Víctor Manuel Gutiérrez spoke to Congress and said: 'One can live without tribunals, but not without lands.'[40] The President, with approval from Congress, dismissed the dissenting members of the Court and replaced them with judges more favourable to the new outlook.

In civil law countries, says Stern, this lack of judicial review is not unusual.[41] Nevertheless, this new action indicated to all that the President would brook no opposition in the realization of the fundamental aim of his Government. The landowners were stunned. There were discussions and declarations by law students and lawyers throughout the country. Most supported the President's action.

The ultimate interest of the agrarian reform was the good of the peasants, but this was not obvious to many of the peasants themselves. Some were able to interpret it, but others were convinced by local authorities, landowners, and even the clergy that land reform was not for their benefit. Still others, in their haste for land, were upsetting the opera-

38. *La Hora*, 2 February 1953.

39. Rosenthal, Mario, *Guatemala, The Story of an Emerging Latin American Democracy*. New York: Twayen Publishers, 1962, p. 247.

40. *La Hora*, 6 February 1953.   41. Stern, op. cit., p. 237.

tion by invading the property of people as poor as themselves.

Monseñor Mariano Rossell y Arellano, Archbishop of Guatemala, deeply concerned with the inroads being made into the established social order by the Government of Arbenz, launched a far-reaching procession that carried the venerated image of Christ of Esquipulas along dusty roads, into towns and remote villages. He accompanied the procession himself and everywhere large gatherings were produced where he led prayers to end the 'communist' régime.[42] He said that the Christ of Esquipulas would not return to His altar until the Government was changed. Then, on 4 April 1954, the Archbishop published a Pastoral Letter denouncing communism and thus releasing a storm of governmental protest and the applause of the Opposition. These acts, perhaps more than anything else, awoke and solidified opposition to the Arbenz programmes.

From January 1953 to June 1954, when Arbenz was finally overthrown, a total of 1,002 plantations were affected by expropriation decrees. Only eleven of these were expropriated in their totality for being either *colonias de mozos* or for having been completely leased. The total area of all the affected plantations was 1,091,073 hectares (2,694,950 acres) but only fifty-five per cent of their land was taken, or 603,615 hectares (1,490,929 acres).[43] This was considered to be 16·3 per cent of the country's total idle lands in private hands that should be available for cultivation.[44] The value of the indemnization bonds for the expropriated properties amounted to Q8,345,544.[45]

The three Departments most affected were Escuintla, Alta

42. Guatemala: Secretaría de Divulgación, *Así se Gestó la Liberación*, 1956, p. 93.

43. CIDA, op. cit., p. 41.

44. Paredes Moreira, José Luis, *Aplicación del Decreto 900*. Guatemala: Facultad de Ciencias Económicas, 1964, p. 16.

45. CIDA, op. cit., p. 41.

Verapaz and Izabal. The twenty-two largest farms in the whole country were all located in Escuintla, where a total of 176 *fincas* were affected, yielding 24·9 per cent of the total lands expropriated. In Alta Verapaz, 117 *fincas* yielded 15·6 per cent of the lands expropriated, while Izabal provided 13·7 per cent from fifty-three *fincas*. It is interesting to note that forty per cent of the total lands expropriated were owned by twenty-three persons in lots of more than a hundred *caballerías* (10,980 acres) each.[46]

Along with the expropriation of private *fincas*, the national *fincas* were also being distributed. Although their production provided the largest segment of Government income, it had been decided that they would be given out to the peasants who were working on them, either in usufruct or on a co-operative basis.

In December 1952 the National Fincas were declared to be in their liquidation phase.[47] Three men were named to the liquidation commission. They were instructed to take the necessary measures to safeguard the interests of the nation. They were also instructed to make the liquidation as quickly as was feasible and to encourage the peasants to organize in co-operatives as often as possible. Many of the *fincas* had been run as large industrial enterprises and the yield of money crops was more readily assured if they were not divided into small holdings but worked as co-operatives.

A total of 107 national *fincas* were distributed, sixty-one to 7,822 farmers in lots of from five to ten hectares of cultivated lands and fifteen to twenty-five hectares of uncultivated but cultivatable lands. Another forty-six farms were given to the peasants to work as co-operatives.[48]

46. Paredes, op. cit., p. 16.
47. Azurdia, vol. 71, p. 617.
48. Fuentes Mohr, A., 'Land Settlement and Agrarian Reform in Guatemala', *International Journal of Agrarian Affairs*, January 1955, p. 34.

In January 1953 one of the big problems that arose was the fact that in forty-six national *fincas* that were being distributed, the peasants had not been paid their usual salaries, amounting to Q255,000, and many of them were afraid that they might be left out of the land distribution and deprived of their back salaries as well.[49] It was organizational failures such as these that caused much of the unrest in regard to the application of the law.

49. *La Hora*, 2 January 1953.

CHAPTER 5

Sweet Fire, Small and Alone

One day, the apolitical intellectuals
of my country will be interrogated
by the simplest of our people.
They will be asked what they did
when their nation died out,
slowly,
like a sweet fire,
small and alone.

OTTO RENÉ CASTILLO[1]

When Arbenz addressed Congress in March 1953, he spoke
strongly about the land reform :

The most important point in the Government's programme,
as well as that of the October Revolutionary Movement, is that
which is related to a profound change in the backward agricultural production of Guatemala and which will be realized by
means of an agricultural reform that will end *latifundios* and
semi-feudalistic practices.[2]

There was no doubt that the principal object of this agricultural reform would be the United Fruit Company, largest
latifundista in Guatemala. UFCo., with more than 500,000
acres in its possession, was affected by the law in four different decrees of expropriation. On 2 and 5 March 1953, 209,842

1. Guatemalan poet killed by Government forces in April 1967 in
the ambush of a guerrilla band.

2. Nájera Farfán, Mario, *Los Estafadores de la Democracia*. Buenos
Aires : Editorial Glem, 1956, p. 156.

acres were taken from their properties in Escuintla; on 17 October, 5,900 acres in Suchitepéquez were expropriated and given to the peasants as private property; on 25 February 1954, it was 171,159 acres in Izabal. This made a total of 386,901 acres.[3]

Although the expropriation had been feared, it was still a shock to UFCo. once it became a reality. The US State Department addressed the Guatemalan Ambassador on the subject in August 1953, after the first expropriations had been made. Their principal objection was in regard to the indemnization offered. The State Department claimed: 'The fixing of the amount of bonds on the basis of tax value of the properties, especially in the light of tax evaluation procedures followed in the present case by the Guatemalan authorities, bears not the slightest resemblance to just evaluation.'[4] The State Department went on to cite the obligations imposed by international law whereby a government is called to pay a just or fair compensation at the time of taking the property of foreigners. International law, they said, cannot be abrogated by local legislation, even though they had suggested identical compensation in the case of Ubico's takeover of the German *fincas*.

The property that was expropriated was registered in the name of 'Compañía Agrícola de Guatemala', a Delaware Corporation duly registered to do business in Guatemala and a completely-owned subsidiary of UFCo. The result of the action of expropriation, according to the State Department, was the undermining of the confidence of foreign investors.

It is interesting to note that of the 209,842 acres expropriated by the first two decrees, the Company claimed that a total of 111,567 acres were leased to two individuals for cattle, and to another for agricultural purposes. They also stated that

3. Paredes, op. cit., p. 30.
4. *U.S. Department of State Bulletin*, 14 September 1953, p. 357.

another 11,500 acres were for the growing of vegetables for consumption in the Company mess-halls and hospital.[5] The Government claimed that these extensions were grossly exaggerated, as well as falling within the category of 'leased lands'. UFCo. felt otherwise, as did the US State Department.

The Company was offered $612,527 for the 209,842 acres that were taken. This amounted to $2.86 an acre, while the Company had paid $1.48 an acre when they bought the same land. Most of the land on the Atlantic side had been awarded to the Company in exchange for finishing the railroad of which they were also given complete ownership.

The President of UFCo. had said in the *Times Picayune* of New Orleans that he would ask the State Department to make some kind of claim in regard to the expropriation of UFCo. land, should this occur.[6] When it did in fact happen, the State Department acceded to the request. On 20 April 1954 there was a formal claim filed against the Government of Guatemala for $15,854,849 in indemnities. The value of lands and improvements in Tiquisate were said to be $6,984,223 and the damages to other lands, including severance damages, were figured at $8,737,600.[7]

The same claim went on to say that, in 1928, 302,000 acres had been purchased for $3,130,634 and that subsequently, from 1936 to 1952, they had invested a total of $25,942,026 for facilities and the improvement of the lands. The one million dollars that they were being offered for land expropriated under all four decrees did not compare with the fifteen million dollars that they were demanding.

The UFCo. claimed that they needed great amounts of

5. ibid., p. 358.
6. Selser, Gregorio, *El Guatemalazo*. Argentina: Editorial Iguazú, 1961, p. 32.
7. *U.S. Department of State Bulletin*, 3 May 1954, p. 678.

reserve lands because the 'Panama disease', which attacks bananas, necessitates flood-fallowing of lands before they can be used again. However, on the Atlantic coast they had only 4,000 acres planted and had a reserve of 88,000 acres. Even if they doubled their production and did not effect flood-fallow, they had enough reserve land for 110 years more.[8] Guatemalan agriculturalists pointed out that bananas wear out the soil more quickly and more radically than any other of Guatemala's crops.

When Arbenz addressed Congress in March 1954 his main concern was again the application of the agrarian-reform law. He expressed the fear that the law and its implementation would be the excuse for foreign intervention in Guatemala's internal problems: 'The cause of political controversy and social struggle in 1953 was principally the agrarian question.'[9] He rejoiced in the positive results reached even in so short a time. He stated that some new land-holders had received a profit of more than Q1,000 in their first year of ownership in comparison with the Q200–300 which were the average incomes previously. The law had not produced the ruin or the misery of the peasants, as some had claimed, but rather development for those who had been favoured by it so far. Then he asked, almost seeming to plead with his fellow citizens, 'Aren't there better possibilities for the future of thousands of Guatemalans with the expropriation of these United Fruit lands?'[10] He gave the totals of what had been expropriated and distributed up to January 1954: total hectares distributed, 247,833 (612,148 acres) to 55,734 peasants; 133 national *fincas* to 16,200 peasants (a total of 175,418 acres); and 44 national *fincas* given as co-operatives to 6,634 peasants.[11]

He did recognize the weaknesses of the application of the

8. Fuentes Mohr, op. cit., p. 34.   9. Azurdia, vol. 73, p. v.
10. ibid., p. vii.   11. ibid.

law and he hoped that the Government would put forth greater effort to correct these:

There have been some radical deviations in the application of the law such as the illegal occupation of lands or the invasion of the lands of others by some peasants in detriment to others. These questions are being corrected by the agrarian authorities, but it is necessary that the directors of the peasant organizations themselves take care that the application of the agrarian reform law be done according to its fundamental tenets, orientating the agricultural workers adequately for their own good. There have also been deviations to the Right but these are less grave because the law itself provides for the correction.[12]

He also mentioned to Congress that the US Department of State had sent two representatives asking that greater consideration be given to UFCo. in regard to the expropriation and indemnizations. The President had answered that the law was legitimate and constitutional, that foreigners were just as subject to it as were nationals, and that no type of preferential treatment would be given to anyone.[13]

A very important aspect of the law was the need for a bank to handle the credits to the new class of small farmers that was being created. The Agrarian Bank (Banco Agrario Nacional) was approved by Congress on 8 July 1953, but the National Mortgage Bank (Banco de Crédito Hipotecario Nacional) handled all the transactions from March 1953 until the new bank was ready to function in October of that same year. In the eighteen months that these two banks operated, they made loans to 53,829 small farmers, amounting to Q11,881.431.[14] Of the beneficiaries, 87.4 per cent were men who had received lands under the agrarian reform programme, and the rest were small farmers who had never before received the benefit of credit. The National Mortgage Bank alone had loaned more than three million dollars from March 1953 until

12. ibid., p. ix.   13. ibid., p. xxiii.
14. CIDA, op. cit., p. 43.

June 1954 and it had recovered ninety per cent of these loans by July 1954. This was an unprecedented and never yet equalled movement of Guatemalan capital in small loans.

The law was in effect for only two years and was actually implemented for only eighteen months. Its immediate benefits can be enumerated, but its long-range benefits, those that the law was primarily meant to effect, were annulled before they could even be observed. Its errors were present for so short a time that it was not possible to correct them before the law itself, judged by many as one of the best agrarian-reform laws that have ever actually been put into effect, was cancelled.

About 100,000 families received lands, which amounts to approximately half a million people. The amount of private land distributed was 603,615 hectares (1,490,929 acres), besides the 101 national *fincas* that were given out.[15] This signifies that the plots of land received by these peasants were sizeable and together with available credit, destined to eradicate the *minifundio* and the *latifundio*, and to establish a large class of small farmers: farmers who would produce that which would provide them with cash crops either on their own small farms, or in co-operatives on the large coffee and sugar plantations.

The 1945 Constitution and the First and Second Governments of the October Revolution did not establish different regulations for Indians and *ladinos*, but very definitely the Government did not agree that the Indian should continue to live as a foreigner in his own land. The 'Instituto Indigenista' had been founded by Arévalo to study specific Indian problems and to look for ways and means to aid the Indians within their own culture. 'Principally, the Government of the Revolution accuses the Indian of not consuming enough and it disputes his right to continue dying of typhus. It also

15. CIDA, op. cit., pp. 40, 42.

denies him his traditionally accepted right not to possess land, a really serious matter.'[16]

The land-reform programme was accused of taking the Indians away from the protective *patrón-peón* relationship and putting them at the 'mercy' of the State. It was asked if the Indian would be capable of being his own boss. One of the differences was that under the new programme, they would pay three to five per cent of their annual harvest as interest to the State instead of one third to one half to the *patrón*. It perhaps occurred to many that the State's 'mercy' was more beneficial than the *patrón*'s 'protection'.

An effect of the agrarian reform was that it created an 'agrarian climate' in other Departments of the Government. Public health began to broaden its services to previously neglected rural areas. The national educational system inaugurated two regional schools for the training of rural teachers – many of whom spoke the Indian dialects; a programme for the study of Indian languages was begun. A hospital in San Juan Sacatepéquez began to train auxiliary rural nurses. Roads to many villages were constructed, giving the small coffee-growers freedom to choose their buyers. Joaquín Noval, a Guatemalan anthropologist, concludes this list of 'Indian projects' by saying : 'Who knows whether the poor rural *ladinos* or the poor urban people should envy the Indians or vice versa? With the new factors now at work in Guatemala, they may emerge together as a better nation.'[17] One thing was certain : if the Indian was to be envied, it was indeed a social revolution of fantastic proportions.

As more peasants began to get better income from their new lands, they came to form part of the money economy. They changed from subsistence farmers to consumers. As a result,

16. Noval, Joaquín, 'Guatemala, The Indian and the Land', *The Americas*, March 1954, p. 6.

17. ibid., p. 43.

many small merchants began to appear in Escuintla, Retalhuleu, Mazatenango and Coatepeque.

The minimum wage in the national *fincas* had been set at
80 centavos a day. When the agrarian reform made labour
more scarce for the large landowners, they were forced to
increase the wages to their workers. Previously, the Government attempted to enforce the minimum-wage law artifi-
cially. Now, the law of supply and demand began to take
effect.

It is no great criticism of the Arbenz Government to admit
that the principal defect of the law was mainly in its implementation. The agrarian committees had a difficult time controlling the peasants. There were invasions of small farms by
peasants so that the poor were demanding land rights from
the poor. In San Miguel Petapa such a scene took place on
11 June 1953. A local agrarian committee took lands belonging to the village of 2,500 people and gave them to sixty
peasants from other towns. The people, small farmers themselves, appealed to the Government for redress of the injustice
and the Government sent a representative to hear the facts
and try to correct the abuse.[18] On 12 February 1952 it was
announced in *La Hora* that any agrarian committees that
committed errors would be fined. The newspapers later reported that the threat had been carried out, with the firing of
some officials and the fining of others.[19] The explosiveness of
the need for land was the real cause of the turmoil and it is
difficult to look back even now and to say how it could have
been avoided.

The second most noteworthy deficiency was the tendency
of the law to punish the more generous landowners. Some of
the landowners who had given better treatment to their

18. Guatemala: Dirección General de Asuntos Agrarios, *La
Evidencia de los Hechos*. Guatemala: 1957, p. 99.

19. *La Hora*, 29 May 1954.

colonos, and provided them with larger and better plots for their personal crops, suffered more than those who were more selfish, since the law stipulated that plots being used by *colonos* were to become their property. Another point of contention was the stipulation that where fifteen or more families were living together on a plantation the site of the houses was to become their property and the area designated as a municipality, so that the settlement was made into a rural village. Land had to be set aside for this. These two points of the law tended to divide property since most of the landowners had their *colonos* living on one side of the plantation and the lands assigned to them might be on any other part of the *finca*. When these lands were expropriated in favour of the *colonos*, the owner found himself with split property, which made it difficult to maintain a unified farm.

The vested interests of the landowners constituted the major reason for their condemnation of the law. It was declared unconstitutional because the right of appeal was limited and an owner who believed himself cheated had no recourse which would favour him. This accusation of unconstitutionality was found to be erroneous after Arbenz was overthrown and the issue brought before the Supreme Court (*El Imparcial*, 10 August 1954).

The price being paid for the expropriated lands, determined by the tax declarations made before May 1952, suited none of the landowners. Hernán Santa Cruz, regional director of FAO for Latin America, said:

An agrarian reform always carries with it an element of confiscation in the general interest of the society, and for this reason long delayed payments must be accepted at no less than twenty years payment, with low interest rates and at prices much lower than the market values, which in Latin America are usually much inflated.[20]

20. Paredes, op. cit., p. 16.

Raúl Branco, of the Center for Development Planning of the United Nations, states:

Given the assumption that land reform will be carried out by due legal process, who would pay for the land confiscated and how would payments be made? Since the landless peasants are by definition poor, the government will have to pick up the tab, even if only to finance the sale to the peasant. If the 'rights' of the landowning class were fully taken into consideration, payments would tend to be made in cash and at rates far above the capitalized value of the land. Obviously, no country could afford to carry out an extensive land reform program with such a procedure. Thus, payments must be necessarily made mostly in bonds, which will be strongly resisted by the present landowning class. Even if a compromise is reached involving limited land reform with a part of the compensation paid in cash, I fail to see the economic rationale of using scarce government funds to finance the transfer of ownership titles of existing inmovable assets, when the same funds could be used for financing the creation of new productive capacity.[21]

The formation of co-operatives was compared by some,[22] not unintentionally, to the Russian kolkhozes, and they were generally feared, as were the rural unions that had been encouraged since the time of Arévalo. The agricultural labour unions had been one of the first tools used by the Government to provide the rural workers with an effective lever with which to demand their rights from the landowners.[23] The landowners historically had had the protection of the Government for securing plenty of cheap labour. This was the second government (and the last, unfortunately) that had given preferential treatment to the workers and peasants.

21. Branco, Raúl, 'Center for Development Planning', *Journal of Inter-American Studies*, vol. 9, 1967, p. 234.

22. Nájera, op. cit., p. 157.

23. Adams, Richard, *Cultural Surveys of Panama, Nicaragua, Guatemala, El Salvador*. Washington: Pan American Sanitary Bureau, 1957, p. 297.

The unrest felt by the landowners was made evident by the political pressure they tried to use in order to change the state of affairs. One of their most effective weapons was the use of the label 'communist' to discredit the Government, especially its agricultural reform programme, as well as to put fear into the minds of the peasants. For the latter, they found particularly good allies in the Church and its ministers.

There is no doubt that there were Marxists in the Guatemalan Government. Two of them were particularly active in the formulation and the administration of the agrarian reform law: Víctor Manuel Gutiérrez and José Manuel Fortuny. Carlos Manuel Pellecer, another Marxist, was the head of the agrarian committee in Escuintla. The Guatemalan Labour Party (Partido Guatemateco del Trabajo) established during the Government of Arévalo, was the communist party in Guatemala. The US Department of State published a study about communist 'intervention' in Guatemala in August 1954 in which they describe the PGT as follows:

The PGT is a party of young ladino intellectuals of the lower middle class. Its founders and present leaders are young school teachers, ex-university students, journalists, white collar workers and former employees of U.S. and foreign enterprises in Guatemala. This was the sector of society most frustrated under the archaic social structure of Guatemala ... which, until after World War II, remained a backward dictator-ridden agricultural country where two per cent of the landholdings covered seventy per cent of the arable land and over half of the population consisted of illiterate Indians living apart from the currents of twentieth century life.[24]

The Party members, during the First Government of the Revolution, had become involved in the reform programme initiated by Arévalo, and had invited experienced men from other countries to help them in the organization of these pro-

24. U.S. Department of State, op. cit., p. 36.

grammes, especially in the fields of labour and education. The General Confederation of Workers of Guatemala became a member of the World Federation of Trade Unions (WFTU).[25] They worked very hard under the guidance of Víctor Manuel Gutiérrez and the special tutelage of Lombardo Toledano, a highly respected Marxist from Mexico, to establish unions and educate the workers in organization. Lombardo Toledano, as head of the WFTU's Mexico-based affiliate, the Confederation of Workers of Latin America, was instrumental in bringing the Guatemalan Confederation into the WFTU.

One would have to consider membership in the General Confederation of Workers (CGTG) or the National Confederation of Workers (CNTG) or the National Confederation of Peasants (CNCG) to be identical with membership of the communist party, in order for the list of peasants from San Raymundo qualified as communists in the House Hearings Report of the Eighty-third Congress to be considered a valid accusation.[26] The names of the peasants listed there are all Mayan names. It hardly seems possible that illiterate

25. The WFTU was founded shortly after the Second World War by the British Trade Union Congress, the North American Congress of Industrial Organizations (CIO), the French General Confederation of Workers and the Soviet Trade Unions. The American Federation of Labor (AFL) refused to join the WFTU because of Communist participation in the new organization and set about gathering support to oppose the WFTU. This organizational campaign, with US State Department backing, eventually resulted in the formation of the Interamerican Organization of Workers (ORIT), which, as a Sub-committee Report (published 15 July 1968, p. 8) of the Senate Foreign Relations Committee says: 'has never quite solved the problem of emphasis as between fighting communism and strengthening democratic trade unions'. ORIT later endorsed the CIA-sponsored overthrow of President Arbenz.

26. House Hearings, *Ninth Interim Report on Hearings Before the Sub-committee on Latin America on Communist Aggression in Latin America*. Washington, D.C.: U.S. Printing Office, 1954, p. 271.

Mayan men, just four years after the founding of the labour confederation, could have been converted to and instructed in political communism in so short a time.

In 1952 the labour and peasant confederations joined forces and began to work more closely together. In May of that year there were 568 unions and in February 1954 they had grown to 1,758.[27] Even the Department of State Report admits that 'the PGT exerts its influence to a somewhat lesser degree over the CNCG than it does over the CGTG'.[28] This same Report goes on to explain the plans of the communist party:

The International affairs, the party (PGT) has emphasized as its first task the 'Peace Campaign' which is defined as preventing the harnessing of Guatemala to the 'war chariot of imperialism' – i.e. preventing Guatemala from taking its role in the defense of the Western Democratic community grouped around the United States. As the corollary in domestic Guatemalan politics, the PGT has announced as its first task the implementation of Guatemala's 1952 agrarian reform law which is designed to transfer much of the country's potential arable land to new small farmers, and as its second, the heightening of the struggle against U.S. 'monopolistic' companies operating in Guatemala. These domestic programs tend toward the breakdown of the established order and are simultaneously adapted to the immediate objective of weakening Guatemala's position in the Western community and the ultimate objective of preparing the ground for the communists coming to power.[29]

In even clearer terms the Party outlined its *Camino Guatemalteco* (Guatemalan Way) into seven points to be followed after their May 1953 plenary session:

1. The application of the agrarian reform must be carried on.
2. Intensify the fight against the foreign monopolies and in-

27. Schneider, op. cit., p. 169.
28. U.S. Department of State, op. cit., p. 39.
29. ibid.

crease the anti-imperialistic sentiment of our people, especially against UFCo., IRCA, and the Empresa Eléctrica.[30]

3. Denounce the counter-revolutionary activities of feudal imperialistic reaction.

4. Give increased support to progressive measures undertaken by the democratic Government of President Arbenz, such as the highway to the Atlantic which will allow Guatemala, by competing with U.S.-owned IRCA, to free itself from monopolistic exploitation.

5. Improve the living conditions of the people, especially by struggling for a minimum daily rural wage of 80 centavos and an urban wage of Q1.25.

6. Cultivate and strengthen organic unity and united action in the working class, by fighting against diversionism in labor organization.

7. Tighten the alliance between the workers and the peasants.[31]

The party membership was difficult to ascertain. The director of the Departamento Nacional Agrario was Major Alfonso Martínez Estévez, considered to be an opportunist non-communist. But seven inspectors of the DNA were publicly registered as Marxists and seven others had been identified as such. Another twelve out of the 350 employees of the DNA were 'known' to be communists: a possible total of twenty-six Marxists in all.[32]

US Ambassador John E. Peurifoy had come to Guatemala in the early 1950s from Greece, where he had been very active and successful in fighting 'communism'. When he appeared at the Congressional hearings in August 1954, after the Arbenz overthrow, he claimed that 'the communist party used the agrarian reform as a weapon to gain political control over the farm workers and the landless peasants'.[33] This

30. Electric Bond and Share, sole owner of electrical power in the Capital.
31. U.S. Department of State, op. cit., p. 66.
32. ibid., p. 70.
33. House Hearings, op. cit., p. 115.

was the cry of the expropriated landlords, and the United States Government obviously agreed.

Nathan Whetten, travelling through Guatemala during the time of the agrarian reform, observed the following:

The communists were under strict discipline. They worked day and night to put their program across. They travelled throughout the country under difficult conditions in order to learn the problems of local and national concern. When there was land to be distributed to peasants by the government, they were the first to arrive on the scene and the last to leave. They seemed to accumulate more information about local problems than anyone else; and the peasants gradually began looking to them for advice.[34]

He also describes a visit to the headquarters of the CNCG, where the men were available at all hours of the day and night to counsel peasants with great patience and solicitude.

The Government of Guatemala was not a communist government. Communists held only four out of fifty-six seats in Congress. There was much political activity and freedom and the newspapers of that time indicate that there was also freedom of the Press and free elections for Congress. There was much made of the fact that José Manuel Fortuny, a very well-known and active communist, lost the election to Congress in 1952. And President Arbenz had continually reiterated his intentions of converting Guatemalan economy from 'feudalism' to capitalism, hardly a communist goal.

The US Government had followed the expropriation of UFCo. lands with great concern. When the first expropriations had taken place in March 1953, the State Department had sent a message to the Guatemalan Embassy in Washington on 25 March, saying:

The Government of the United States sees with great concern the way the agrarian reform law of Guatemala has been applied

34. Whetten, Nathan, 'Land Reform in a Modern World', *Rural Sociology*, vol. 19, 1954, p. 334.

to the property of the United Fruit Company in Guatemala....
The Guatemalan Government seems to be applying the law in
such a way as to make impossible the continuation of UFCo.
activities in Guatemala.[35]

Viewing what UFCo. activities had been, there is no reason
to doubt the truth of this allegation.

Guatemala answered this message as follows:

The agrarian reform law is a general law, applicable equally
to a person, natural or juridical – national or foreign – who owns
rural lands in the national territory. Its application constitutes
an act of inalienable sovereignty, therefore the Government of
Guatemala cannot consider at present, nor in the future, the
possibility of converting this business into a matter for international discussions.[36]

The expropriations of UFCo. land continued. But several
attempts against the Government were made. Arms were
found on UFCo. property. The struggle between the Guatemalan Government and the Company became more and more
evident.

In March 1954 the tenth Interamerican Conference was
held in Caracas, Venezuela. The US Secretary of State, Mr
John Foster Dulles, attended the Conference until a seven-
teen-to-one vote had been passed whereby the countries of
Latin America agreed to their unity and the mutual defence
against 'commmunist aggression'. Guatemala voted against
the agreement, which gave the United States freedom to intervene anywhere in the Americas in the defence against
communism. Mexico and Argentina abstained, and Uruguay
voted in favour, but its representative told reporters afterwards that they were very unhappy about it but felt forced
to vote because of US pressure.[37] Actually, after Mr Dulles
left, the Conference was to run for two more weeks. They
had just begun to work.

35. Toriello, op. cit., p. 58.
36. ibid.   37. *New York Times*, 7 March 1954.

The Latins are not unaware of the threat to their security implied by International Communism, but they have long felt that they cannot solve effectively their social and economic problems, which are indeed the breeders of communism, without substantial help from one or more of the great industrial and capital exporting nations. This was the problem they had come to Caracas to discuss and Mr Dulles' proposal received their support because the present U.S. administration has made it reasonably clear that only nations which take approved views of International Communism can expect to be recipients of economic aid or technical assistance without much American grumbling. ... Mr Dulles' departure was, in their eyes, tantamount to saying that he was concerned only with their support, and could not take time to discuss Latin American internal problems since they were not of sufficient importance.[38]

A month later, in April 1954, the Department of State made a formal claim to the Guatemalan Government for $15,854,849 for the UFCo. lands that had been expropriated. The Guatemalan Embassy in Washington answered in May and said, among other things:

If the Government of the United States continues to act in favour of the illegitimate pretensions of these companies, the Government of Guatemala cannot but consider such an attitude as the insistence of intervening in the internal affairs of the Republic of Guatemala, contravening in this way the most solid principles of the Inter-American community.[39]

Mr Dulles held a news conference on 25 May 1954 after receiving Guatemala's answer to his claim in favour of UFCo. He accused the Guatemalan Government of being infiltrated with communists. He based his judgement on three significant factors: first, Guatemala was the only Latin American

38. **Taylor**, Philip B., 'The Guatemalan Affair', *American Political Science Review*, September 1965, p. 791.

39. Toriello, op. cit., p. 258.

state that did not ratify the Treaty of Rio during the Caracas Conference; second, Guatemala was the only country that voted in Caracas against the statement that the domination of the political institutions of any American state by the international communist movement would constitute a threat to the sovereignty and the political independence of the American states; and third, Guatemala was the only American state that had been the recipient of a shipment of arms from behind the Iron Curtain.[40] It is obvious that Guatemala could not vote for a treaty that was tantamount to giving foreign governments permission to intervene in its internal affairs. Nor did Mr Dulles make a distinction between national and international Marxism, something that Guatemalans and most Latin Americans seem to have no problem with. As a matter of fact, there are many sincere non-communist nationalists in Latin America who see the United States as a greater threat to their sovereignty than the USSR, if for no other reason than proximity.

The Secretary of State failed to mention that the shipment of arms from behind the Iron Curtain was precipitated because the United States had since 1948 maintained an effective embargo on arms to Guatemala from all nations in the US sphere of influence,[41] and later it was openly supplying arms in 1953 and 1954 to the Governments of Honduras and Nicaragua, as well as to Guatemalan exiles in these countries and in El Salvador for the express purpose of overthrowing the Arbenz Government.

Dulles then went on to quote a statement by Guillermo Toriello, the Guatemalan representative to the Caracas Conference, and to refute it:

The Guatemalan Government boasts that it is not a colony of the United States. We are proud that Guatemala can honestly say that. The United States is not in the business of collecting

40. *U.S. Department of State Bulletin*, 7 June 1954, p. 873.
41. Toriello, op. cit., p. 143, and Taylor, op. cit., p. 794.

colonies. The important question is whether Guatemala is subject to communist colonialism.[42]

As the United States continued to arm and train the Castillo Armas forces in Honduras, Guatemalan protests in the United Nations were met by the US delegate and acting President of the Security Council, Henry Cabot Lodge:

While the reports that we receive on the situation in Guatemala are incomplete and fragmentary, the information available to the United States thus far strongly suggests that the situation does not involve aggression but is a revolt of Guatemalans against Guatemalans.[43]

On 30 June 1954, when the military invasion against Arbenz had succeeded, Dulles addressed the United States in a radio and TV broadcast:

Communist agitators ... dominated the social security organization and ran the agrarian reform program. The judiciary made one valiant attempt to protect its integrity and independence. But the communists using their control of the legislative body, caused the Supreme Court to be dissolved when it refused to give approval to a communist-contrived law.[44]

We must remember that the communists were only four out of fifty-six in Congress, hardly 'control of the legislative body'. The Secretary of State continued:

Throughout the period I have outlined, the Guatemalan Government and communist agents throughout the world have persistently attempted to obscure the real issue – that of communist imperialism – by claiming that the US is only interested in protecting American business. We regret that there have been disputes between the Guatemalan Government and UFCo. We have urged repeatedly that these disputes be submitted to an inter-

42. *U.S. Department of State Bulletin*, 7 June 1954, p. 873.
43. U.S. Department of State, op. cit., p. 14.
44. ibid., p. 31.

national tribunal or to international arbitration. That is the way to dispose of problems of this sort. But this issue is relatively unimportant.[45]

If this issue was 'relatively unimportant', Dulles had not made the basic issues any clearer by making such insistent demands in UFCo.'s favour. Nor did he think it very important that the issue of the fifteen-million-dollar payment be submitted to an international tribunal. UFCo.'s word was sufficient for the United States to back their claims. The fact of the matter is that Dulles, as a senior partner of the Cromwell–Sullivan law firm, UFCo.'s lawyers, had been personally instrumental in drawing up the contract between the United Fruit Company and Dictator Jorge Ubico in 1936, and his continued support of the Company's claims left his motivation open to criticism.

Castillo Armas was the man chosen by the US State Department to be the beneficiary of arms, money, planes, pilots and advisers. He was to be the hero of the day, the man who would push back the tides of the 'international conspiracy' that had prompted this 'communist-contrived' law. He was to be the saviour of the landowning class and the protector of the United Fruit Company's interests. And so, with complete disregard for the freedom and self-determination of the Guatemalan people, the United States added one more page to its long history of intervention in Latin American affairs under the banners of the highest idealism, while seeking principally the furtherance of US economic interests at the expense of Guatemala's poorest.

45 ibid., p. 32.

CHAPTER 6

Misery in the Name
of Liberty

The United States appear to be destined by Providence to plague
America with misery in the name of liberty.
SIMÓN BOLÍVAR

Colonel Carlos Castillo Armas, despite the fact that he was
obviously strong-willed, was in many ways a helpless figure.
Caught up in the turmoil of strong cross-currents of political
ideologies, Guatemalan economic and social backwardness of
abysmal proportions, with ties to powerful national and international blocs not always of his own choosing, he took the
reins of Guatemalan government in the early days of July
1954 until his assassination in August 1957. That he managed
to survive at all at the head of his Government for three years
is a tribute in itself.

Castillo Armas became official head of the new Government through an election held within the reigning military
Junta on 7 July 1954. He had already been included as a member of the five-man military Junta owing to the 'Pact of El
Salvador',[1] which had taken place on 2 July under the
auspices of the President of El Salvador, Col. Oscar Osorio.
Present also at the meeting were José María Peralta, President of the National Congress of El Salvador, Archbishop
Genaro Verolino, Apostolic Nuncio of the Vatican in Guate-

1. Azurdia, vol. 73, p. 69.

mala and El Salvador, Col. J. Alberto Funes, Ambassador of El Salvador in Guatemala, Col. Elfego Monzón, reigning member of the military Junta which had taken over after Arbenz had stepped down, and Col. Carlos Castillo Armas, head of the 'National Liberation Movement'.

After Castillo Armas had won his 'military victory' at Chiquimula, he had returned to El Salvador to await arrangements for his inclusion in the new Government. This was effected by the 'Pact of El Salvador', at which time it was agreed that an election would take place within fifteen days from among the Junta's five members (besides Monzón and Castillo Armas, they were Cols. Cruz Salazar, Dubois and Oliva) and a new head of the Government would be declared. It was a foregone conclusion that the winner would be Castillo Armas, which is exactly what occurred in Guatemala on 7 July. At the same time, Cols. Cruz Salazar and J. Mauricio Dubois resigned.

We refer to the 'military victory' of Castillo Armas at Chiquimula for want of a better expression. It is doubtful that much of a battle took place. The Guatemalan newspapers of those days are filled with photographs of the Liberation Army's soldiers lolling around in the sun, conversing lazily in the shade of tropical trees or simply practising marksmanship. Nowhere is there a picture that resembles a military encounter. The foreign Press was excluded from the 'battle area' for unexplained reasons, one of which may be that there was no real battle. It is true that skirmishes occurred, but their limitation seems to be reflected in Castillo Armas' own words:

In the wars of all times and countries, that which counts and makes history is not the number of effective soldiers or the quality of its armaments, but the socio-political results which are obtained as a consequence of victory; and in this case, the Battle of Chiquimula has national importance, because it was there that the liberty of Guatemala was won.[2]

Even the radio address of Arbenz on 27 June, as he handed over the Government to a military junta headed by Col. Enrique Díaz, did not reflect a preoccupation with the military capacity of the Liberation Army:

> The military situation of the country is not difficult; quite the contrary. The enemy, the foreign mercenary bands recruited by Castillo Armas, are not only weak but incapable and cowardly. We have proved this in the few battles we have sustained. The enemy managed to advance and capture the Department of Chiquimula only because of the attacks of the mercenary aviation. I do not think that our Armed Forces will encounter great difficulty in defeating them and expelling them from the country.[3]

There is much contained herein that is still shrouded in mystery. If Arbenz did not fear a military defeat, why did he resign? Some claim it was sheer cowardice. Those who know him best claim he is incapable of cowardly conduct. Another explanation was that he feared imminent and massive United States participation (the bombings had already demoralized the population), and felt that he could best avoid this by stepping down himself and turning his Government over to Col. Enrique Díaz, his Minister of Defence, and two other colonels. Most observers feel that the reason was that Arbenz could not induce the Army to fight, nor would it agree to arm the thousands of peasants who were ready to duplicate the feat of repelling counter-revolutionary forces as they had done for Arévalo in July 1949. The President apparently thought that Col. Enrique Díaz might have more influence at this time with some of his fellow officers to at least arm the peasants, if not fight themselves.[4] Díaz imme-

2. Azurdia, vol. 74, p. 44.   3. ibid., vol. 73, p. 68.
4. Baker, op. cit., p. 48.

diately stated his firm intention of expelling Castillo Armas from the national territory and almost as immediately was replaced by Col. Elfego Monzón, the second member of the new Junta. The manoeuvring of the US Ambassador, John E. Peurifoy, played a big role in this substitution. He was present when the change of power occurred,[5] and there is little doubt that he promised and threatened that the United States would see Castillo Armas in the President's chair and that the Junta had better accept it.

Arbenz and his followers today admit that he made a grave mistake in not remaining to fight.[6] There was at least one peasant force already assembled in Cobán in central Guatemala, preparing to leave for the battle front, that wept openly upon learning of the President's resignation.[7] There is no question that Arbenz could have obtained ample support if he had gambled for time. One thing is certain, that when he did resign, he did not believe that Castillo Armas would be successful.

One of the elements that Arbenz mentions in his speech is the 'foreign mercenary bands' and 'the mercenary aviation'. He was referring to the fact that the forces of Castillo Armas had been trained, equipped and financed by the United States Government and his Air Force (six P-47s) was donated and flown by personnel of the Central Intelligence Agency, then under the direction of Allen Dulles, brother of the Secretary of State. Despite Cabot Lodge's disclaimer in the United Nations, the US interference in Guatemala was public knowledge and its brazenness shocked many US allies. The former English Prime Minister Clement Attlee wanted to know 'how US support of an anti-communist faction in Guatemala

5. Taylor, op. cit., p. 797.

6. Guillen, Fedro, _Guatemala, Prólogo y Epílogo de una Revolución_. Mexico: Cuadernos Americanos, 1964, p. 72.

7. From the authors' personal interview with a participant.

differed from, say, Chinese support of a communist faction in Vietnam'.[8]

Many authors have since minimized US military participation, yet the CIA Air Force was better equipped than Guatemala's own, the head of which, Col. Rodolfo Mendoza Azurdia, had already been induced to desert to Salvador by the former Deputy Air Attaché at the US Embassy. Nor should the psychological impact of the threat of massive intervention by the world's strongest military power in a nation of just over three million people be minimized. US participation was significant enough, in that President Dwight Eisenhower, after his retirement, listed the defeat of 'communism' in Guatemala as one of the highlights of his administration.

But to say that Castillo Armas was only the tool of US foreign policy in Guatemala would be an exaggeration. He had proved his capabilities and sentiments in late 1950 when he attempted a military *coup* against the Arévalo Government and was condemned to death. His dramatic escape from prison put him high on the list of *macho* heroes for many Guatemalans. But we cannot ignore the fact that he had received much help and support from the United States and thus became a participant in the international cold-war battle between the US and Russia, between the 'international communist conspiracy' on one side and the 'democratic free world' on the other. He could not now ignore a moral debt of gratitude, nor, for that matter, his monetary obligations to the Government of the United States.

It would therefore be incorrect to suppose that his anti-communism was generated by US sponsorship of his movement, as well as to think that he was indifferent to the US's

8. Stebbings, Richard P., *The U.S. in World Affairs, 1954*. New York: Harper Brothers, published for the Council on Foreign Relations, 1956, p. 383.

applause for his anti-communism. He was obviously a firm advocate of, if not necessarily a believer in, the international conspiracy concept and a cold-war gladiator in his own right. His *Plan de Tegucigalpa* which had been formulated the preceding year in the capital city of Honduras as a general statement of his aims, indicated that the primary principle of his movement was the *desovietización*[9] of Guatemala. In one of his first statements as head of the new Government, he declared he would 'satisfy the needs of the people, destroying the arguments that communism uses to rob the world'.[10] Almost all of his legislation contains preambles denouncing the 'communism' of the Arbenz Government. All his public statements attempt to show that the failures of the preceding Government were such because they were communist-inspired and communist-directed, and that he would be successful by not only avoiding that route but vigorously closing it to others.

The danger of viewing all social reforms through the cold-war prism lay in believing that all measures passed by the Arbenz Government were bad because they were inspired by Russians for the purpose of turning the country over to Russia. Who actually believed this, and who merely stated it because it fitted his own purposes, is hard to tell. But the AGA (General Association of Agriculturalists) proclaimed it as their official doctrine. That it fitted their purposes there is no doubt. To prove to themselves, to all Guatemalans and to the world that the land-reform programme of Arbenz was an integral part of the international conspiracy, was the order of the day, every day.

There is no question that the members of AGA, along with UFCo., were the staunchest opponents of the Arbenz agrarian reform, as the ones most affected by it. They gave money, food and men to the Castillo Armas crusade, for they were the ones to benefit most by his success. After the Castillo

9. Azurdia, vol. 73, p. xii.　　　　10. DGAA, op. cit., p. 7.

Armas triumphal entry into Guatemala City (on a flight from El Salvador in the US Ambassador's plane) the AGA made a big fuss over sending food and supplies to the victims of the battles in Chiquimula.

It was a formidable array of opponents for Arbenz and backers for Castillo Armas: the US Government, the United Fruit Company, the General Association of Agriculturalists, the Catholic Church and every self-proclaimed anti-communist on the two continents. Emotions had been heated to boiling-point, and when Castillo Armas finally managed to take over, many people were not just looking to him for action, but were demanding it of him.

Despite the fact that Castillo Armas had said that 'In this crusade, there joined together men and women of all groups and social sectors; old fighters and young enthusiasts; professional people, workers, peasants, soldiers, farmers, businessmen and industrialists',[13] it is certain that his support was not as broad as that. His Army was estimated at 1,000 men, most of them political exiles living in Honduras, El Salvador and Nicaragua, plus the few peasants that he had picked up on his journey from the Honduran border.

Castillo Armas recognized the lack of support among the peasants and this is shown by the fact that one of the new Junta's first decrees was the cancellation of the voting franchise of illiterates. This effectively closed the door to seventy-two per cent of the Guatemalan population to participation in the Liberation Government, and it served as a warning to the peasants as to how Castillo Armas regarded them – certainly not as supporters.

Castillo Armas was in power only a few days when his régime had to face the fact that some of the landowners had already begun to take 'justice' into their own hands and reclaim their expropriated lands, as is evident from newspaper accounts. On 12 July, 'Anti-communism Day', in his

13. Azurdia, vol. 74, p. 42.

first public discourse, Castillo Armas found it necessary to say that:

> For national recuperation and for the establishment of social justice, the immediate collaboration of the *finqueros* and *patronos* is indispensable. It ought to be understood that the MLN cannot be a pretext for committing injustices and taking vengeance. Those who do it, far from co-operating to heal the country, are sabotaging our Movement. Neither the firing of workers nor the recuperation of lands can serve as a base for a just restructuring of the nation. To eradicate communism does not signify to persecute the worker and the honest peasant who in every case merits the protection of the Government.[14]

That such a stand was necessary is corroborated in the newspaper accounts of those difficult days. *El Imparcial* for 2 July states that 'seventeen workers were killed in Tiquisate by anti-communists'. 6 July reported a fight between 'four hundred communist Indians and anti-communist *ladinos* of San Juan Sacatepéquez in which seventeen Indians were killed and many wounded'. On 8 July the Minister of the Interior, Jorge A. Serrano, says that the jails are full of 'aroused peasant farmers', and on 13 July he announced that 4,000 'communists' were in jail throughout the country. *El Imparcial* of 9 July tells of the 'arrest warrants against the humble peasants of Progreso as communists'. Who was a communist and who was not, who had received a piece of land legally and who had not, who was being excessively vengeful for personal reasons and who was not, were the problems of those days and the Head of State was not finding it easy to solve them.

An interesting study was made at this time of a sampling of 250 prisoners in three Guatemala City jails from a total of 1,600 who were there accused of communism. The study was conducted immediately after the fall of the Arbenz Government by 'Stokes Newbold', who has since been identified as

14. Azurdia, vol. 73, p. 71.

the American anthropologist, Richard Newbold Adams, an authority on Guatemalan affairs. The study is called 'Receptivity to Communist Fomented Agitation in Rural Guatemala' [15] and accepts the basic premisses of the cold-war conflict:

This awareness of a new sociological potential had its distinct ideological aspects; the sociological changes themselves involved vast alterations in the traditional ways of thinking. It was probably of little importance to the rural people involved in this process whether it was done under one name or another; what was important was that there was, for the first time, a series of channels of communication and permissive activity between themselves and authority. That communism abused these channels to the point that a change in government was brought about through revolution is a tragedy of history.[16]

Actually the study proves just the opposite of 'communist abuse' of the channels of communication, but since the survey was obviously made with the co-operation of the Castillo Armas Government, perhaps these conclusions were meant to be proved by the investigation. One wonders why such an eminent scholar should use an alias for the study, which is actually very objective. In describing the political orientation of the interviewees, the author states:

I gradually started to believe that many, if not all, the persons who claimed ignorance of the issues actually knew little or nothing about them. Support for this is to be found in the fact that a person who claimed not to recognize the name of the communist labor leader, Víctor Manuel Gutiérrez, would also not recognize Mariano Rossell, the Archbishop of Guatemala. By the way in which some of the questions were answered, it was quite apparent they had actually not heard of the 'struggle between the classes',

15. 'Newbold, Stokes', 'Receptivity to Communist Fomented Agitation in Rural Guatemala', *Economic Development and Cultural Change*, vol. v, No. 4, 1957, pp. 338–361.

16. ibid., p. 361.

the 'dictatorship of the proletariat', the 'Communist Manifesto', and various other ideas and organizations mentioned. ... All the interviewers agreed that voluntary responses on the part of the interviewees consisted principally in comments to the effect that (1) they knew nothing; (2) they were poor, illiterate people; (3) they were in favor of the government in power; (4) they wanted only to return to their families and work, and (5) they were Catholics. The 'know nothingness' was apparent throughout the interviews. In response to a question as to whether they thought (an opinion, not a statement of fact) the new government would continue with the agrarian reform, the labor code and the labor unions, 67 per cent, 66 per cent and 84 per cent of the persons said they did not know; when pressed, most said they would not presume to say what the government would do.[17]

The author then goes on to show some of the ideas that the prisoners had picked up since 1944:

There is little doubt that some of those interviewed were not so concerned by the change in government as they were that they had landed in jail as a result. On the other hand, there were also seventy (and there may well have been more who felt it may not have been politic to give such an answer) who said that 'a government selected by the people' was an important part of a democratic country. This was the second most popular response to the question concerning the characteristics of such a country; 'protection of the poor' was first. In view of the common opinion that illiterate people are apolitical, it is of interest to note that 62 per cent of those who chose 'a government selected by the people' as a characteristic of a democracy, were illiterate. It would appear that the efforts of the post-1944 governments did have some effect in putting this idea into circulation.[18]

All in all the study proves to be a strong indication that there was little political manipulation or indoctrination of the peasants with communist ideology by the Arbenz Government.

Castillo Armas knew he had to undo Decree 900 because

17. 'Newbold, Stokes', op. cit., p. 352.   18. ibid.

this promise was the basis of his movement, but he didn't know exactly how to go about it. He had to move slowly enough to prevent organized resistance on the part of the peasants, and fast enough to avoid the precipitous actions of the landowners. On 20 July he made another appeal to the nation for calmness and to the landowners not to take justice into their own hands.[19]

But it seems that his efforts were not very successful.

The General Confederation of Workers compiled a list in February 1955 of names and places where murders had taken place in those first few weeks of the 'Liberation'.[20] It lists 217 persons and states that thirty-eight peasants were killed in Las Cruces, forty-nine peasants killed in Rio Shusto, eighteen killed in Los Cimientos, twenty-nine peasants killed in San Juan Sacatepéquez, two members of the agrarian committee killed in San Juan Acasaguastlán, and other labourers, truck drivers, train workers and soldiers murdered. It goes on to state that 'lists of people assassinated in other areas of the country are being compiled and will be published as soon as the data can be verified'.[21] The exact figures will never be known because the Government made sure that no open investigations were ever made.

It was in an effort to accomplish the mandate that he had been given in Honduras, to return the expropriated lands to their original owners while still avoiding chaos, that Castillo Armas promulgated Decree 31 before he was a month in office. It was meant to be 'translated into a gradual but firm repeal of the agrarian reform as institutionalized by Decree 900 of the national Congress'.[22] Decree 31 was enacted on 26 July 1954. It denies categorically that the agrarian-reform law produced any benefits but then it goes on to admit im-

19. El *Imparcial*, 20 July 1954.   20. Toriello, op. cit., p. 331.
21. ibid.
22. Monteforte Toledo, *Guatemala: Monografía Sociológica*, p. 437.

plicitly that there were benefits by stating in its first article that the peasants and agricultural workers who had received parcels, credits and other benefits from the application of the agrarian reform would remain under the same conditions and obligations, in possession, use and usufruct of the same, until a new agarian-reform law was enacted.

Perhaps the fairest index of the new Government's mentality would be to quote the preamble of the new agrarian decree. It reads as follows:

Considering that the agrarian-reform law promulgated by the previous Government bequeathed to the nation grave problems whose immediate solutions are demanded by all sectors of our society ... and that it converted the Guatemalan peasant into a political instrument by tying him to the Government and to the oligarchic groups within the official political party ... and that it overtly tried to destroy the institution of private property, upon which the social structure of Guatemala lies, producing a lack of confidence in the economic sector and the flight of capital necessary for the development of our resources; and despite offering to the peasants and Indians that by means of the agrarian reform they would obtain immediate benefits in the economic order and an improvement in their standard of living, the reality showed that instead of improving, their situation tended to become more and more precarious and anguishing ... and that the sectarian application of Decree 900 gave results radically opposed to an increase in our agricultural production, producing discontent in our labour relations and a sharp struggle between classes in the rural sector.[23]

Here is the rationale that was used by the new Government to begin whittling away at Decree 900 and its agrarian reform. It is doubtful that Castillo Armas believed all that is stated here, but it is certain that he wanted everyone else to believe it and hammered constantly at these points. They are worth examining.

23. *Revista de la Facultad de Ciencias Jurídicas y Sociales*, op. cit., p. 803.

There is no question that the attitude of the Arbenz Government had produced a lack of confidence in the economic sector that resulted in the flight of capital of the wealthy, especially foreign capital. It is also obvious that the Decree was never meant to stimulate harmony between the peasants and landowners, since their interests were diametrically opposed. It was blatantly untrue that 'it converted the Guatemalan peasant into a political instrument' to a degree that did not exist before nor exists now as a result of the Liberation Government's measures.

The peasants' economic situation is just too precarious for them to maintain any marked degree of political independence. Their vote continues to be bought and sold with impunity, often for a package of cigarettes. For this to be done by a government for a piece of land, cannot be taken as a serious indictment of the Arbenz Government.[24] Could Castillo Armas's revocation of the voting franchise to the unlettered be considered any less sectarian?

To claim that the institution of private property would have been destroyed by Decree 900 is also untrue. The Decree did allow for the continuance of private property up to seventy acres and even more, if such lands were producing. It also allowed for the development of a new landowning class, awarding ownership titles to more than a quarter of the recipients who benefited by the Decree. To say that the right of private property is not absolute, and one that could be curtailed by the Government, would be more exact. No one claims, for instance, that the conversion of fifty per cent of Mexico's lands to the public sector in the formation of *ejidos*

24. According to John D. Powell, the function of the Venezuelan land reform for the Government in power was also to gain the votes of the peasants. This system had a 'political payoff to the parties in the form of rural votes and campesino payoff in the form of goods and services provided in the government's agrarian reform program' (Preliminary Report on the Federación Campesina de Venezuela, Land Tenure Center: University of Wisconsin, 1964, mimeo, p. 71).

destroyed the institution of private property in that country. We think that the key phrase in this accusation would be the reference 'upon which the social structure of Guatemala lies'. In preceding chapters of this study, we have shown that the whole socio-political and economic system of the country depends upon a small landowning class and a large landless class. The destruction of this relationship was bound to effect basic changes, and indeed was the very reason for the law's enactment and implementation. If Castillo Armas was protesting the destruction of the *status quo* as it had existed in Guatemala since the arrival of the Spaniards, he was correct in his assertion. To equate this to the disappearance of the 'institution of private property' is quite another thing.

Arbenz did not offer the peasants and Indians 'immediate benefits in the economic order and an improvement in their standard of living'. Indeed, any student of human nature knows that such fundamental changes as those envisioned by his law, as well as the new tensions produced by its implementation, could hardly have resulted in immediate benefits. The new landowners had to learn many skills and acquire management techniques that had never been demanded of them as migrant labourers or subsistence farmers. John Powelson says:

It is scarcely possible to carry out any change in land tenure without adverse effects on production. ... The upheavals of any agrarian reform are such that farmers must grit their teeth and expect early losses.[25]

This is an obvious consequence of any drastic programme such as that implemented by Arbenz. It really should not surprise anyone that Decree 900 could have produced, according to the preamble of Decree 31, 'results radically opposed to an increased agricultural production'. Yet its effects were

25. Powelson, John P., *Latin America: Today's Economic and Social Revolution*. New York: McGraw-Hill, 1964, p. 65.

not very devastating, and in many cases were quite the opposite.

The legal effect of the new law was not to abrogate Arbenz' law but merely to stop any further execution of it, while giving the landowners the permission to begin turning the clock back. It declared that all expropriations made under Article 91 of Decree 900 were invalid. It was this particular article that had caused so much *furor* by giving the Government the power to expropriate in their totality and without indemnization the lands of those owners 'who oppose the application of the agrarian reform by violent or subversive means'.[26] It was felt that 'subversion' was a term with too indefinite a meaning and could apply to anyone who merely protested.

The law returned to the original owners 'all dwellings built at their expense' and gave all those who suffered expropriation of lands the right to appeal on the decision to the newly created 'Dirección General de Asuntos Agrarios' (Department of Agricultural Affairs). Nathan Whetten says that on the basis of this, 'in most instances, decisions were made favorable to the landlords. The agrarian recipients were gradually removed and the land returned to the original owners.'[27] He concisely notes where the Government's heart is:

In some cases, agrarians who felt that they had received the lands in good faith from the previous government, resisted evacuation and were removed by force. Some observers declare that during the Arbenz regime the government was invariably on the side of the peasants and workers in any dispute involving the landlords; in the post-Arbenz period, just the reverse was true.[28]

This was bound to be true since under the Arbenz Government the agrarian committees did not have landowner repre-

26. Azurdia, vol. 71, p. 30.
27. Whetten, *Guatemala*, op. cit., p. 166.   28. ibid.

sentation, while under the Castillo Armas Government, following Guatemala's historical pattern, it was the peasants who had no representation. Decree 31 declared that the Departmental Agrarian Committees would be composed of the Governor of the Department, who is a presidential appointee, the Mayor and the first *síndico* (trustee) of the departmental capital. The latter two would be elected officials, but almost certainly members of the landowning class, due to the population make-up of of departmental capitals.

The new Decree stated that any recourse against a decision of the DGAA had to be made to the Minister of *Gobernación* (the Interior) and beyond him there was no recourse. Since Miguel Ortíz Passarelli was Minister of the Interior and the owner of huge properties in Alta Verapaz, some of which had been affected by Decree 900, it was obvious on whose side his loyalties lay. So, though Arbenz had been roundly criticized in international circles, namely the United States, for not allowing appeals on expropriations to be made to anyone other than himself, Castillo Armas effectively blocked any objective recourse to the revocations executed by his Government by giving Ortíz Passarelli (winner of fraudulent presidential elections in 1957) the same power.

The same Decree also abolished the two laws of 'forced rental' of the two previous governments and gave the tenants until 31 March 1955 to get off the lands. This was so that they would have sufficient time to bring in the crops that had already been planted. A number of times it is stated in the law that its implications must be explained verbally to the peasants affected by it. Such foresight recognized that many peasants would not understand the new Government's attitude after ten years of official recognition as full-fledged citizens.

It was obvious that the new law was almost exclusively negative in its propositions. It was clear what this meant for the future of the Guatemalan peasant. Under the Liberation Government, he began by losing his vote, and now he was losing his new-found lands. Whetten, with the ring of prophecy, said:

There are many campesinos who received lands under the agrarian law of 1952 only to have them taken away again after the fall of the Arbenz government. They might be receptive to any revolutionary scheme that promises to restore to them the land of which they were the proud possessors for such a short time.[29]

It was perhaps with a similar glance at the future that Castillo Armas did offer a hope of sorts to the *campesino* in what he calls the 'fundamental principles' of Decree 31, even as he must have recognized the obvious contradiction of these principles with the articles of the law itself. In the first one, he states:

Every Guatemalan has the right that the land necessary to insure his economic subsistence and that of his family, be given to him and fully guaranteed as his private property. Such property so created by virtue of this norm shall be considered as family patrimony, and shall enjoy all protection and support.[30]

He thereupon indicates how and where this would be done:

By opening up those regions of the national territory that have remained at the margins of the national economy for lack of communications, irrigation, healthful conditions and inhabitants. Consequently, it will be a fundamental policy of this Government ... an intense colonization of the national territory.[31]

It was clear that he was talking about the Petén. The AGA had been vociferously demanding such a programme ever

29. Whetten, *Guatemala*, op. cit., p. 356.
30. *Revista de la Facultad de Ciencias Jurídicas*, op. cit., p. 804.
31. ibid.

since Arévalo started talking about agrarian reform, even though the latter's attempt at Poptún had shown the costs to be prohibitive.

The third fundamental principle of this Decree does recognize that there are huge tracts of idle lands in private hands and that something should be done about it: 'consequently, the government will take every opportune measure necessary to reduce it'.[32]

Perhaps the most humane principle of all, but one that must be regarded as demagogic in view of the cancellation of the two laws of forced rental, is that which declares:

Every type of gratuitous labour in the fields, wounds the Guatemalan as a free man in the most profound depths of his human dignity; workers will never be obliged to fulfil any contract of work or duty in exchange for compensation of services of any kind.[33]

Despite Castillo Armas's criticisms of Decree 900 and the man who preceded him in the presidency of Guatemala, Powelson was able to say:

The Reform Law of 1952 was based on the Constitution of 1945, introduced after the overthrow of the Dictator Ubico and the restoration of a popular government. The Agrarian Law provided for the liquidation of feudal properties, prohibition of all forms of servitude and distribution of lands to the landless. It was no more radical than what would be acceptable today under the Alliance for Progress.[34]

Thus it was that Castillo Armas began the legal and physical process of *desovietización* of Guatemala. These are not very bright days in the history of that nation nor of the new Government.

On 20 August, three weeks after the first agrarian decree was issued, the new Government promulgated its second

32. ibid.   33. ibid.   34. Powelson, op. cit., p. 55.

agrarian law. If anyone had any doubts where the new régime was going and what its intentions were, this law effectively served to enlighten the nation once and for all. It called the rehabilitation of the National Plantations into the patrimony of the nation. The reasons for such a move are stated clearly in the law itself, but again Castillo Armas was exaggerating in his attempts to make Arbenz look bad and himself look good.

Decree 57 begins more or less with the same broadsides that all the other laws of the Liberation Government contained:

Considering that the partitioning of the National Fincas ... favoured only that sector that was most militant in its communism and created a state of discrimination among the *campesinos*, who in their majority have categorically shown their willingness to return to a system of salaries ... also produced negative results in fomenting anarchy and consequently brought about a reduction in the national production and the destruction of the enterprise as an economic unit, the majority of the plots being found in total abandonment ... and that the goods of the nation ought to bring general benefits to everybody and not go astray for motives of partisan politics, as occurred in the application of the agrarian-reform law.[35]

But not everyone believed what was said, even if they had to obey these decrees.

In order to give credence to this infamy, the dictatorship had the audacity to deduce that the *campesinos* in their majority 'wished to go back to a system of salaries' and in order to aid in this fallacy, proceeded to take away the plots of land on the National Fincas that the Government of the Revolution had distributed, and along with them took away 'their movable property, their ripening harvests, animals, houses, constructions, installations, vehicles, machinery, seeds, fertilizers, tools, equipment of whatever type, products in storage and all other goods'. All this in exchange for being 'liberated from international communism',

35. *Revista de la Facultad de Ciencias Jurídicas*, op. cit., p. 812.

the peasant has the exciting prospect that the DGAA, on its own judgement will give them in 'concrete cases' some compensation for the work and improvements that they had effected.[36]

This was written by Guillermo Toriello, who, as Foreign Minister under the Arbenz Government, had spent months in the United Nations trying to mobilize action against the US's arming of Castillo Armas in Honduras.

And even as a member of Castillo Armas's administration, temporary Minister of *Gobernación*, Jorge A. Serrano, in speaking to reporters of the number of people in jail, admits that very few of them, if any, were communists.[37] It is difficult even to this day to imagine any group of Indians anywhere in the country who would know what communism is. Certainly the US Ambassador to Guatemala didn't know what it was when he testified before the Senate Subcommittee:

AMBASSADOR PEURIFOY: Communism, in my opinion, is a religion, Mr Feighan. I don't think there is any doubt about that. And anyone who thinks it is a theory –

CONGRESSMAN FEIGHAN (Ohio): It is a religion. It was originated in hell, with the assistance of Satan and all the evil forces.

PEURIFOY: That is a better definition than mine.[38]

It seems that the new Government judged as communists those who were most in favour of the land-reform programme – on such a basis, it is fair to assume that three quarters of the total population were also 'communists'.

It is difficult to believe that the peasants did want to go back to the 'system of salaries', as Castillo Armas states in the preamble of this law. It would not have been difficult to convince them that their best interests lay in being paid a salary, in view of the new Government's attitudes toward

36. Toriello, op. cit., p. 202.
37. El *Imparcial*, 8 and 13 July 1954.
38. House Hearings, op. cit., p. 131.

'agrarianists'. It is evident that these people were very much afraid of what the Government would do to them, as is shown by the fact that many had already fled, leaving their plots in 'total abandonment'. But to maintain that their best economic and social interests actually were procured by taking back the lands from them and returning the people to dependence on salaries from the Government, flies in the face of Guatemala's history.

There is no question that there were difficulties on the National Fincas. Many of the *colonos* thought that the *fincas* should be exclusively theirs and resented the intrusion of the newcomers, some of whom received more and better lands than the *colonos* themselves. Disputes broke out, and these perhaps represented the 'anarchy' that the new law refers to.

The real crux of the problem, though, lay in 'the reduction of national production and the destruction of the enterprise as an economic unit'. During Arévalo's presidency, these plantations were producing as much as eight million *quetzales* for the national budget in 1947 and though it dropped to five million *quetzales* by 1950, this represented from ten to fifteen per cent of the total Government finances. This was just a little bit too much money for Castillo Armas to lose. Arbenz may have considered taxing the country's oligarchy to replace this source of income, but this was something that Castillo Armas could not consider doing.

This law declared that all *fincas* be returned to the national patrimony no matter in what form or to whom they had been given, be they individuals or co-operatives.[39] It also stated that all the belongings of the *fincas*, such as those mentioned by Toriello, also be returned, and that the peasants be paid for any work or improvements that they had made, since the harvests would belong to the Government. It was recognized that injustices would be committed in carrying out this law.

39. *Revista de la Facultad de Ciencias Jurídicas*, op. cit., p. 813.

The juridical personality of all co-operatives existing on these plantations was cancelled, while giving the ex-members the choice of staying on and working for a salary like any other worker. It is perhaps from this time on that the official toleration and unofficial disdain of co-operatives dates. In many quarters of Guatemala, to this day, co-operative is synonymous with communism.[40]

This decree had a somewhat ominous tone when it stated that the law was 'of public order and has the character of a security measure',[41] which means that arrests could be made and individuals held without the usual right of bond and hearing if the Government so decided.

It was about this time that many observers were becoming aware of the fact that the Liberation Government was not only anti-communist but was using this label as an umbrella to protect itself from the fall-out that was bound to come in its attempts to return the country to pre-1945.

It was one thing for the Junta to return expropriated properties to UFCo. and powerful national interests. It was quite another to take back even the Government's own plantations. If the workers on these farms wanted it that way, perhaps that is the way it should have been. But why, then, did this law need to be considered 'of public order and a security measure', if everybody agreed it was the best thing to do? It seems at this point that Castillo Armas was more interested in fighting 'communism' than in legislating for the welfare of the poverty-stricken of the nation.

40. One of the authors was instrumental in the founding of more than a dozen co-operatives, including the National Federation of Credit Unions of Guatemala. It often takes more than a year to get official recognition of a co-operative's statutes, while Government bureaucrats examine the purposes of the co-operative and the backgrounds of the prospective members.
41. *Revista de la Facultad de Ciencias Jurídicas*, op. cit., p. 814.

The dissolution of the co-operatives was a step consistent with the policies of the new Government. All worker and peasant organizations were suspect. One of the earliest creations of the Liberation Government was a 'National Committee for the Defence Against Communism', whose job it was to ferret out 'communists' and 'communist sympathizers'. This was meant to take the witch-hunting activities out of the hands of landowners, who had been taking the administration of 'justice' unto themselves, and put it into the hands of the Government. The labour movement had been the principal object of attack of the landowners and industrialists. The seven leaders of the United Fruit Company's Labor Union had been some of the first to be murdered,[42] and they were followed by many others. Partly to forestall repetition of these incidents and partly to rid the country of its 'subversive' elements, before the month of July was out, Castillo Armas had ordered the Confederation of Workers (CGTG) and the Confederation of Peasants (CNCG) to be disbanded. He cancelled the legal registrations of 533 unions and amended the labour code so as to make effective unionization impossible.[43] Two of the first unions to be dissolved were SETUFCO and SETCAG, both of which were worker syndicates of the United Fruit Company. The Company's assistance in the overthrow of Arbenz was being rewarded.

A few days after the National Fincas were returned to the patrimony of the nation, another decree was promulgated, under the title 'Preventive Penal Law Against Communism'. It was this law, called 'savage' by the editors of *Christian Century* magazine,[44] that legislated the death penalty for a series of 'crimes' that could be construed as 'sabotage'. It was a concept broad enough to include labour organization and strike activities. Under its umbrella, even those laws left

42. El Imparcial, 2 July 1954.
43. Huizer, op. cit., p. 207.

standing in the labour code could not be effectively enforced by worker pressure. Minimum wages were effectively abolished, the work week was again extended to forty-eight hours and paid vacations were terminated. Firing for 'political reasons' was encouraged and no indemnization was granted for such a loss of employment. A report made by the United-Nations-sponsored International Labour Organization in 1965 mentioned that only sixteen peasant unions existed in Guatemala at that time, portraying a 'deficient and almost non-existent syndical organization'.[45]

Castillo Armas's persecution of those who had participated in the reforms of Arbenz, or who had worked in rural unions, resulted in passive resistance in large areas of the rural sector.[46] This passive resistance is translated even today into peasant distrust for any reform programme in many parts of Guatemala. Union organizing is often as feared by the workers themselves as it is by the landowners.

Other laws governing the agrarian situation were enacted. In September a decree was promulgated which effectively terminated the operations of the National Agrarian Bank as a source of credit to small farmers who otherwise had inadequate security.[47]

By December 1954, when through Decree 170 the landowners were again permitted to pay their workers by lending them small plots of lands for their seasonal crops, there was no question that Castillo Armas would fulfil all his commitments to the plantation owners. In order to make the law seem more palatable, the proprietors of extensive holdings were told that they had the 'obligation of providing gratui-

45. Oficina Internacional del Trabajo, *Informe al Gobierno de Guatemala de la Misión Interagencias sobre Colonización e Integración de Poblaciones Indígenas.* Geneva: OIT, 1965, pp. 46–9.
46. Huizer, op. cit., p. 207.
47. *Revista de la Facultad de Ciencias Jurídicas,* op. cit., p. 817.

tously that land to which their *colonos* were accustomed'.[48] With the removal of the minimum-wage enforcement, the fact that the lands were given gratuitously had no meaning whatsoever, since the wage agreement reached was again governed by the mutual understanding between owner and labourer. The lands lent to the *colonos* would again play a major role in determining such understandings, 'maintaining at the same time the workers' dependence on the landowner'.[49] The law also stated that in no case would such lands be the object of expropriation. The assurance was superfluous.

An interesting insight is given in the preamble of this law into Castillo Armas's claims against Arbenz and the effects of his own policies:

> Considering that the agrarian reform and other dispositions dictated by the previous régime in relation to agriculture, ruined totally the national agricultural production, causing a positive and evident injury to the economy of the country . . . the alarming and progressive decline of the production of articles of prime necessity in the Republic, is one of the most felt effects of the above mentioned dispositions, as is shown by the decrease, since 1950, of four million quintals of corn, which constitutes the staple of our people's diet. . . .[50]

The part that is blatantly inaccurate in this statement is the figure of a four-million-quintal decline. In 1950 the Guatemalan harvest yielded 8,217,000 quintals of corn; in 1952 it increased to 10,711,00 quintals; in 1953 it descended to 9,400,000 quintals and then in 1954 to just under 9,000,000 quintals, but still far above the 1950 yield. However, in 1955 the total dropped almost one million quintals from what it had been in 1954, and continued to drop further in 1956.[51]

48. Azurdia, vol. 73, p. 170.

49. CIDA, op. cit., p. 46.

50. Azurdia, vol. 73, p. 170.

51. *Guatemala en Cifras*. Guatemala: Dirección General de Estadisticas, 1944–1957.

It seems that the Liberation Government saw what was happening to the corn production because of its own policies, and thought it could blame this decrease on its predecessor. The mistake that Castillo Armas made was in miscalculating the loss at four million quintals, which would have been of famine proportions, instead of the one-million-quintal loss that actually occurred.

The four Departments that were most affected by the agrarian reform, Escuintla, Alta Verapaz, Izabal, and Quiché, all experienced marked increases of corn production in 1953–4 over the preceding years, and big drops the following year, the first of Castillo Armas's régime.[52]

The Liberation Government had been in power six months as the year 1954 came to a close. It had accomplished what it had set out to do, that is, stop the 'sovietization' of the nation. It had done this mainly by reversing the land reform policies of the previous Government. Now it was time to look towards some positive measures of its own, something to combat the social problems that had been building up for centuries. The impetus of a negative movement that is only anti-something is not sufficient to justify the existence of any government. It was now a case of producing, or turning the government over to civilians, something Castillo Armas was obviously not prepared to do.

In October 1954 the Junta had asked for a demonstration of popular backing by holding a plebiscite and giving Guatemala's literate electorate the opportunity to say either yes or no to the new caudillo's accession to the presidency. Journalists estimated that no more than 400 negative votes were cast out of a total of 470,000,[53] but what methods they used for making such calculations is not known. Certainly it was not safe to admit publicly that one was voting against Castillo Armas.

52. ibid.　　53. Johnson, Kenneth, op. cit., p. 193.

CHAPTER 7

Stones or Bread?

Would anyone of you, fathers, give his son a stone,
when he asks you for bread?
Or would you give him a snake, when he asks you for a fish?

MATTHEW vii, 9

On 30 December 1954 the first step was taken towards a positive programme of land legislation drawn up according to the principles of the Liberation Movement. A commission was established to study the situation and present suggestions for a new agrarian law.

The new commission was to be made up of five members, picked by five different entities: the Ministry of Agriculture, the DGAA, the AGA, the banking institutions, and the National University of San Carlos. The first two were therefore appointees of the Government, the next two were appointees of big money interests, and the last one can be considered a neutral party. The neutral member of the commission, the appointee of the University of San Carlos, can be regarded as the only one of the five who might represent the interests of the peasant and not be threatened by what was done by the previous régime. There is no question where AGA and the banking institutions stood on land reform. The Ministry of Agriculture and the DGAA were the Government and cannot be viewed as any less anti-communist, any less anti-Arbenz, or any less anti-Decree-900, than Castillo Armas himself.

The *Acuerdo* (agreement) that establishes this commission is also interesting in that it lays down the 'fundamental principles' that will govern the MLN land reform :

The land will be given as private property; technical and financial assistance will be given to those who receive lands; the under-populated areas of the country will be converted into centers of agricultural labor, by means of internal migration; so that there be an effective increase and betterment of the national agricultural production; that the idle lands of the government be justly distributed; that agricultural zones be opened by means of new roads or the betterment of the means of communication already existing; that the latifundios be taxed in a reasonable and progressive way so as to effect their disappearance in the least possible time; that with the intention of forming new agricultural and cattle units, long term credits be given at low interest; that in the political–social order true harmony be established for the sake of the national welfare.[1]

As can be seen, these principles are the basis for an adequate programme of colonization, not of land reform. The problem is that even here we must question the sincerity of the Castillo Armas Government since they were obviously ignoring the socio-economic and political reasons that have caused the *latifundismo* in the first place, and will continue to propagate it since the Government has accepted the basic premises of such a social system. This, despite the fact that they admit that the *latifundios* must 'be taxed in a reasonable and progressive way so as to effect their disappearance in the least possible time'.

After more than a year of work the agrarian commission presented its findings to the newly elected Congress. On 25 February 1956, Decree 559, the Agrarian Statute, was

1. Johnson, Kenneth, op. cit., p. 494.

promulgated. It confirmed the DGAA as an official governmental entity, replacing once and for all the now defunct 'Departamento Agrario Nacional' and entrusting it with the realization of the new agrarian legislation of the Liberation.

The DGAA, because of the National Liberation Movement, substituted the ex-DAN. Its efforts since that time are too many to enumerate, but they can be synthesized in two fundamental aspects: first, liquidation of the policy of attack in the rural area, which in the name of Decree 900 found ample and irresponsible support from the Government; second, the creation of new lines, conveniently harmonized, of an adequate agrarian policy. In both of these aspects, it has worked with determination, counting on the collaboration of diverse entities and persons, and has come a long way on these points: it is about to liquidate the situation inherited and there is now in progress a new programme that, without going to the extreme of despoliation, is realizing the rehabilitation of the peasant within a framework of legality that is his best guarantee for both the present and the future.[2]

What made the Castillo Armas Government's policies more legal than the Arbenz reform is not indicated. On 10 August 1954, after Castillo Armas's accession to power, the Supreme Court had declared Decree 900 constitutional on the basis of the Constitution of 1945. Perhaps this is the reason that Castillo Armas felt obliged to suspend the 1945 Constitution and why he asked Congress to enact a new one. Only on this basis was the new agrarian Statute 559 legal and constitutional while the old one was not.

Since the 'inherited situation' was about to be liquidated we might expect a more positive attitude on the part of the Liberation Government. In this light, Decree 559 states:

The DGAA, consequently, has all the attributes, both sufficient and final, to permit it to develop with efficiency the principles contained in the new agrarian statute which, in synthesis,

2. DGAA, *Tierra en Propiedad*, chapter 1, p. 1.

has as its object to effect a better distribution of the land and a better use of the same for the benefit of all.[3]

It represents progress to hear the Liberation Government talk about a 'better distribution of the land and a better use of the same for the benefit of all' after hearing its negative pronouncements for almost two years. With the above statement, we can say that Guatemala had been brought through a full circle in little over ten years and was now back to where it started when Arévalo took over in 1945, as far as land problems were concerned. At last, Castillo Armas was going to attempt 'land reform' himself.

The new Decree, despite the propaganda that the Government made to the contrary, was not a revolutionary law. It established three types of lands where the agrarian reform would be effected.

The zones of agrarian development will be established preferably in large unused extensions of land as the following: (a) unused lands that are the property of the nation; (b) the national plantations that have been exploited in a defective or deficient manner; (c) private property that the State may acquire by whatever means after the promulgation of this law.[4]

The private properties to be used for this programme were certainly not going to be the objects of expropriation. The Government would acquire them by what Monteforte Toledo calls '*la vía persuasiva*'[5] and this persuasion was to be effected by taxing idle lands out of existence, forcing the owner to either sell or cultivate. *Time* magazine refers to this taxing proposition as the 'most revolutionary part of the law'.[6] It goes on to say that 'though low, the tax strikes hard at the principle of holding land not for farming, but as an inflation-proof investment'.[7] It also states that if the lands remain idle, the tax will increase by twenty-five per cent the following

3. ibid.   4. ibid., p. 92.
5. Monteforte Toledo, *Guatemala*, op. cit. p. 437.
6. *Time* Magazine, 12 March 1956, p. 40.   7. ibid.

year and keep going up until after five years the tax will be one hundred per cent or twice as much as the original calculation.[8] Powelson, in describing the pitfalls of using taxation as a means of enforcing land reform, states:

One method is to tax idle land at a higher rate than productive land. A major difficulty, however, is the definition of productive land. How much of a crop does a landowner have to plant in order to avoid the high idle-land rate? Will a few stalks of corn scattered here and there be enough? If so, the introduction of this tax would soon lead to the extinction of all land registered as idle but not to increased production. This problem should not be minimized by the suggestion of certain criteria or controls. They will have to be pervasive, and rigid inspection will be necessary to see that lands are properly categorized. Often the difference between idle and productive will be a matter of opinion, and underpaid tax-assessors may be susceptible to monetary persuasion. ... Finally, the implementation of a land tax will be no better than the tax machinery with which the country is equipped. So long as the tradition of tax paying is not established, land surveys not made, books and records not adequately kept, and officials subject to bribery, taxation will not be an effective instrument of agrarian reform.[9]

The first 'loop-hole' provided to the landowners was contained in the law where it gave them the right to classify their own lands. Gerardo Guinea, a defender of the Government and its policy, in reference to this privilege granted to the landowners, says:

One might believe that such a measure, because of the special circumstance of leaving it to the responsibility of the farm owner to classify his own lands, lends itself to fraud and trickery designed to avoid the tax he is obliged to pay. But no. The DGAA will make a study of the data contained in the sworn declarations and will verify them if it deems it necessary.[10]

He does not state how the DGAA will judge a statement as

8. ibid.   9. Powelson, op. cit., p. 60.
10. Guinea, op. cit., p. 86.

false, and it is doubtful that this entity had the money, man-power or will to do anything about it anyway. It is a fact that Guatemalan landowners have known for generations how to skirt or avoid the tax laws, aided by the lack of any real tax-collecting system or agency, that made the possibility of taxing the large plantations out of existence highly unlikely. Even to this day, Guatemala lacks the good land survey neces-sary for anything but minimal taxation.

The lands that were to be given the agrarians from national lands or *fincas* were to be paid for over a period of ten years. The price was to 'be decided by DGAA and in no case was it to be greater than the price, at the time of concession, that would correspond to other lands of the same quality in the same area'.[11] That is to say that the new owners would have to pay for their lands the market price which, according to economists, is inflated beyond its real value in all Latin America because of its almost unique role as insurance against inflation in the economy.

The Government describes the types of land-holdings that the new law will create:

(a) economic-type farms and (b) subsistence-type farms. The farms of an economic-type classification are those that, because of their extension, offer the possibility of becoming farms of great productive capacity. It is thought that the peasant who receives a farm of this type ought to have a true dedication to agricultural activity since the land will demand from him and his family a maximum effort. The results will repay him abundantly as he makes himself into an economically independent rural owner. The subsistence farms are those that will have an undetermined area that will always be smaller than the economic-type farms. These will be given to peasants who have incomes from small manual industries or salaries that they receive as labourers in some enterprise. It is, in sythesis, a complement to the economy of the rural worker.[12]

11. ibid., p. 94.   12. DGAA, *Tierra en Propiedad*, chapter 4, p. 1.

It is obvious that the second type of land-holdings created by the law are nothing else but *minifundios* for a continuation of subsistence farming. It is hypocritical of the Government to attempt to explain them away by saying that they are only meant to supplement the peasant's income. It has been shown that it is because of a lack of any real income, other than insufficient amounts from farming, that the vast majority of the population lives in poverty. To give landless peasants a less than subsistence plot does not eradicate the poverty and misery of the beneficiary.

The law also clearly states that the recipients of the new lands will be Guatemalans, between the ages of eighteen and sixty, mentally and physically capable, and not already possessing lands that allow them and their families a decorous subsistence livelihood.

Since the Government recognized that the people fulfilling these qualifications were many more than the lands to be given, preference would be given to those people who fulfil the greatest number of the following conditions:

(a) those who have farming or husbandry experience or knowledge; (b) those who live in the area or a neighbouring area of the agrarian zone to be partitioned; (c) those who habitually live in the rural areas; (d) those who have families that are dependent upon them, giving preference to those with small children; (e) those who have tools or animals or other things that would facilitate the exploitation of the land.[13]

The selection of the beneficiaries according to these qualifications seems justified with the possible exception of 'those who live in the area or neighbouring area of the agrarian zone'. People living in an area where large extensions of land go untouched are not apt to be as badly off as those living up in the highlands. It is the Indians who have been forced back up into the mountains with only the most miserable plots to

13. Guinea, op. cit., p. 111.

sustain themselves who are most in need of lands. And this provision eliminated them.

One other aspect of this Decree that we might examine is the fifth chapter, where it states : 'For this reason, the DGAA will answer directly to the President of the Republic and its jurisdiction will extend to the whole of the national territory.'[14]

It seems that Arbenz's idea of having the agrarian policies of the country under his own eye and control had not been lost on Castillo Armas. There was here no accusation of unconstitutionality, as there could not be. The new law was written to conform to the new Constitution. Castillo Armas need not be afraid of submitting any disputes that might result from the application of this law to the judiciary, because its provisions effectively looked out for everyone's interests but those of the landless peasant. The danger of a peasant taking any landowner or the Government to Court to force the State to protect his rights as a citizen was minimal, if not absolutely non-existent.

Thus it was that Guinea could, on this basis, make the comparison between Decree 900 and Decree 559 :

The big difference that exists between one and the other 'instrument' is immediately obvious. Juridically, the Agrarian Statute is delineated by the constitutional precepts that guarantee respect for private property. The President of the Republic is no longer the supreme organ of the law, but rather the authorities who, by constitutional right, have the obligation to watch out for the application and observance of the laws of the executive branch.[15]

Nevertheless, Castillo Armas did make the agrarian policies his special domain by determining that the DGAA would answer directly to him.

A few weeks after the law was promulgated, Castillo

14. ibid., p. 87.   15. ibid., p. 82.

Armas appeared before the Congress, on 14 March 1956, to render his first 'state of the Union' message to his new colleagues in government. The speech he delivered at that time was a ten-thousand-word document, of which less than three hundred words were devoted to the explanation of his agrarian policies. They are worth quoting here since they are so concise:

The third phase of the plan is for the effective development of agriculture and cattle, and although it is obvious that such development ought to be the concern of private enterprise, the Government has the obligation to create an environment in the economic, social and institutional orders that is conducive to the work of individuals. With such a concept, State action in favour of agriculture and cattle raising is directed toward technical assistance and the services of colonization and the distribution of lands, without underrating the aid of credit on the part of the Government banks and the stabilizing of prices. The colonization and distribution of lands are aimed at giving farms to 25,000 families, with an extension of twenty hectares of useful land each. Credit will be obtained by capitalizing the National Agrarian Bank, INFOP and the National Mortgage Bank with fifteen million *quetzales* that the Government will give them. Finally, five million *quetzales* will be assigned to begin the control of prices of grains, in order to prevent extreme fluctuations. The total investments to promote agriculture and cattle raising that are assigned to this plan are forty-two million *quetzales*.[16]

Special emphasis was being put on the amounts of money and technical aid to be invested in colonization, as well it might be. It was obvious to everyone who had thought about the project that this activity was to be a very costly endeavour. Castillo Armas was not afraid to face the prospect since he could count on his good friends to the North to supply him with monetary and technical help, an advantage that was never available to his two predecessors.

16. Azurdia, vol. 75, p. 20.

The main vehicle for US technical assistance in the programme was the Interamerican Cooperative Service for Agriculture (SCIDA) that had been established in Guatemala during the Second World War when Roosevelt was trying to line up opposition to the Germans. It disappeared under Arévalo and Arbenz but was revived in order to aid Castillo Armas carry out his new programme. By the end of 1956 its personnel had been expanded to include twenty specialists from the US and 215 Guatemalans.[17] Under succeeding governments, the programme ran into difficulty when the Ministry of Agriculture 'made repeated assertions that the US was dominating the programme and ignoring the wishes of Guatemalans in some of the projects'.[18]

Meanwhile the International Cooperation Administration (ICA) was funnelling money into the colonization programme as fast as it could be absorbed. By the time Castillo Armas presented his plans to Congress, the US had already given him $2,400,000 for land resettlement[19] and during the succeeding five years a total of $12 million was expended on the programme.[20]

The new law made provision for avoiding the re-absorption of lands given to the peasants by contrary agrarian pressures that tend to reconcentrate the newly acquired property in a few hands, as had repeatedly occurred in other moments of Guatemala's modern history. This was assured by denying the beneficiary the right 'to mortgage, alienate or divide in any manner, for twenty-five years, the lands that he had received'.[21] This, of course, was an excellent idea, meant to guarantee the children of the beneficiary the *patrimonio familiar* that the large landowners had always been so adept at swallowing up. The Government's good resolution to protect the small-holding lasted until the end of June 1957,

17. Whetten, op. cit., p. 171.   18. ibid.
19. *Time* Magazine, 12 March 1956, p. 40.
20. Hildebrand, op. cit., p. 358.   21. Guinea, op. cit., p. 95.

when a law was passed that gave the new landowners the right to sell their farms for 'industrial purposes, paid for by shares in the Company or in cash'.[22]

So it was that the Liberation government recognized that 'the greatest need ... is a vigorous program of land colonization, reclamation and resettlement. It is argued that families needing land should be colonized on land not in use, instead of disrupting the productive enterprises that are already in operation'.[23]

The figures on the distributions vary among different authors and can become very complicated. The CIDA report gives the figures that seem to be the most faithful to what actually happened. There are three types of holdings worth noting and a fourth, which is included in the statistics, but which was never meant to remedy the agricultural situation, consisting of 68 titles to urban plots averaging ·11 hectares each.

The CIDA work classifies the three agricultural types of holdings as: agrarian zones, microplots and communities.[24] The first category, agrarian zones, is the colonization programme about which much propaganda was made by all the friends of the Liberation Government as they contrasted it with the Arbenz programme. This was the most promising of the three types and its objectives can be summed up as comprised of four stages: (1) redistribution of landed property; (2) credit for an adequate exploitation of the redistributed land; (3) technical assistance; and (4) social assistance that may attain higher material and moral levels of life.

With such ends in view, 2,814 families received landholdings that averaged 19·2 hectares (5·1 acres) in the agrarian zones, qualifying them in this category. There is little record of financial credits being given to these peasants that would

22. Azurdia, vol. 76, Decree 1187, Article 89.
23. Whetten, op. cit., p. 166.   24. CIDA, op. cit., p. 49.

enable them to obtain the designs held out for them by the Government. In fact, in later years it was made obvious that some of this credit was forced and onerous. From the photographs reprinted in government publications and taken at Nueva Concepción, it can be supposed that the Government did carry out its promise for some technical help. Upon visting the area in 1963–4, the authors found that many lots were being rented out to sublessees for the price of clearing the jungle growth from the lands, and very little technical aid was available. There was no evidence of 'higher material and moral levels of life' among the new landowners.

In the second category, small individual plots of land were distributed in an attempt to liquidate the agrarian programme of the Arbenz Government. As noted previously, after the overthrow of Arbenz most of the expropriated properties were returned to the previous owners. 'This second type of holding was a matter largely of granting titles to persons permitted to keep some of the land allotted to them by the Arbenz regime.'[25] There were 3,953 recipients with an average of 2·6 hectares (6·4 acres) per family.

The third type of holdings were described thus: 'small farms were distributed to the workers, each to be operated on a collective basis with ownership in common. The land in this programme amounted to 45,834 hectares (113,210 acres) which were distributed to 8,590 recipients, an average of about 5 hectares (12·4 acres) per family.'[26] These are what CIDA calls *comunidades* and would be similar to either co-operatives or the Mexican *ejidos*.

It is not correct to call this an agrarian reform and we should not rate even these totals against what Castillo Armas said he would do. Many of these distributions were made before Decree 559 was passed by Congress, recognizing *de facto* distributions made by Arbenz, and Castillo Armas lived less than eighteen months after its promulgation in which to

25. Whetten, *Guatemala*, op. cit., p. 170.   26. ibid, p. 169.

put it into practice. Yet the Government insisted on making propaganda on its own behalf, mixing all these totals together, confusing the actual amount of land distributed and then talking about 15,000 families or more as having received their own farms. We can best see what the law actually accomplished by examining the meaning of the totals.

CHART 1   *Land Distribution by the Liberation Government*

Year	No. of lots Avg.* Agrarian zones		No. of lots Avg.* Microparcels		No. of lots Avg.* Communities		No. of urban lots Avg.*	
1955	153	19·2	1,663	2·0	251	3·5	0	0·00
1956	1,262	19·2	1,838	1·8	1,972	10·0	402	0·11
1957	1,399	19·2	452	8·0	5,876	3·3	226	0·11
TOTAL	2,814	19·2	3,953	2·6	8,099	5·0	628	0·11

* Average size of lot in hectares.

Of the titles given out in communities, only the 1956 distribution was of family-sized farms and can be considered as part of a legitimate agrarian programme. These recipients, plus the 2,814 who received lands in the agrarian zones during the Liberation Government's three years, total 4,786 beneficiaries of the Castillo Armas programme. This does not mean that all the recipients were landless peasants, however. When Rodolfo Castillo Armas was fired as head of the DGAA (General Headquarters of Agrarian Affairs) after his brother, the President, was assassinated, eighty-seven people immediately had their titles cancelled for not having fulfilled the conditions of the law (they were not poor peasants) and another 214 were investigated, 'among them ... judicial police, military men and public employees'.[27]

The land distribution worth noting during this period was effected on 3 July 1956 on the second anniversary of the

27. *El Imparcial*, 11 March 1958.

installation of the new Government Junta. It was the fourth distribution to be made and involved over 50,000 hectares (123,500 acres) on twenty-two different plantations. Property titles were said to have been given to 3,346 families, who received lands averaging 15·1 hectares (37·3 acres) each. This was close to the planned size set by the Government. The largest area of land was at Nueva Concepción, a tract of 34,909 hectares (86,225 acres) that had been obtained by the Government from the United Fruit Company under terms that were never made public. Twelve hundred families were supposed to be situated there, receiving twenty hectares (49·4 acres) each, and the rest of this land was to be utilized for communal and urban facilities and roads. Actually 1,194 farms were distributed there, but in the list of new proprietors published by the Government, only 849 names appear,[28] or 351 less than the projected aim, which results in over 7,000 hectares (17,290 acres) being 'misplaced', or given to people whose names could not be listed.

The distribution at Nueva Concepción was considered the beginning of the colonization programme based on the *zonas agrícolas* idea. In its publication *Tierra en Propiedad*, the DGAA demonstrates the Government's plans to provide for the complete human development of the settlers by building schools, clinics, storage facilities, recreation halls, offices, roads and other installations.

It is obvious that a lot of money was being invested. No one could fault the Government for such a programme, but it must be considered in perspective. Where would the money come from to help, on this same scale, the numbers of people who actually needed help in Guatemala? The high cost can be seen further from a governmental *Acuerdo* dated 20 June 1956 that authorized the DGAA to purchase the plantation, 'Trapiche Grande', in the Departments of Retalhuleu and Suchitepéquez, from the Guatemala Plantations Aktiebolag

28. DGAA, op. cit., chapter 4.

Company for the price of $500,000.[29] This too, was to be made a *zona agrícola*. If such an amount of money can be used to purchase lands, one might judge that the Castillo Armas programme was not meant to go very far, and would not go very far without massive transfusions of money.

A comparison between the Arbenz agrarian reform and the Castillo Armas agrarian programme would be a valid basis for judging the two Governments. CIDA makes a rather mathematical comparison between the two when it notes that the Revolutionary Government distributed an average of 33,500 hectares a month while the Liberation régime gave out 19,000 hectares a year.

A better contrast can be seen from the goals both Presidents set for themselves. In his annual message to Congress in 1954, Arbenz stated that there was no reason why every Guatemalan should not have a family-sized farm before he (Arbenz) finished his term of office in 1957. At the rate his programme was going, there is no question that he would have attained his goal. Castillo Armas said that his Government would distribute lands to 25,000 families in five years, a defeatist programme not intended to keep pace with the population increase, and certainly not a remedy for the existing problem. Even this minimal pace he was unable to maintain.

Castillo Armas constantly accused Arbenz of political manipulation as the motivation of his land reform. The basis for the charge was that Arbenz gave the land for life-long 'usufruct' and not as 'private property'. It is doubtful that a piece of paper registered as a private title would make peasant manipulation any more or any less difficult. Such a view flies in the face of the Indians' historical experiences at the hands of most national governments, and certainly Castillo Armas himself proves this point by the ease with which he abrogated another piece of paper – the Constitution.

29. Azurdia, vol. 75, p. 240.

Yet, in spite of all the *furor* over private property versus usufruct, Arbenz gave out more private property titles (approximately 27,000) in his year-and-a-half programme than the Liberation Government intended to do in five years. This fact, plus the circumstance that over ninety per cent of the Guatemalans have no other legal title to their lands than 'usufruct', gives a better perspective to the 'Liberator's' charges.

In early August 1957 the reins of Guatemala's government were snatched from Castillo Armas's hands just as he had taken them up – through violence. He was shot down in the presidential palace by a member of his personal guard, who in turn succumbed to an immediate hail of bullets fired by members of the President's staff. It was generally conceded that the young soldier was not the author of the assassination plot and rumours flew that individuals very close to Castillo Armas were responsible. The immediate death of the assassin sealed his lips for ever, but, in so doing, only managed to inflame imaginations that speculate dangerously to this day. But just as the deaths of Col. Francisco J. Arana (1949) before him and Mario Méndez Montenegro (1965) after him, remain shrouded in the shadows generated by political passions, so too, the real source of the bullets that ended Carlos Castillo Armas's life will probably never be known. He will long be remembered in Guatemala's history as the great saviour of the landed oligarchy, as an 'authentic martyr' of the Catholic Church[30] and as a typical President to the poverty-stricken masses.

30. Proclaimed such by Archbishop Mariano Rossell.

CHAPTER 8

A Corrupt Age

In a corrupt age, greatness can be attained only by immoral means.

MACHIAVELLI

It had just not been the year for the ex-Ubico *aide*, General Miguel Ydígoras Fuentes, to throw his hat into the electoral ring against Colonel Jacobo Arbenz Guzmán in 1950. It had been obvious then that the former had inherited much of the conservative support that would have gone to the assassinated Col. Francisco J. Arana, but Guatemala was still feeling heady over the social implications of the 1944 Revolution, and that year, 1950, conservatism was not the wave of the future. January 1958, however, was a completely different story. The presidential elections that followed in the wake of the Castillo Armas assassination were produced to order for Ydígoras Fuentes. The reactionary forces that had been set loose across the land by the Arbenz overthrow were still impossible to contain. The murder of Castillo Armas, if it had any effect on conservative passions, had only inflamed them more.

A quickly called and obviously rigged election gave the presidency in October 1957 to Miguel Ortíz Passarelli, heir apparent and ex-Minister of the Interior under Castillo Armas. Ydígoras cried out in outrage and threatened the capital with reprisals at the hands of faithful followers if Congress did not annul the results. The deputies heard the message and complied, calling for new elections in January 1958.

This second election proved indecisive since none of the three candidates obtained the absolute majority of votes needed for election.[1] The decision was then thrown into the unicameral Congress, and the deputies themselves were given the honour of selecting the next President of Guatemala. Ydígoras again made threatening noises as to what his followers would do to the capital if he were not chosen, and Congress, in what is called a 'secondary election', again bowed to the threats of the 'Old Fox'.

It is not difficult to characterize the Government of 'Redemption', as Ydígoras called his régime. It was ideologically conservative, blatantly dishonest and consistently erratic. He had enemies on the Right who charged him with being soft on communism, among them Ortíz Passarelli[2] and later his own Minister of Defence, Col. Enrique Peralta Azurdia. He had enemies on the whole spectrum of the political Left, all of whom he himself accused of communism, including the municipal authorities of Quezaltenango, Guatemala's second city;[3] Galich, the Mayor of the capital;[4] and Mario Méndez Montenegro, his opponent for the presidency, whom he graphically denounced as having inflicted some grotesque tortures on political prisoners under the two revolutionary Governments.

Not many people believed his protestations of anti-communism, least of all Monseñor Mariano Rossell, the Archbishop of Guatemala :

These are not the anti-communists who have sealed with their

1. Ydígoras – Redención: 190,000; Cruz Salazar – MLN: 138,000; Mario Méndez Montenegro – Partido Revolucionario: 134,000. *El Imparcial*, 6 February 1958.
2. *El Imparcial*, 24 September 1959.
3. ibid., 12 August 1958.
4. ibid., 8 December 1958.

blood their conviction that Guatemala had to be freed from the atheistic ideology of Marxism. These are not the anti-communists faithful to the ideals of the caudillo of the Liberation, creator of the plan of Tegucigalpa and sincere protagonist for social justice and for a New Life, a better life for his people: Carlos Castillo Armas, whom for these same ideals, we count today among the martyrs of an authentic anti-communism.[5]

And in case the new President didn't understand that the Archbishop had little admiration for him, he concluded this same speech:

When will the day come that Guatemala may merit another energetic and sincere defender of the interests of the poor, of the weak, of the exploited, of the same calibre as Castillo Armas? [6]

Perhaps the Archbishop didn't believe that after refusing to aid Castillo Armas in the invasion, Ydígoras still had the right to call himself an anti-communist.

The General disagrees and offers us the following description of himself in his autobiography, *My War With Communism*:

I fought Castro-Communism from the outset and from the first days of 1959, I was a victim of Fidel Castro's aggression. I frustrated his invasion of Panama in March of 1959; I broke off relations with his government in April of 1960; I withstood two military uprisings inspired by his money and his agents; I cooperated with anti-Castro groups to train 2,000 Cubans and launched them against the Soviet bastion in the Caribbean; I put down an incipient civil war in March, April and May of 1962; I swung a submachine gun around my shoulder in November of 1962 and put down a rebellion of the Guatemalan Air Force.[7]

5. ibid., 8 July 1958.
6. ibid.
7. Ydígoras Fuentes, Miguel, *My War With Communism*. New Jersey: Prentice-Hall, Inc., 1963, p. 2.

Many observers of the Guatemalan scene will question the historical accuracy of the above description, including people high in the Ydígoras Government itself. Ralda Ochoa, who acted as his Vice-President, says that his putting down the uprising in November 1960 is a good joke.[8] In any case, although Ydígoras was no friend of Castillo Armas's political party, he did not consider himself to the Left of it. He therefore continued the general outlines of the Liberation Government's agrarian reform. He did this, however, without the co-operation the US Government had afforded to his predecessor.

It is not clear exactly why Ydígoras was not appreciated by the Eisenhower administration, as he also attests in his book. He complains of the chilly reception given him by John Foster Dulles during his visit to Washington while still President-elect in February 1958, and compares himself and his trip to the ice-breaker that was working in the Potomac River at the time. Foster Dulles is quoted as greeting Ydígoras with a very curt speech :

We welcome President-elect Ydígoras Fuentes. We want him to know that it is our desire to maintain our friendship with Guatemala, united to the efforts to fight the common enemy : international communism.[9]

Even though Ydígoras replied that it was his intention to organize a Government on 'strict anti-communist lines to stand shoulder to shoulder with the US at all times in the war with Communism', it may well have been a doubt about this very point that had provoked the hostility. Ydígoras had not been as co-operative as the US apparently desired when it had been time to arm Guatemalan exiles against Arbenz in 1953 and 1954. He tells how it happened :

8. *Prensa Libre*, 3 March 1969.
9. Ydígoras Fuentes, op. cit., p. 61.

A former executive of UFCo, now retired, Mr Walter Turnbull, came to see me with two gentlemen whom he introduced as agents of the CIA. They said that I was a popular figure in Guatemala and that they wanted to lend their assistance to overthrow Arbenz. When I asked their conditions for assistance, I found them unacceptable. Among other things, I was to promise to favor the UFCo and IFCA; to destroy the railroad worker labor union; to suspend claims against Great Britain for the Belize territory; to establish a strong-arm government, on the style of Ubico. Further, I was to pay back every cent that was invested in the undertaking on the basis of accounts that would be presented to me afterwards. I told them that I would have to be given time to prepare my conditions, as theirs seemed to me to be unfavorable to Guatemala. They withdrew, promising to return; I never saw them again.[10]

Ydígoras goes on to say he found out a short time later that Castillo Armas had accepted the conditions and was being prepared for the invasion in Honduras. A 'gentlemen's agreement' was arranged with Carlos Castillo Armas as to what role Ydígoras would play in the new Government (he was to participate in elections shortly after the take-over) but Castillo Armas did not abide by the agreement and Ydígoras remained outside the country during the Liberation Government's rule.

This antagonism between him and Castillo Armas can perhaps explain some of the difficulties the new President was having with the US, especially the financial ones. He speaks of his meeting with Eugene Black, Head of the World Bank, during the same visit to Washington. Black told him he could expect 'not one cent of help from the US or world banks', and cited among other reasons that 'previous governments of Guatemala were indebted to certain American citizens and corporations' and that he, Eugene Black, 'acting on instructions from President Eisenhower had loaned Castillo Armas the amount of $18,200,000'.[11]

10. ibid., pp. 49–50.   11. ibid., p. 63.

Ydígoras says that it was made clear to him that if he didn't make good 'on these oppressive claims', the doors of all banks would be closed to his Government. To make matters worse, he was approached at this same time by some men whom he describes as follows:

A group of sinister individuals, all dressed in black, informed me that they were representatives – and members of – a Washington law firm. They told me that they had financed the 'liberation movement' of Castillo Armas, who had committed himself to certain payments. On his death he still owed them $1,800,000, and as they considered me to be his 'heir', they held me responsible for payment of this monumental debt.[12]

The President-Elect sent them packing according to his account, despite the threats that retaliation would be made against his Government in the Department of State and in the US Press.

Yet Ydígoras writes his book as a great friend and admirer of the US and his charges cannot be written off as an anti-American diatribe. Although there are many statements in the book that can be questioned, there is no doubt that his Government was often in serious financial difficulties.

It is possible, also, that this lack of US financing played more than a small role in his decision to lend Guatemalan territory to the CIA to train the Bay of Pigs invasion force, despite strong domestic opposition; a concession that got him in very serious trouble.

When Ydígoras became President in March 1958 he continued the same general lines of the agrarian policy of the previous Government. In October 1959 he announced that he was having a new agrarian law drawn up by a Spanish technician. When it was presented to Congress, it was intensely criticized, particularly because a foreign technician, who 'didn't understand the national situation', had drawn it up.

12. ibid.

It was obstructed especially by the Christian Democrats, who wanted a real reform law. They presented a counter-proposal emphasizing the social function of land, but Ydígoras said: 'I will give land to all who need it without touching what others have inherited.' [13] The law was discussed and set aside.

At a land-distribution ceremony in January 1960 Ydígoras said: 'The agrarian reform being realized is a scientific one due to the help of USICA (United States Interamerican Cooperation Administration)'.[14] In June 1960 Enrique Peralta Azurdia, then Minister of Agriculture, appealed to Congress to approve the four-fold agrarian reform plan still pending their consideration. It consisted of four laws: (1) Law for land distributions in lots; (2) Law for agrarian development zones; (3) Law regulating idle lands; and (4) Law for INTA (Instituto Nacional de Transformación Agraria).

The law establishing INTA was discussed again in Congress, with the Christian Democrats still pushing their version. AGA (General Association of Agriculturalists), the large landowners' lobby, wrote a detailed public letter to the Christian Democrats and complained especially about the articles dealing with the definition of idle lands and with expropriation. The Association of Economists said that the new law being discussed would have good results since it was improvised, empirical and was looking for the economic progress of the country apart from the consideration of the misery of the majority of the population. Congress was discussing details of the articles, they charged, without even considering their false base.

On 28 September 1962, in four hours, Congress approved the remaining 248 articles after it had been discussing the first thirteen on and off for three years. A Christian Democrat Congressman, René De León Schlotter, said:

The articles approved in this manner, against the regulations

13. El Imparcial, 2 November 1959.
14. ibid., 1 February 1960.

(there was no opportunity given to propose amendments) are null and void. The law will be inoperable and it is only being published so that the government can ask for money from the Alliance for Progress programs.[15]

On 17 October 1962 the new law was finally published. The President described it as 'an anti-communist and Christian answer to Decree 900'.[16]

If the INTA and DGAA laws are compared, not many differences can be noted. The size of the *fincas* subject to expropriation was raised to those over 100 hectares (247 acres) that had more than 50 hectares of idle lands. Regulations for agrarian zones, credits and family patrimony are similar. Expropriation procedure is a little more difficult. In fact, the CIDA report states:

Especially in the regulations relative to taxation and expropriation of idle lands, it can be said that the new law represents the most conservative expression that has ever been known on this subject in Guatemala.[17]

The two laws determine four types of holdings for the lands to be distributed:

(1) Zones of agrarian development are colonies of family-type farms established by DGAA and INTA on large extensions of idle lands from national *fincas*, Government land or lands which are purchased from private estates and which need Government resources to initiate their exploitation. These parcels are given to landless peasants or to those who have insufficient land.

(2) Family patrimonies are individual farm lots, large enough to support a family and to market produce, given out from cultivated farm-lands that have been donated to the Government, that have been expropriated, or that are from national *fincas*.

(3) Agricultural communities are lands to be exploited com-

15. El *Imparcial*, 29 September 1962.
16. ibid., 17 October 1962.
17. CIDA, op. cit., p. 52.

munally whose topography doesn't permit their partition into lots.

(4) Urban lots are for building homes and are given out in urban zones or in agrarian zones where urbanization is desired.

Perhaps the best analysis of the Ydígoras attempts at agrarian reform can be made from a study of what he did with the National Fincas. It will be remembered that Arbenz had distributed these during his reform programme, only to have Castillo Armas take them all back a few weeks after he took over the government. When Ydígoras came to power in March 1958 the State owned 132 of these plantations which could have been used to alleviate the needs of many landless peasants. On 25 April the new President named three large landowners to take charge of selling or otherwise disposing of the National Fincas: Julio Héctor Leal, Roberto Berger and Manuel Ralda Ochoa.[18] The latter two are the largest cattle ranchers in the country. Approximately twelve of these *fincas* were used for agrarian distributions.[19] Others were given to Government or public agencies, either to be sold or to be managed in order to supplement the agencies' budgets.

The Department of Agrarian Affairs suggested that some of these lands be given to those employees who had lost their jobs when the new administration had taken over.[20] The Association of University Students (AEU) demanded that the National Fincas be given to the peasants living on them.[21] Back in 1957, in a public debate on the National Fincas, the Association of Economists and Public Accountants had declared itself in favour of using these *fincas* to solve the peasants' need for land.[22] But the Fincas continued to be returned to their original owners, to be sold to pay Government debts and to be given to individuals in exchange for

18. El *Imparcial*, 19 February 1958.
19. ibid., 9 September and 5 December 1959.
20. ibid., 28 April 1958.   21. ibid.
22. CIDA, op. cit., p. 52.

goods and services.[23] Ydígoras stated that the confiscation of German properties had been a 'national shame' and since the 'State was a bad administrator', these lands should be sold.[24] They were worth Q150,000,000 and could therefore greatly help resolve the Government's budgetary problems.[25]

The Revolutionary Party [26] said that they were opposed to the sale of these plantations since a correct distribution of these lands could substantially help to solve the agrarian problem.[27] Some of the first 'buyers' were 200 military officers who received urban lots from two *fincas* on the outskirts of Guatemala City. The price: five centavos a square metre.[28] Congress complained, but to no avail.

The production of corn threatened to be low in 1959. A shortage of this basic staple affected the whole nation. Coffee growers must feed their harvesters and a daily ration of corn is necessary. Ydígoras made a public plea that idle lands on National Fincas be rented free and that private lands be rented for the legal fee. 'It would be a national shame to have to import corn.' [29] But a plea carries no executive force.

In October 1959 five peasants came representing forty others to ask Ydígoras to sell them two small National Fincas on credit. 'We have never been able to have any economic security or convenience. We are not asking for a gift. We will pay for this land.' [30] The President's declarations on land reform had reached their ears and they had mistaken political promises for sincere concern. Their petition was ignored.

The President had spoken the truth when he had said that the State is a bad administrator. Disinterested public service is not common. When Nery Rendón, the cashier for the

23. El Imparcial, 26 October 1960.
24. ibid., 6 June 1958 and 31 October 1958.
25. ibid., 31 October 1958.
26. The PR, political heirs of Arévalo and Arbenz.
27. El Imparcial, 6 November 1958.   28. ibid., 22 December 1958.
29. ibid., 25 March 1959.   30. ibid., 28 October 1959.

National Fincas, announced that there were some shady business deals going on, especially in the *finca* 'Palo Gordo', he was immediately fired and his accusations were declared false.[31] The public, however, was not fooled, nor was it surprised when on 12 January 1960 Alfonso Alejos, personally representing Ydígoras, earned a neat Q5,800 in one day at the coffee auction where he sold 58,000 quintals (hundredweight) of National Finca coffee charging a ten-centavo autioneer's fee per bag. He had a lot of answering to do but his profit was not declared undue or illegal.

The Department of National Fincas had bought two cargo ships in August 1959. They constituted the beginnings of the Flota Mercante Gran Centroamericana. Guatemala could begin to use its own freighters and not have to depend exclusively on foreign shipping. However, Congress questioned the constitutionality of a Government agency's unauthorized expenditure, especially when the National Fincas were consistently declared to be functioning at a loss.[32]

The Minister of Agriculture, Col. Peralta Azurdia, clarified this concept. He said the Fincas Nacionales were producing well, better in fact than when the Germans owned them. From 1954 to 1959 they provided more than Q6 million for the public treasury.[33] (This was Q6 million in five years. In 1950 alone it had been Q5 million.) Still, Congress, on 18 February, declared that the purchase of the freighters had been unconstitutional despite the availability of money.

Peralta had been trying to consolidate the agricultural enterprises of the Government. He felt it was the duty of the Minister of Agriculture to direct the agrarian policy of the nation. He was finally successful on 14 June 1960, when the DGAA (Dirección General de Asuntos Agrarios) and the Nacional Fincas both came under his administration. The next day it was announced that three more *fincas* were to be sold

31. ibid., 9 December 1959.   32. ibid., 2 February 1960.
33. ibid., 13 February 1960.

so as to come under private enterprise. He appointed a new director for DGAA, Crisóstomo Castillo, who in turn announced a new policy for the Department:

The policy of agrarian development has produced few results. Lands must now be given to the middle class. Native peasants lack sufficient preparation, laboriousness and a spirit of initiative.[34]

Peralta supported him in his declaration and a week later added that the purpose of selling the national *fincas* was to benefit the middle class.

In spite of increased profit, an announced Q2,500,000 in each of the two previous years, it was decided to cut back on the number of employees in both the DGAA and the Fincas Nacionales.[35] Both groups went on a short-termed strike to protest. Nevertheless, the budget of the National Fincas was cut in half. Their normal allotment had been Q10 million from the BNA (Banco Nacional Agrario). They had almost 20,000 workers and totalled sixty-one *fincas* in all at this time.[36] Of the country's 11,094 coffee plantations, 327 produced from 1,000 to 5,000 quintals of coffee; and of these, forty-five were National Fincas. Another thirty produced more than 5,000 quintals and of these sixteen were National Fincas. The latter, therefore, were among the most productive in the nation. The average profit was Q6.00 a quintal.

Four months later, on 26 October 1960, Castillo was out and Angel Augusto Pellecer replaced him. A conflict had developed over the sale of the National Fincas. The same policy, however, was to continue, as Pellecer declared:

The granting of lands to the middle class is an established policy I will continue according to the economic possibilities of the Department and according to the international agreements signed by the Guatemalan and the U.S. Governments through the ICA (International Cooperation Agency).[37]

34. ibid., 30 June 1960.   35. ibid., 7 September 1960.
36. ibid., 8 September 1960.   37. ibid., 2 November 1960.

At the same time he announced that six more *fincas* were up for sale. Castillo's mistake had been that of arranging for personal friends of his to receive preferences and advantages in the sales.

The corn shortage was again a threat in 1961 and again a plea from the Minister of Agriculture went out to landowners to rent their idle lands so that landless peasants could plant corn.

On 13 November 1961 it was finally decided to transfer the incipient shipping enterprise, Flota Gran Centroamericana, into private hands.

On 27 June 1961 Congress discussed the problem of the National Fincas. From 1954 to 1956 there had been a Q14 million profit and now they had a debt of Q9 million. The explanation Congress received was that payment on the debt was not due until 1962 and there were enough products in the *fincas'* storehouses to pay at any moment. Besides, the high 1954–6 profit had been due to the fact that it represented the harvesting of products planted by the peasants who had received those lands under Decree 900 and which had then been returned to the national patrimony, plus the high price of coffee. Previous administrators had approved a removal of Q1,200,000 for the political campaign of Ortíz Passarelli, the purchase of the two freighters for Q2,500,000, as well as the acquisition of a fleet of cars and an aeroplane for the use of the Department. Twenty-five plantations more had now been given out.

A month later, Montenegro, who had followed Peralta as Minister of Agriculture, resigned because he felt he was not given sufficient authority over the National Fincas.[38] Once out of office, he declared that these *fincas* should be used to resolve the problems of the peasants and not be sold to private individuals. Pedro Mombiela, a well-known cattle-rancher, was named the new Minister of Agriculture.

38. ibid., 5 July 1961.

The public debate about the National Fincas reached a high pitch when on 4 January 1962 it was announced that the Department would cease to exist by 31 March. Sixteen *fincas* were being returned to Nottebohm, one of the dispossessed Germans, who had won one of his suits before an international court in Geneva. Eight of these alone were valued at Q2,791,170. INFOP (Instituto Nacional de Fomento de la Producción) was to receive plantations worth Q8,200,000 and the BNA Q7,000,000.[39] Others were to be given to the Banco de Crédito Hipotecario and the rest were to be sold. someone finally remembered that these *fincas* had workers living on them. Twenty thousand families would be affected. Their daily wage was supposed to be eighty centavos but in the transfer it was often reduced to sixty centavos or less. Food allotments, customary on coffee *fincas*, were reduced, as was the amount of land each family could use for its own crops. The administrators and agronomists would simply be fired. As an editorial on 5 January in *El Imparcial* affirmed, many people were bothered with the obvious personal benefits being taken by unscrupulous persons who as buyers or intermediaries were obtaining profits that could only hurt the national patrimony.

Nevertheless, the sale and personal business deals continued. On 11 January 1962 it was made public that Juan Mini was to receive plantations valued at Q953,260 in exchange for the land he had ceded to the Government on the outskirts of Guatemala City for the construction of the Roosevelt Hospital. The evaluator, Ramiro Samayoa, a cinema magnate and personal friend of Ydígoras, received one *finca*, Xolhuitz, worth Q239,960 for his services.

'Palo Gordo', the centre of the dispute between Willy Dorión and some sugar growers, was finally to be sold to a 'co-operative' of large sugar producers, 200 shareholders, with Alfredo De la Hoz as President. Ramiro Samayoa received

39 ibid., 5 April 1962.

another plantation, 'El Perú', valued at Q435,580 in exchange for the 'Rancho Nimajay', an old hotel in Antigua, Guatemala.[40] 'Concepción' and 'Castañaz', the first being one of the largest *fincas* in the country, went to Herrera, Dorión and Co. All these were valued at Q25,000,000.

In all, the Ydígoras Government disposed of 115 plantations as follows : eleven went to public entities, some of these for distribution; thirty were exchanged for lands and for constructions that were given to the Government; four were for 'personal services'; sixteen were returned to previous owners : dispossessed Germans or Ubico politicians; and seventeen were turned over to the BNA to pay obscure Government debts. The destiny of thirty-seven other *fincas* is impossible to trace. This left seventeen plantations in the hands of the Government by April 1963 with a total of 22,548 hectares (55,694 acres) in spite of the March 1961 goal to be rid of them all.[41]

There is no question that these dealings involving the National Fincas were not motivated by concern for the needs and rights of the nation, nor were these transactions legal. This can best be seen by the actions of the Peralta Government that followed Ydígoras, and its attempts, often successful, to repossess these plantations for the State.[42]

As early as June 1958, when the Ydígoras Government was not four months old, an accusation had been made in the newspapers that forty-five sales of Government properties had already been consummated for 'laughable prices', including

40. ibid., 5 April 1962.   41. CIDA, op. cit., pp. 52–3.

42. On 19 June 1963 the Peralta Government passed Law 52, which ordered a re-examination of all the transactions involving the National Fincas effected by the Ydígoras Government (El Imparcial, 30 June 1963). By 7 July, sixteen plantations had been reclaimed (El Imparcial, 22, 25 June and 7 July 1963). In January 1964 eighty-nine *fincas* more were brought under investigation. Peralta ordered Ydígoras extradicted from the United States, but the then ex-President left Miami and was welcomed in Costa Rica.

one piece of land that was sold for Q200 and then mortgaged the following week for Q48,000.[43] There were many other accusations of fraudulent deals, some of them involving the President's son, Miguel Ydígoras Laparra.[44] However, some of the money must have found its way into the Government treasury to alleviate the dire need for funds, as indeed this was one of the reasons that had been suggested for the sale of the National Fincas.

Marroquín Rojas, the first Minister of Agriculture, had made this proposal on several occasions [45] as a solution to aid the President in raising Q40 million that he had been requesting from Congress. The Legislature had rejected the request since Ydígoras refused to divulge what he wanted the money for. Then, in October 1959, the President made a public declaration to the effect that he no longer needed the Q40 million from Congress,[46] and although Marroquín Rojas presented his plan for the sale of some of the *fincas* to raise this money, and the plan was subsequently studied by Congress, Ydígoras maintained his stance of indifference. Marroquín shortly resigned and later said: 'I refused to be a labourer for the North American foreman who is governing us.' [47]

It is not easy to understand: Ydígoras needed money, and his requests for Q40 million had been insistent; he also needed to effect at least a token land reform. Yet he sold the Government plantations to private individuals at 'laughable prices' which effectually closed the door to the use of these *fincas* to solve one or both of these problems. But apparently his need for money disappeared in October 1959, as he himself stated. It is not clear where the money came from. Subsequent events, however, seem to indicate that a new understanding was reached with the Eisenhower administration, and this might be sufficient explanation.

43. El Imparcial, 28 June 1958.   44. ibid., 17 September 1959.
45. ibid., 11, 23 and 24 November 1959.
46. ibid., 30 October 1959.   47. La Hora, 3 March 1966.

In April 1960 public outcries appeared in the papers saying that Cuban exiles were being trained in the *finca* 'Helvetia', property of a friend of Ydígoras, wealthy Roberto Alejos. Ydígoras labelled the charges as false and invited the OAS to send an inspection team to verify his denials.[48] His protestations were not universally believed, despite the invitation to the OAS. He either thought they would not come, or, if they did, that they would not make their findings public. He published his own assertions that Cuba was preparing to invade Guatemala, until a Congressman, Villagrán Kramer, in a telegram to the OAS,[49] denounced the whole thing as a farce and an attempt to divert attention from what Guatemala herself was doing against Cuba.

A camp was also established in San Juan Acul in the Petén region for training frogmen in demolition techniques. This was difficult to hide, especially when the camp was discovered by chicle harvesters and the newspapermen reported that '500 armed guerrillas were in the area'. When two US pilots, who were flying the men in and out of the base, were killed in a crash, it was impossible to hide the truth.[50] The Government covered up by claiming that they had captured twelve Castroite guerrillas in the Petén area,[51] and that all was again normal in that region. Roberto Alejos repeated Ydígoras's invitation to the OAS to send an investigating team to his plantation to verify that the comings and goings of the huge Globemaster planes and the presence of US military advisers was only to supply and train Guatemalan soldiers in counter-insurgency.[52]

48. El *Imparcial*, 25 April 1960. 49. ibid., 8 December 1959.
50. ibid., 23 September 1960. 51. ibid., 13 August 1960.
52. ibid., 1 January 1961.

CHAPTER 9

A Disorganized Society

Once society becomes disorganized, military power becomes one of the few effective means for obtaining political goals.

HENRY BIENEN

The fate of the National Fincas is one measuring-stick of the orientation of the Ydígoras Government and the meaning of its agrarian programme. Another frame of reference is the number of people who lost their lands (or what they thought were their lands) while the 'Redemption Government' was in power.

On 2 June 1958, less than three months after stepping into office as head of the DGAA (General Headquarters of Agrarian Affairs), Col. Enrique Peralta Azurdia announced that all people living on United Fruit Company lands must get off, but he denied the charge that he had already used violence against the peasants in Bananera and Tiquisate (the two areas of UFCo. operations) to accomplish this end. A few months later, 'several peasants' complained that they were expelled from the lands of a National Finca, where their parents had been born while it was still under German ownership, for the 'crime of communism', in this case: voting for the Revolutionary Party.[1]

In May 1959 two peasants were killed and another three were wounded when the owner of 'La Campana' drove his

1. ibid., 15 October 1958.

tractor through the cornfields of eighty families, ploughing the fields to sow cotton.[2] The owner himself received a *machete* cut on the hand and a bullet in the stomach. The lands had been given to these people by the Government of Arbenz and though the Castillo Armas régime had decreed that the expropriation was invalid, for some reason it was never enforced. The DGAA had warned the peasants that they had no right there, and then finally the owner had taken matters into his own hands, with the results noted above.

On 3 June 1959 Col. Peralta Azurdia again denied that he was using soldiers to expel Indians from the plantations 'Palmar', 'Aurora', 'Naranjo', 'Campana' and 'Cadiz'. He stated that the peasants were leaving willingly after receiving their indemnization. Two weeks earlier, referring to the expulsion of fifty families, a public letter written to the DGAA had been published in the newspapers:

My most sincere gratitude for the magnificent job done on my plantations, 'Bolivia' and 'Aurora', located in Masagua, Escuintla, as regards the evaluations you made of the permanent crops and homes of those people, who, aided by the calamitous Decree 900, have been occupying my above mentioned lands ever since, and now the whole affair has culminated with the removal of these invaders by means of the indemnization payment. Gonzalo Palma C., Owner.[3]

That same month, when the DGAA was accused of expelling people from lands in 'Navajoa' and 'Santo Tomás' in Izabal, both National Fincas, it was claimed by DGAA that the people were 'invaders' and had no right to the lands.

A few weeks later, when the Minister of the Interior was asked by a reporter why twenty-seven families had been expelled from the lands of the Government *finca* 'San Andrés Osuna', he was told that only the police of Escuintla knew.[4]

2. ibid., 4 May 1959.   3. ibid., 16 May 1959.
4. ibid., 22 June 1959.

In August of that same year, DGAA expelled 200 families from the lands of Ricardo Berger in San José where they had lived for twenty years.[5] The peasants maintained that when they had established their homesteads there, they were told that the lands belonged to the Government and not to any private individual. No indemnization was made on this occasion.

That same month, 500 familes invaded Government lands on the outskirts of Guatemala City, stating: 'We cannot wait around with folded arms until the Government takes care of us, since we know from experience that the colonies are given out to relatives and friends of Government officials.'[6] Police gave them three days to get out even though they had already constructed their shacks. When they marched *en masse* on the presidential palace, Ydígoras said that he would give them until 31 December to find some other place to live.

During 1960 the same type of incident was reported from time to time in the Press.

In early January 1960 it was announced that 1,000 families who had occupied UFCo. lands in Izabal (Bananera) were to be expelled. They had been there since 1954 when Arbenz had given them the lands, and the Castillo Armas Government had been paying rent to the Company ever since, to avoid perhaps the implications of an expulsion.[7]

In February the judicial police moved into Los Angeles, Escuintla, where they captured one peasant while others escaped. 'Their crime was trying to defend the 200 families that the DGAA was expelling from lands that they had received in 1954.'[8] The police threatened to hold the wives as hostages until the other peasants gave themselves up.

In November 1960, 48 families were expelled from another Government *finca*, 'Bárcenas'.[9] And then in June 1962 the

5. ibid., 27 August 1959.
6. ibid., 19 August 1959.
7. ibid., 5 January 1960.
8. ibid., 23 February 1960.
9. ibid., 25 November 1960.

United Fruit Company expelled 200 families from 'El Semillero', Escuintla. The Governor of the Department of Escuintla had received orders to remove them and to pursue the men. The Director of the DGAA later denied the report of this order as ridiculous. 'The Governor is not a subordinate of the Company.' The peasants, he suggested, should take their case to Court.[10]

In that same month a group of approximately fifty young military officers decided that they had had enough of the Ydígoras Government and tried a barracks revolt. The reason for the attempted overthrow, according to Ydígoras, was international communism:

The entire picture, starting with the urgent objective of destroying the anti-Cuban bases in Guatemala; the seemingly pointless overpowering of a barracks in the capital to flee with arms to the coast; the knowledge that Colonel Rafael Sesán Pereira was receiving money from Cuba that caused his dismissal; the intervention of the known communist, Mario René Chávez García; the admission in the revolutionary manifesto that 'a free country, which is truly sovereign' gave the movement support and cooperation; the intercepted message from Cuba; and the fact that the movement was the culmination of months of political agitation, are all powerful indications that the movement was not Guatemalan in its essence.[11]

Ydígoras admits that the 'local and international press were incredulous as to the hand of international communism in the affair'.[12] However, President Eisenhower did believe the Guatemalan President and he sent the aircraft carrier 'Shangri-La' to wait off the Atlantic Coast so as to 'discourage any invasion attempt'.[13] One thing is certain, though: all participants in the original plot were Guatemalan Army men and they, along with many segments of the population, had

10. ibid., 23 June 1962. 11. Ydígoras, op. cit., p. 169.
12. ibid. 13. ibid., p. 167.

plenty of reasons to find the Ydígoras Government intolerable.

Lt. Marco Antonio Yon Sosa, one of the leaders of the revolt, differs from Ydígoras in his view of the incident, and he relates it through Adolfo Gilly, an Argentinian writer who spent several months with the guerrilla leader in the mountains of Northeastern Guatemala:

The aim [of the coup] was to clean up the Government, not to destroy capitalism. The Ydígoras administration, which had risen to power as a result of the electoral fraud of 1958, not only devoted itself to the defense of imperialism and the latifundistas [owners of large landholdings], but also lined its pockets with national treasury funds. ... It was the movement's intention to prevent Guatemala's utilization as the base for aggression against Cuba, as planned by the U.S.[14]

When the plotters arrived in Zacapa and captured that military base, Gilly tells us:

Eight-hundred peasants presented themselves at the Zacapa barracks and asked for arms with which to fight against the Government. This was not in the program, nor was it even anticipated by the rebels, who could not make up their minds to arm the peasants. ... There were no facilities for holding organized discussions and making decisions; but in Guatemala, as in Honduras and in El Salvador [where many of the rebels fled], all the peasants helped and protected the rebels, tried to influence them and win them to their side. The peasants' motives were not only to offer solidarity but also to win allies and leaders in their struggle for the land. ... Many of the rebels did not respond but the effort was not in vain; the influence was felt by some, but not immediately. Yon Sosa and Alejandro de León and their 'compañeros' did not jump to conclusions; but little by little, the peasants won them over.[15]

Ydígoras does admit that the rebels were able to 'recruit

14. Adolfo Gilly, 'The Guerrilla Movement in Guatemala'. *Monthly Review*, May 1965, p. 13.

15. Gilly, op. cit., pp. 14–16.

over 300 civilians',[16] but that their 'ardor was cooled by the unappealing and unintelligible speech of a loyal government pilot who was obliged to address the meeting with a ·45 revolver pressed to his ribs'. Why the rebels would have a loyal officer address the crowd is not clear. In Zacapa, according to Ydígoras, 'two light planes had dropped thousands of leaflets inciting the people to support a revolutionary movement'.[17]

It is difficult to know how much peasant support the revolt of 13 November 1960 actually had, but that it had peasant support, and that it still has peasant support, is shown by the fact that Yon Sosa was still fighting and hiding in the mountains of Izabal nine years later – an impossibility without broad peasant co-operation. That this support is based on the struggle for land there can be no doubt. In February 1962 Yon Sosa's forces were fighting in the Sierra de las Minas mountains under the name 'Guerrilla Movement, Alejandro de León, 13 November', named for a dead leader of the revolt and the date of the uprising. By April 1964 the name had been changed to 'Revolutionary Movement, 13 November'[18] to indicate the new orientation of the struggle, now not just for a change of government but rather for a total change in the social, economic and political structure of the country.

The United States Government recognized the threat to the stability of the Guatemalan political, social and economic institutions that this movement represented and in May 1962 established a Counter-insurgency Base in Mariscos, Izabal, under the leadership of two officers and five enlisted men of the US Special Forces, all trained in Laos and of Mexican or Puerto Rican descent. Fifteen Guatemalan soldiers trained by the US in Panama were also part of the teaching personnel.[19]

16. Ydígoras, op. cit., p. 168.
17. ibid., p 164   18. Gilly, op. cit., p. 20.
19. El Imparcial, 17 May 1962.

New jet airplanes (T-33s), transport planes (C-47s) and pilot training were given to the Guatemalan Air Force.[20]

A pacification programme was begun in the Zacapa area under the auspices of the US Defense Department, comprising the digging of wells, the establishment of clinics and the distribution of lunches to schoolchildren.[21] Generals Andrew O'Meara and Theodore Bogart of the US Carribean Command flew in for a three-day look at the situation.[22] A C-47 without any markings on it made a forced landing in Guatemala City – the pilots were Guatemalans, and the passengers were US paratroopers.[23]

No further reports of peasant expulsions from lands appear in the Press during the years 1961, 1962, 1963, except for some difficulties on the UFCo. lands in Tiquisate, on the Pacific Coast. It is possible that no actions of this kind were executed on the Atlantic Coast so as not to antagonize the people or the guerrillas in that area, or else the publication of such actions was discouraged for obvious reasons.

An example of local peasant struggles for land is the case of Huitzizil, Tiquisate. The first notice of the conflict there appeared in the Press in January 1961, when it was announced that 'only 82 families, not 400' were to be put off the UFCo. lands.[24] In February, the AEU (Association of University Students) interceded for the families, stating their right to remain there after twenty years of occupation.[25] In May, Linwood Adams, a director of the United Fruit Company, was murdered in his office by one of the peasants.[26] The DGAA maintained that all the peasants wanted to move but that communist agitators wouldn't let them. Three days later the Army moved in and escorted 105 families off the lands under heavy guard of machine-guns and rifles.[27]

20. ibid., 4 January 1963.   21. ibid., 4, 26 and 29 January 1963.
22. ibid., 26 January 1963.   23. ibid., 14 January 1963.
24. ibid., 18 January 1961.   25. ibid., 10 February 1961.
26. ibid., 17 May 1961.   27. ibid., 20 May 1961.

The peasants protested that they had paid over Q3,000 to Congressman Carlos Enrique Jiménez Peralta because he had promised that he would obtain for them legal title to their lands, having charged each family first Q10, then Q15 and finally Q8 for honorariums.[28] On 29 May the DGAA announced that the problem in Huitzizil had been solved with the distribution of 108 new farms in the agrarian zones to the 'invaders of UFCo. lands'. Many others were said to have returned to 'their place of origin', and all of them were advised that if they wanted compensation for their homes and crops they would have to take their cases to Court.

In August an announcement was made that all was still not well with the peasants of Huitzizil. UFCo. denied any responsibility, maintaining that they had given the Government land in 1954 to resolve just such problems.[29] On 26 August the Army moved in and burned the homes of the peasants.[30] In September Ydígoras made a special appeal to UFCo. to go slow until the legal position of the peasants could be defined.[31] A week later one of the peasant leaders was in jail at the request of the Company.

In February 1963 the peasants of Huitzizil hired a lawyer, Alfonso Bauer Paiz,[32] to defend their interests. He maintained that they had no place to live, no place to work.[33] A week later the Minister of Agriculture said that the situation in Huitzizil was an exaggeration, and that everyone there had received farms in the agrarian zones. Nothing more is heard of the matter until five years later, in March 1967, when the Government of Méndez Montenegro offered to pay Q50,000 to García Salas to buy the Huitzizil lands that had apparently been sold to him by UFCo. The Government planned then to sell the lands to the peasants, thus solving 'the problem of 13

28. ibid., 20 May 1961.   29. ibid., 24 August 1961.
30. ibid., 27 August 1961.   31. ibid., 3 September 1961.
32. A Congressman killed by Right-wing terrorists in 1968.
33. El Imparcial, 4 February 1962.

years duration, which had begun with Arbenz and Decree 900'.[34] A month later, the MANO (a Right-wing terrorist group) had their own way of solving the problem. They 'executed' Leopoldo Castillo and Arturo Schellenger in Huitzizil and announced their motive: 'To stop their communist demands to government agencies.'[35]

Ydígoras did manage to give out more lands during his five-year administration and his policies were not exclusively negative in this field. He used the same propaganda ploy that the Castillo Armas Government had used, that is, lumping all types of distributions together without regard to size or purpose, and thus effectively distorting the real picture. In mathematical terms his distributions consisted of 2,451 farms in the agrarian zones, 3,982 in communities, 371 microplots (*minifundios*) and 2,175 urban plots.[36] As with Castillo Armas we again have to discount the latter two categories from a meaningful agrarian programme. As regards the other two groupings, the communities were lands distributed in co-operative holdings to peasant villages, but even here the ratio of land to people puts the extension in the *minifundio* class, for an average of 2·5 hectares (6·18 acres) per family.[37] The agrarian zones were sufficiently large family farms, averaging 19·5 hectares (48·17 acres) each; we must note, however, that not all of these were given out to landless and needy peasants, as the cancellations made by subsequent Governments attest, as well as other revocations which should have been made (such as the land given to the Bishop of Quezaltenango) but which for political reasons were never effected. The situation of these agrarian zones, as was discovered during the Peralta Government (1963–6), will demonstrate that they are not maintained as well as the Government Secretaries of Information would have us believe.

34. ibid., 29 March 1967.
35. CIDOC, *Dossier No. 21.* Cuernavaca, Mexico: 1968, p. 4/282.
36. CIDA, op. cit., p. 49.   37. ibid., p. 49.

Ydígoras continued to alienate large segments of the population, owing largely to the open corruption of his Government. He had made an uneasy ally of the US mostly through his participation in the Bay of Pigs invasion. He attempted to gain the backing of the Catholic hierarchy and clergy and was only moderately successful, certainly never to the degree that Castillo Armas had been. The 'Old Fox', as he was popularly known, began by giving the Archbishop, Mariano Rossell, Q5,000 for his birthday and was promptly 'repaid' five days later when Pope Pius XII sent a special blessing to Castillo Armas' Liberation Party.[38] But Ydígoras did not despair, he could not afford to, and was able to push through Congress a number of laws favouring the Church, including the right to teach religion in state schools,[39] civil recognition for religious marriages[40] and, finally, juridical personality for the Church,[41] which again allowed it to own property for the first time in seventy-five years. Pope John XXIII responded by sending a special papal decoration to the President's wife.[42] Thereafter, Ydígoras felt enough confidence to demand that every Catholic, in fulfilment of his Christian duty, vote for his political party 'Redemption'.[43]

But his difficulties multiplied, and according to many their provocation was intentional, to distract the nation from more fundamental problems. He precipitated international incidents by ordering Mexican fishing-boats strafed by his Air Force P51s and then severing diplomatic relations with Mexico in the resulting furor. Claiming British Honduras to be Guatemalan territory (rightfully, it seems), he entered unannounced into that country, began an inspection tour and had to be requested to leave. He recommended that 'every Guatemalan soldier should go to bed every night and get up every morning, thinking about Belice [British Honduras]',

38. El *Imparcial*, 20 and 25 July 1958.   39. ibid., 3 November 1958.
40. ibid., 6 May 1959.   41. ibid., 11 July 1959.
42. ibid., 5 May 1959.   43. ibid., 5 December 1959.

and even threatened to go to war with England over the matter. He fought with El Salvador over the waters of Lake Güija on their common border. He promised to use the powers of his office to obtain the canonization of Hermano Pedro Betancourt, a historical religious figure in Guatemala with a wide popular following.

The economy rapidly deteriorated due to his graft and incompetence but he steadfastly maintained that Guatemala's only salvation lay in the Central American Common Market; he wanted to be known as the 'Great Unifier' even as Bolívar was known as the 'Great Liberator'. He tried to block Congress' criticisms of his underhand dealings by accusing the Legislature itself of graft, then he enjoyed the injured protests of outraged innocence that the public could compare to his own.[44] His police burned the ballots of the congressional election,[45] and so the Revolutionary Party (PR) claimed electoral fraud and demanded that he resign.[46] He retaliated by imprisoning Mario Méndez Montenegro and other leaders of the Revolutionary Party on charges of communism.[47]

Bombs were exploding all over the capital city and many people openly accused Ydígoras himself of responsibility for them, in his attempts to excite the populace against his political opponents. He trucked in 7,000 workers from the National Fincas for demonstrations in favour of his Government and when 200 peasants refused to participate, he fired them.[48] University and high-school students took to the streets demanding his resignation and protesting at the fraudulent congressional elections. The resulting military repression produced scores of deaths, several hundred were wounded and hundreds more went to jail.[49]

The Church hierarchy showed only limited concern, protesting that the chaos was weakening the nation and leaving

44. ibid., 8 September 1959.   45. ibid., 11 December 1961.
46. ibid., 12 December 1961.   47. ibid., 25 January 1962.
48. ibid., 3 April 1962.   49. ibid., 13 April 1962.

the door open to communism.[50] The Christian Democratic Party, basing its argument on the Bishop's Pastoral Letter, demanded the immediate resignation of Ydígoras.[51] Then the Catholic Bishops finally came out with an even stronger Pastoral Letter, on 15 August 1962, recognizing in its starkness, the agony of the nation:

Large sectors, with just aspirations, now living in the most miserable and overworked state, aspire for their human dignification and their institutional liberation. There is the problem of housing; there is the economic plight of beggars, the lack of urbanization and the absence of schools. On the plantations, the peasant is frozen in by customs hundreds of years old and submerged in conditions of blatant inferiority, receiving salaries that hardly permit him to avoid death by starvation. Also, these salaries are not paid with regularity but rather are doled out weeks and months late, leaving him without the hope of decently clothing his children and unable to provide them with an education befitting human beings and free citizens. Especially grave is the standard of living of thousands and thousands of workers on State and privately owned plantations. Besides the conditions of their work, they live collectively in wooden shacks, without light, without windows, without interior walls for privacy, generally without sufficient and adequate sanitary systems, without the possibility of intimate family life nor morality, in situations closely resembling concentration camps rather than the homes of free human beings, upon whom rests precisely the national wealth. It is here that infant mortality triumphs, reaching astonishing ratios, as well as sickness and social disintegration.[52]

The Bishops went on to encourage the peasants and workers to form their labour unions, but to be on their guard that they not be used for 'political or atheistic purposes'.

Meanwhile, Juan José Arévalo, living in exile in Mexico, declared that he was ready to 'assume the leadership of all revolutionary forces in the country'.[53] Ydígoras responded by

50. ibid., 24 April 1962.
51. ibid., 27 April 1962.
52. ibid., 21–8 January 1963.
53. ibid., 3 January 1962.

demanding his extradition from Mexico.[54] Early in 1963, Arévalo announced his intention of returning to Guatemala to participate in the approaching presidential elections. The Minister of the Interior then declared that Arévalo would be prosecuted for the assassination of Col. Francisco J. Arana.

Arévalo had often been castigated for not having conducted a more thorough investigation of the murder, but he had never before been so openly accused by Right-wing forces of Arana's death. That accusation had always been reserved for Arbenz.

Ydígoras then let it be known that he was prepared to allow Arévalo to participate in the elections, though it was believed that the 'Old Fox' was only trying to outflank some of his political opponents. Mario Rodríguez, a US scholar who has written numerous books and articles on Guatemala, said that Arévalo would have been an easy victor if he had been allowed to run.[55]

The former interim President, Flores Avendaño, stated that Arévalo's entrance into the country would only mean civil war. The House of Representatives of the United States made an announcement in mid-March that was duly publicized in the Guatemalan press :

The basic position of the United States is that if any Government requests aid to avoid being overthrown by communists, they will receive help. We are militarily prepared in anticipation of any Government's request for this aid.[56]

Arévalo's feelings about the United States' role in the overthrow of Arbenz in particular and the Monroe Doctrine in general had not been in doubt since he had written his widely read book, *The Shark and the Sardines*, which charac-

54. ibid., 6 April and 25 May 1962.
55. Rodríguez, Mario, 'Guatemala In Perspective', *Current History*, December 1966, p. 340.
56. *El Imparcial*, 15 March 1963.

terized the US as the Shark swallowing up Latin American Sardines.

Nor were the US feelings about Arévalo exactly a secret, when the US ambassador John O. Bell described the former president as 'a communist and thus unworthy of the presidency'. Rodríguez describes the remarks as 'indiscreet' and says that it 'made it appear that the US Government was officially opposed to the ex-President'.[57] As the official voice of the US Government in Guatemala, Bell's remarks would be considered more than indiscreet by Guatemalans, and no attempt was made by the Embassy to give a contrary impression.

On 20 March all the Central American Presidents met with President John F. Kennedy in Costa Rica to discuss mutual interests. Ydígoras told Kennedy that:

The hour of armed invasion is passed [referring to Cuba]. Now it remains for the U.S. to give effective and immediate help to the countries of Central America. Resolving our urgent economic problems of housing, education, sanitation and agriculture, we will be able to laugh at communism and subversion; thus we will terminate once and for all the agitation that is used as a flag by national and international communists to maintain our peoples in anxiety.[58]

Kennedy responded that their plans and projects would be studied, but a week later gave what is believed to have been the green light for the overthrow of Ydígoras by his Minister of Defence, Col. Peralta Azurdia.[59]

57. Rodríguez, op. cit., p. 339.
58. El Imparcial, 23 March 1963.
59. Miami Herald, 24 December 1966.

CHAPTER 10

A Constitution
of the Worst
Possible Type

Our aim in founding the commonwealth was not to make any one class especially happy, but to secure the greatest possible happiness for the community as a whole. We thought we should have the best chance of finding justice in a state so constituted, just as we should find injustice where the constitution was of the worst possible type.

PLATO

When Col. Enrique Peralta Azurdia decided that the country could no longer sustain the disaster of supporting a man such as Miguel Ydígoras Fuentes in the presidency, he took matters into his own hands. He did so knowing he would be applauded by the nation's politicized minority of almost every stripe and orientation. Ydígoras, in describing what happened on the night of 30 March 1963 tells us that he was 'betrayed by the enemy within'.[1] Nine hundred soldiers and six tanks under the orders of Peralta Azurdia stormed his residence, guarded only by six loyal officers, but he did not surrender until a 'tank crushed the weak doors of my home and aimed a cannon at my very face'.[2] And so, 'an emergent democracy was ruthlessly crushed'.[3] Peralta Azurdia was not seven days in power when the new 'Head of Government', as he requested that he be called, decreed his 'Fundamental Charter',[4] which was meant to temporarily replace the 1956 Constitu-

1. Ydígoras, op. cit., p. 2.   2. ibid.
3. ibid., p. 3.   4. Azurdia, vol. 82, p. 21.

tion, abrogated by the very act of his *coup*. Herein lies the basic rationale of the overthrow and the new Government's intentions: the Army assumed control in an 'absolutely disinterested way and without the slightest desire of perpetuating itself in power'[5] and the sole object of its action was to avoid an 'imminent civil war and the establishment of a communist regime'.[6] He promised, at the same time, 'to prepare a favorable political climate that will permit the Guatemalan people a free election of the person who will direct the destiny of our country without pressure of any kind'.[7]

He followed this up two days later with the promulgation of his 'Law for the Defence of Democratic Institutions', which reflected the first troubled days of Castillo Armas:

Communism denies God, the human personality and the highest values of the spirit, which is contrary to the traditions and aspirations of the great Guatemalan family. ... Communism is an international doctrine by means of which the minorities in power sell the national sovereignty and independence and give over their peoples to the most opprobrious slavery.[8]

He then decreed two years in prison as a penalty for passing out 'communist literature', five years for making explosives, ten years for belonging to the Communist Party and fifteen years for terrorism. Execution was the penalty for anyone involved in an act of terrorism that resulted in the injury or death of another.[9] The application of this decree was extremely arbitrary and it was used to make it a crime even to speak out against unjust social conditions. It was also used to persecute 'communist' labour organizers and union members.

The ultimate event to trigger the military intervention was Arévalo's making good his threat to return to Guatemala from his Mexican exile to participate in the campaign for the presidency. Ydígoras must have been in on the plot to have

5. ibid.   6. ibid.   7. ibid.
8. ibid., p. 24.   9. ibid., p. 25.

Arévalo enter Guatemala, for he says in his incomprehensible way:

> The situation was climaxed by the plans of the extreme Left, the moderate Left, the Center and others, to use the figure of former president Arévalo to unite all the extremists and to again impose a communist government on the country.... They [Peralta Azurdia and followers] had no faith in the people of Guatemala; with no historic precedent, nor basis in fact, they assumed that the entire country would rise up like one man to support the leftist demagogue, Arévalo.[10]

To sort out the details of the various plots and counter-plots is next to impossible, nor perhaps is it necessary. Ydígoras apparently arranged the return of Arévalo in the hopes of seeing him beaten in an 'open' election. Whether Peralta Azurdia ever agreed to this is not certain, but he could have done it either for the purpose of capturing Arévalo on his arrival or to afford himself the excuse he needed to topple Ydígoras. Many people maintain that this last was the actual plan, executed with Ydígoras's connivance, to give the old General a way out – what is known in Latin America as an *auto-coup* or an *auto-golpe*.

There is no question that Ydígoras was an adroit political schemer (thus his nickname, the 'Old Fox') and a man who had survived many attempts against his Government. He had always managed to play one power bloc off against another, and in times of political earthquakes, when the dust lifted, there he would stand in the middle, straight as a rod, the rubble of political opponents spread around his feet. It is this fact that prompted many to think that he could have survived Peralta Azurdia's attempt if he had so wished. It certainly did not take him by surprise since the *coup* was talked about around the capital quite openly for weeks in advance.

There is another ramification to this theory. It is believed that Peralta received John Kennedy's go-ahead for the over-

10. Ydígoras, op. cit., p. 5.

throw without JFK's understanding that Ydígoras himself was implicated. This was an attempt to compromise the young US President as a responsible party to a *coup* and thus to commit him to further financial aid to the new Government.

Ydígoras did give Peralta his blessing a few days after the latter was seated in the President's chair and even went so far as to declare he was in voluntary exile and to name Peralta as his 'personal representative'.[11] He says he did this to save the country from 'confusion and communism' and not because he agreed with the *coup*. The situation was one that demanded clarification by Peralta. His fellow countrymen could understand much of the political dynamics, and were happy that Ydígoras was gone, but it was also necessary for him to justify his action to the world, to receive diplomatic recognition, especially that of the US, and to declare his political creed. Everyone realized that the basic principle of any military government in Guatemala had to be 'anti-communism', as Peralta had stated in his 'Fundamental Charter'. But this was not enough, since his predecessor had also been rabidly 'anti-communist' and yet the country was in a very sorry plight. Something more was needed, some virtue that had not been practised by Ydígoras, something that was anti-Ydígoras even as Castillo Armas had been anti-Arbenz. It was not difficult to decide what that virtue would have to be: honesty.

Peralta Azurdia adopted the name *Operación Honestidad*, Operation Honesty, as the theme of his administration. He would attempt to bring 'honesty' back to public life. To this purpose he took a reduction in his own salary, fired all 'phantoms' on the Government payrolls and quickly decreed Law 52.

Decree 52, promulgated on 20 June 1963, declared that all the transactions of State properties that had been made by the Redemption Government were illegal and subject to in-

11. ibid., p. 6.

vestigation. Peralta immediately began a process of recupera-
tion of these properties and eventually tried unsuccessfully
to bring Ydígoras back to the country to stand trial along
with five of his colleagues, who had already been jailed for
malversation of public funds.

When we speak of Peralta's agrarian reform, or rather what
he characterizes as his agrarian reform, we must not lose
sight of his declared orientation : anti-communism and
honesty. He maintained that his rule was only temporary, so
it stands that no long-range planning could be undertaken.
His was a caretaker Government. He stayed in office three
years. Most observers believe that his Government was relatively free from graft and corruption. He did prevent a 'communist take-over', if in fact one had been imminent. He
therefore did fulfil the goals that he set for himself, and thus
justified the rationale of his *coup*.

But what of the people? What of the great landless masses
who every day were becoming more and more conscious of
their misery, of the injustice of their situation? Was the new
Head of Government unconscious of their rights, their aspirations, their history and the social dynamics then at work in
Guatemala?

On 28 September 1963 he announced what the agricultural
policy of his Government was to be. He said that Guatemala's
fundamental problem was the low standard of living of the
peasant population. The goal of his Government would be
'to raise this standard so that well-being might flow to the
rural areas'.[12] But this would be done gradually, by stages,
with a socio-economic programme that respected private
property.

It would be a mistake to base our agrarian policy on a régime
of massive expropriations of private lands, since this would produce inconvenient emotional reactions and have sterile effects

12. *El Imparcial*, 28 September 1963.

that are incompatible with the financial resources of the State.[13]

He announced that in order to demonstrate his Government's sincerity, he had placed at the disposition of INTA 'the extensive and magnificent State lands of Quiché and Izabal'. Later, other measures regarding the National Fincas would be announced.

Congressional elections were held to establish a 'Constituent Assembly' that would draw up a 'Magna Carta' to substitute for the abrogated Constitution. The Christian Democrats refused to participate in the elections because they did not want to lend an air of legitimacy to a military Government. The Revolutionary Party did participate, as did the Liberation Party, and a document was formulated that was meant to legitimize and give permanence to the legislation issued by the government.

When Congress discussed agriculture, they suppressed the section that said : 'The law shall determine the protection of family patrimony, the better use of the nation's resources, and the limitations of the right of private property that may be necessary for the transformation of idle lands.' [14]

They did approve three articles that contained the basis for future agrarian legislation :

Article 63 : Private property is guaranteed. The State has the obligation of assuring the proprietor the necessary conditions for the development and utilization of his goods. The law will determine the proprietor's obligations and rights.

Article 66 : In concrete cases, private property can be expropriated. It will be paid for according to its actual value within ten years, plus interest. To determine the value, all elements, circumstances and conditions will be considered instead of registrations or official documents.

13. ibid.   14. ibid., 25 March 1965.

Article 116: A programme of agricultural reform will be based on: (1) No lands will be touched that are considered necessary by the proprietor for enlarging his enterprise; (2) While there are national lands that are not yet registered, private lands will not be touched unless they are legally declared to be idle; (3) Idle lands can be expropriated once the State has exhausted all national lands, has given the owner a reasonable amount of time and has paid for the lands in full; (4) Forest land will never be considered idle land.[15]

Even with the assurance of this constitutional protection, the National Agricultural Council [16] was worried and wanted to make sure that the talk of land reform remained just that. They asked that the colonization of the Northern region of the country be declared of public utility and of national urgency. They based their request on the fact that 'all the attempts at reform since Arbenz have failed because they have always been accompanied by agitation and political explosion'.[17] They went on to explain that the 27,000 [sic] beneficiaries of the different attempts at reform had not improved their lot owing to a lack of understanding of the 'idiosyncracies of the peasants' on the part of the authorities. And they added:

The beneficiaries of lots in Government distributions continue being orphans in education, sanitary attention, living in housing that lacks comfort, without water, electricity or the hope of a prompt improvement of their standard of living in which they were placed at a given moment.[18]

15. ibid., 26 March 1965.
16. The National Agricultural Council is formed by: AGA, National Association of Coffee Growers, Association of Lumber Producers, National Association of Sugar Producers, Guatemalan Association of Cotton Growers, Cattlemen's Association and the Chamber of Industry.
17. El Imparcial, 1 April 1965.
18. ibid.

If the expropriations and distribution of private lands were to follow the same pattern as before, they said, there could only come as a result 'political convulsions which are negative to the development which Guatemala needs'. This is the voice of the landowners and those who enjoy the comfort and luxury of a standard of living 'in which *they* were placed at a given moment'. They would like to see some of the landless peasants settled in the Northern regions of the country, away from their own plantations where 60·7 per cent of the lands are temptingly idle.[19] They criticized the lack of technical, sanitary and educational assistance to the holders of lots given them by the Government, but they refused to face a rise in taxes – some of the lowest in the world [20] – and they maintained the workers in their own plantations in far worse conditions.

The National Agricultural Council warned the legislators that the expropriations and distributions of private lands would cause 'political convulsions'. These could only come from themselves, since they were the only ones objecting to land reform. The question remains whether their plans for the development of Guatemala gives these 'idiosyncratic peasants' a positive share in that development.

In the Economic Council of the United States, Michael George, the US delegate, said that only if an agrarian reform has as its primary goal the increase of agricultural production, as well as social and political reform, will its results be socially and politically satisfactory. This statement produced the following remark in an editorial:

At last they [the U.S.] are beginning to realize the danger of the so-called peaceful revolution proposed by the Alliance for Pro-

19. CIDA, op. cit., p. 20.

20. *El Imparcial*, 5 January 1968: out of sixty-four countries listed, Guatemala rated sixty-third, with taxes comprising 7·7 per cent of the GNP.

gress. Rapid reform creates more political and social problems than it solves.[21]

This reference to the Alliance for Progress was becoming a hot point in congressional discussions. Most observers agree that Ydígoras's attempts to bring Guatemalan legislation into line with the demands of the Alliance had been political ploys not meant to effect social change. His Agrarian Reform Bill was a step backwards from that of Castillo Armas, and his Income Tax Law, which replaced other tax laws, amounted to an increase of tax revenues of from eleven to thirteen million *quetzales*, far too little to be meaningful. The Alliance for Progress had been set up a few months after the unsuccessful Bay of Pigs invasion and wisely recognized the popularity of Fidel Castro's agrarian reform. Title I.6 of the Alliance Charter states:

To encourage, in accordance with the characteristics of each country, programs of comprehensive agrarian reform leading to the effective transformation, where required, of unjust structures and systems of land tenure and use, with a view to replacing latifundia and dwarf holdings by an equitable system of land tenure so that, with the help of timely and adequate credit, technical assistance and facilities for marketing and distribution of products, the land will become for the man who works it the basis of his economic stability, the foundation of his increasing welfare and the guarantee of his freedom and dignity.[22]

In December 1964 in Lima, Peru, the Third Annual Meeting of the Inter-American Economic and Social Council at the Ministerial Level was held, and it clarified what was meant by 'Agrarian Reform' in the Alliance Charter. It recognized that 'the majority of Latin American Countries have established legal instruments aimed at bringing about agrarian

21. ibid., 16 July 1965.
22. CIDA, *The Agrarian Reform and the Alliance for Progress.* Washington: CIDA, 1965, p. 2.

reform',[23] but stressed that to be effective such a reform had to produce structural changes. These changes included 'giving the land its social function' and 'modernizing rural life' as well as changing the power structure of the nation.[24]

The concept that land could have a 'social function' became the subject of an acrimonious debate in the Guatemalan Congress.[25] The Congressmen were being pressured by the Chamber of Industry, which maintained that:

Social justice is a dangerous ambiguity. For the communists and socialists, social justice is administered by the State; for Catholics, social justice is left to the conscience of every individual.[26]

El *Imparcial*, the leading daily, published editorials against the concept of social justice every day[27] and the Co-ordinating Committee of the Association of Landowners, Businessmen, Industrialists and Bankers demanded that all references to social justice be struck from the Constitution:

We are not against social justice but rather against the demagogic way this term is used. Private enterprise might collapse if we augment the burdens of the owners.[28]

By the end of June 1965 only one Congressman out of eighty was arguing for the rights of the little man:

It seems that you people need a 'cacique' in order to tell you what it is that you should approve; nothing for the benefit of the worker has been approved by this Assembly.[29]

The Congressman, Mauro Monterroso, complained that he was accused of 'communism' every time he presented one of his motions.[30]

23. ibid., p. 3.   24. ibid., pp. 3–4.
25. El *Imparcial*, 12–16 March 1965.   26. ibid., 2 February 1965.
27. ibid., 12–16 March 1965.   28. ibid., 27 May 1965.
29. ibid., 30 June 1965.   30. ibid.

Finally the 'Magna Carta' was approved and it was signed by all the deputies but one, his objection being not to the fact that all mention of social justice had been excluded but rather that the Archbishop's representative, Monseñor Girón Perrone, didn't like the text and had said, 'No special rights have been democratically conceded that correspond to the Church.'[31] He was answered by José Calderón Salazar of the Liberation Party, who had led the fight for the rights of the Church:

Seven months we fought over this Magna Carta and not a word out of the Church; even when we discussed the topic of social justice, the Catholic Hierarchy could be found toasting at a reception, turning their backs on the religious reality of Guatemala.[32]

The justification for the exclusion of such concepts had been given by Congressman Menéndez Sandoval of the Liberation Party:

The evil phrase, 'the social function of property', gave birth precisely to Decree 900 which was on the point of carrying Guatemala to the greatest disaster in its history, this both in practice and in theory, because the real agrarian problem of Guatemala is not the scarcity of lands but rather that the lands be made to produce more.[33]

In view of the fact that the Alliance recognized the need for changes in the power structure that were based on the ownership of land, the Lima Meeting specified that 'expansion of agricultural production and colonization are not acceptable substitutes for agrarian reform'.[34] Yet colonization was the programme that Castillo Armas had begun with his agrarian zones; the one that was continued by Ydígoras; and

31. ibid., 14 September 1965.   32. ibid.
33. ibid., 30 October 1964.
34. CIDA, *The Agrarian Reform . . .*, p. 4.

it seemed now that it would be the line of least resistance that would be followed by the Peralta Azurdia Government.

On June 11, 1965, Decree 354 was promulgated. Its preamble stated its purpose:

Considering that it is the fundamental obligation of the State to dictate the measures necessary to bring about the greatest possible good for the inhabitants of the nation and that among these measures, one that is urgent is the provision of lands to be dedicated to the production of foodstuffs, in order to satisfy the demands of a minimum diet for the inhabitants;

Considering that the lands of Guatemala that are actually dedicated to the production of foodstuffs will not be sufficient in the immediate future to produce what is necessary for the inhabitants;

Considering that it is urgent to foresee what the consumption of foodstuffs in Guatemala will be, and that this makes it necessary to prepare and colonize new lands, such as those along the banks of the Usumacinta River and its tributaries, which, for ecological reasons are the most appropriate for this purpose . . .

Article One then stated what would be done:

The fixed goal of greatest priority is to obtain, in a time period no greater than ten years, the intensification of the colonization and the rational utilization of the lands of the Department of Petén, and of all the rest that constitute the banks of the Usumacinta River and its tributaries.[35]

The notice of the shortage of primary foodstuffs was something Peralta could not continue to ignore. During the Ydígoras administration, the yearly shortage of corn necessitated the importation of hundreds of thousands of quintals from the US and Mexico, and now rice too, another peasant staple, was being imported. If for no other reason than to

35. *Diario Oficial, El Guatemalteco,* vol. CLXIII, No. 85, 11 June 1965.

maintain a more favourable trade balance, more lands had to be brought into production. However, the banks of the Usumacinta and its tributaries were not the most appropriate for this purpose, as will be discussed later.

The colonization of Petén had been seen as a partial solution to Guatemala's land difficulties seventeen years earlier and had even been·attempted by Arévalo without much success. When Ydígoras had come to power, he proclaimed, as one of the primary goals of his Government, the development of Petén, which comprises one third of the national territory and is covered largely by rain forests. Shortly after Ydígoras took office, Decree 1286 was issued, declaring the economic development of Petén to be of 'national urgency'. This was to be accomplished by the 'scientific exploitation and preservation of its forests and other natural resources, a programme of public health, its colonization and industrialization'.[36] It can be seen, though, from Article 6 that this colonization was not directed for the benefit of the landless and illiterate masses, but rather was aimed:

to stimulate an increase in the population of Petén, organizing industrial, agricultural and cattle raising colonies and to establish new urban communities and tourist centres, looking to the needs that a gradual development of Petén demands. To accomplish this, FYDEP [Institute for the Development of Petén] will study the convenience of bringing in immigrants, preferably those who are specialized in particular crops, techniques of forestry, animal husbandry or industry. . . .[37]

The programme never seriously got under way with Ydígoras and now Peralta decided that perhaps the colonization of the Petén could be the solution to the agrarian problem after all, and he published Decree 354.

There are a number of reasons why the Alliance for Progress technicians would not accept colonization as a substi-

36. Azurdia, vol. LXXVIII, p. 12.   37. ibid.

tute for land reform. Colonization means the opening up of virgin lands that are in the hands of the State. Colonization is meant to avoid touching those unused lands that are in private hands. Where political, economic and social power are very intimately linked to the possession of lands in Latin America, the unwillingness to expropriate excessive lands owned privately represents in reality an unwillingness or inability to change the archaic political, economic and social structures. Furthermore, the mere fact that virgin lands are still in the hands of the State, after more than four hundred years of domination by the Spanish tradition of land ownership, says much about the condition of these lands, as regards their inaccessibility and/or their worthlessness. In addition, to substitute colonization for the expropriation of large, idle, private holdings means a far greater expense in both economic and social terms while not directly affecting the political system, and therefore can be nothing more than a token.

When Castillo Armas began his programme of *zonas agrarias* in 1956, CIDA stated that 'The spirit of the law, nevertheless, gave the new programme all the characteristics of a colonization, rather than a reform.' [38] The reasons for qualifying it as such were that the two main projects of the programme were on virgin lands that had been purchased from private owners: United Fruit gave 'Nueva Concepción' through a special agreement with the Government and 'La Máquina' was purchased for half a million *quetzales*. The implications are that State lands are largely worthless for colonization and that to obtain suitable lands is a very expensive project. Such an expense puts a limit on the amount of help that can be provided by such a solution, as Castillo Armas and Ydígoras well understood. Peralta Azurdia could not have been blind to the limitations of such a programme.

In August 1964 a precursory notice appeared in the news-

38. CIDA, *Tenencia . . .* , p. 47.

papers to the effect that the Ministry of Public Health was fighting a malaria epidemic in the Agrarian Zone of Nueva Concepción. Doctor Ponce Archila, the Minister of Public Health, had to utilize emergency methods to aid the 'more than 10,000 homes in which live more than 38,000 people'.[39] A month later, Col. Pedro Rodríguez Valenzuela, head of INTA, in view of the fact that there were supposed to be only 1,150 farms in the area, ordered an investigation of Nueva Concepción, 'because there are people living there illegally, others are renting their farms, and others have sold theirs, contrary to Decree 1551'.[40]

Part of the difficulty, as we have seen, was that many farms had been given out to undeserving people and that they had obtained *colonos* to work the lands for them. But the real reason that Nueva Concepción had turned into another project of *minifundismo* was that the effort was too modest in view of the overwhelming needs. People flowed into any area where lands were distributed by the Government and it was difficult for the beneficiaries to refuse entrance in the farms to their relatives and *compadres* who were in the same miserable conditions as the fortunate beneficiary had been.

The same thing happened to La Máquina. In October 1967 it was observed that the 'floating population of the zone had reached between 17,000 and 18,000 people'.[41] This figure plus the legitimate population put the total somewhere near 24,000 people on 1,147 farms – another rampant case of *minifundismo*. This should have been some indication of the difficulties Arbenz had experienced in holding back the peasants from illegal invasions once distributions had begun.

That Peralta Azurdia really believed that the colonization of the Northern jungles would solve the agrarian problem may legitimately be doubted. He was not ignorant and his

39. *El Imparcial*, 29 August 1964.   40. ibid., 2 October 1964.
41. ibid., 11 October 1967.

interest in the Petén region dated from his term of office as Head of the DGAA. In June 1963, only two months after his *coup*, he attended a meeting with the directors of the Government Bank and members of the National Economic Planning Commission to study the proposal of F. M. Warren of Coastal Timber and Pulp Company to invest $100,000,000 in Petén's lumber industry. The project was named 'Showcase for Democracy' and the Company wanted timber rights for the entire area.[42] In July another group of US investors went to Guatemala and made counter-proposals of huge investments, one of which was a plywood factory. FYDEP officials were also busy showing Guatemalan cattlemen the treeless savannahs for their livestock that they could purchase for a song.[43]

In December 1964 FYDEP announced the creation of its new Department of Colonization with Col. Romeo Samayoa as its director. His first announcement stated the intention to create 125 farms of 22·5 *caballerías* (62,470 acres) each for cattle raising – not meant for small farms. He mentioned that he already had 2,400 requests for land in Petén and that within eight years the population of the Department would be 70,000 people, or an increase of 45,000 over the existing population. He said that selection of those who would receive lands would be made by lottery so that no second guessing would occur.[44]

A month later, the first official word was given that Petén was being considered as a solution to the agrarian problem, when the economic development plan for 1965–9 stated:

The government contemplates a massive colonization of the Government lands situated in the Northern portion of the country, by means of a system that will take care of the great needs of the Western population, dispossessed of lands, as well as the manner of exploiting the same.[45]

42. ibid., 11 June 1963.　　43. ibid., 4 June 1964.
44. ibid., 17 December 1964.　　45. ibid., 9 January 1965.

A few days later, the first farm of 22·5 *caballerías* (2,470 acres) was given to Pompeyo Del Valle Cano, a native of Petén. He was promised that title would be given later.

In June 1965 J. Philip Murphy, President of Murphy Pacific Corporation of California, went to Guatemala to 'finalize the investment of $30 million in the colonization of the Northern part of the country, forming CIAINSA (Compañia Impulsadora del Norte, S.A.) for Petén and Alta Verapaz'.[46] A week later the Secretary of Information of the Government announced Decree 354 and stated:

Our goal is the intensification of the colonization and rational exploitation of the lands of Petén and all the others that constitute the Usumacinta River basin and tributaries within ten years. These lands are very suitable due to ecological conditions. The Government will stimulate private enterprise to aid in the project.[47]

In October, the National Council of Agriculture, a private organization composed of the various lobbying groups, gave this measure its wholehearted support, declaring:

The colonization of the Petén is of national emergency and public necessity in order to increase the production of basic foods, to relieve the congestion of overpopulation in certain regions, to combat crime and decrease unemployment, to maintain the sovereignty of our territory in the North, to stop the invasions of national lands and to guarantee the respect and inviolability of private property.[48]

A few days later, Col. Peralta Azurdia announced to the landowners that they should not fear expropriation of their properties since the Government had no money to pay them. He also announced that in view of Decree 354, 590,000

46. ibid., 9 June 1965. 47. ibid., 14 June 1965.
48. ibid., 9 October 1965.

hectares (1,457,300 acres) of Petén would be incorporated into the national economy : 330,000 hectares (815,100 acres) for cattle and 260,000 (642,200 acres) for agriculture.[49] That same month, the first two groups of landless peasants went to the banks of the Pasión River in Sayaxché : ninety families formed the co-operative 'Felicidad' from the floating population now grown huge in the Government's agrarian zone of Nueva Concepción; another fifteen families formed the co-operative 'Manos Unidas' from Cabricán, Quezaltenango, a parish co-operative founded by the Maryknoll Fathers.[50] In March 1966 the National Council of Catholic Bishops announced its backing of the colonization programme represented by the Cabricán parish co-operative, and promised that it would lend moral support to the effort to transfer 5,000 families to Petén.[51] AID stated its willingness to lend money to the co-operatives for the cultivation of rubber, but when their technicians analysed the soil they found that the lands given to the peasants had a very high water-table and that the top soil was only a few inches deep. Dr James Walker of the University of North Carolina, a leading expert in this field, predicted that the lands would be swamps within five years if they were given over to agriculture. No money would therefore be given for rubber or any other crop to be sown on the lands along the banks of the Pasión and Usumacinta Rivers. This, despite the fact that the Government was still maintaining that 'these lands are very suitable due to ecological conditions'.

Sebol-Chinajá was another creation of the Peralta Azurdia Government, planned along the lines of the agrarian zones

49. ibid., 15 October 1965.
50. Maryknoll is a North American Catholic missionary society of which the authors were members. 'Manos Unidas' is one of the co-operatives founded by the authors.
51. El Imparcial, 2 March 1966.

and meant to correct the errors of Nueva Concepción and La Máquina. It was organized to settle 25,000 families in the forests of Northern Alta Verapaz at a cost of Q64 million. Since the project was to be developed by INTA, and the lands ran into the Petén, which was FYDEP territory, it was not certain how the obvious conflict was to be resolved. The first public information about the project came in July 1963 with the formation of the Agrarian Zone Fray Bartolomé de las Casas, in which 1,000 families would receive two *caballerías* (219.6 acres) each and 552 families one *caballería* (109.8 acres) each.[52]

In May 1964 the announcement was made that 100,000 families would receive lands 'in the North', that AID would give two million dollars towards the study and that the Guatemalan Government would give eight million for the same purpose. A loan was being made from BID for seven million dollars to start settling 1,000 families, in the Sebol-Chinajá area.[53]

Just as had happened in Nueve Concepción and in La Máquina, as soon as people heard that lands were to be given out they began moving into the area so as to receive preference. In July 1964 INTA warned that those who, without INTA's authorization, moved on to the lands to be distributed, would be considered invaders and would never receive lands. INTA claimed that unscrupulous people were organizing landless peasants to invade the area.[54] In 1965 a UN report on the colonization zone Fray Bartolomé de las Casas stated that there were already 475 single-room houses of rustic poles and palm roofs with damp dirt-floors, housing approximately 3,000 people.[55] The majority of these homes

52. ibid., 17 July 1963.
53. ibid., 16 May 1964.
54. ibid., 18 July 1964.
55. Oficina Internacional del Trabajo, *Informe al Gobierno de Guatemala sobre Colonización*: Ginebra, 1965 (mimeo), p. 89.

had no latrines or baths and all were getting their water from open streams. Control of malaria was most difficult.

In May 1967, when FYDEP and INTA were arguing over which institution would control the colonization of Petén, the Head of FYDEP charged:

The impotency of INTA during these past four years in the land distributions of Sebol, Fray Bartolomé de las Casas, and Puerto Sebol-Chinajá, constitutes an irrefutable case of that paralysis that appears in the distribution of lands suitable to their purposes and it will be much more grave in lands that are not so suitable.[56]

If INTA's purpose was land reform, it could be questioned whether or not these lands were suitable. But when these lands are compared to those of the Petén, the point was well taken. By July 1967, 530 farms had been distributed and already 7,000 people were living on them.[57] The process continued.

The total land distributions made by the Peralta Azurdia Government were: forty-five titles to farms (extension unknown),[58] two hundred urban lots,[59] and five hundred and thirty provisional titles in the Sebol–Chinajá project.

56. El Imparcial, 24 May 1967.   57. ibid., 17 July 1967.
58. ibid., 4 May 1965.   59. ibid., 16 February 1965.

CHAPTER 11

An Aristocratic Government

An aristocratic government has an inherent vigour, unknown to democracy. The nobles form a body, who by their prerogative, and for their particular interest, restrain the people; it is sufficient that there are laws in being to see them executed.

MONTESQUIEU

Since this interim military régime had no other social goal than honesty in the conduct of its business, perhaps we should not expect that it realistically would or could do anything about the outstanding social problems of the nation. Still, we cannot take this to mean that it was completely indifferent to what was going on in the country or that it merely attempted to maintain the *status quo*. There are some indications of Peralta's concern with his Government's prestige in the rural area. One effort was the construction of 191 small but very visible schools, financed tripartitely by his Government, the AID and the local communities. No attempt was made, however, to improve the quality of education, simply a farce in many areas because *ladino* teachers often refuse to instruct Indian pupils.

The expulsions of peasants from lands they had possessed for many years were not as numerous as under the Ydígoras Government, judging from the newspapers. However, the constant 'state of siege' declared by the military Government extensively limited the freedom of the Press. And it can also be recalled that the individual in charge of these expulsions under the Redemption Government had been the then Head of the DGAA, Peralta Azurdia himself. On 29 January 1964 the newspapers record what might have been the first expulsion order under the military Government:

Twenty-five families in El Manchón were told by the Governor of Retalhuleu [1] to leave their homes and burn them, or go to jail. They have lived for thirty years on the lands of the *finca* Buenos Aires and the former owner had left them alone. Two months ago the *finca* was bought by Juan Samayoa, whose son was named military commissioner of the area.[2]

The other reports are more terse: 'Several families were expelled from their homes by the municipal government in Zone 8 of Guatemala City.'[3] 'Fifteen families expelled from their lands in Zone 12. Women and children crying in the streets. The men demand to see the President. They have lived there twenty years and now have no place to go.'[4] 'Ten families expelled from municipal property in Guatemala City.'[5] 'The Association of University Students [AEU] appeals to INTA to investigate the expulsion of thirty families from their lands in Gualán where they have legitimate ownership papers dating back to 1928. The man who claims ownership, Ricardo Miralles, is the brother-in-law of the judge of the Zacapa area, who is accused of falsifying the papers of ownership.'[6] 'Indians in Chipacatox, Baja Verapaz, claim that Fernández Isaguirre has stolen three *caballerías* from them. Fifteen years before he tried the same thing and the Arbenz Government declared that the lands belonged to the Indians. Now he has built a fence around the land.'[7]

1. All Governors of the Departments under the military Government as well as under Méndez Montenegro are Army officers.
2. *El Imparcial*, 29 January 1964.　　　3. ibid., 25 February 1964.
4. ibid., 13 February 1965.　　　5. ibid., 17 May 1965.
6. ibid., 6 January 1966.　　　7. ibid., 16 April 1966.

Perhaps a more serious indictment of the military Government arises from the situation it permitted to exist on the cotton plantations. Ydígoras had been quite generous in extending credits and encouraging the large landowners to devote more lands to cotton, in order to diversify the country's exports. He was successful in this, but just as the *latifundistas* became wealthier on their cotton, the peasants' lives became more miserable on the plantations. On 15 October 1963 the Inspector General of Labour 'energetically warned the cotton growers to build houses for their workers since a great number are obliged to sleep exposed to the weather. There has been much sickness and often this results in the deaths of entire families.'[8]

Warnings such as these, however, do not carry much force in Guatemala. Indeed they are not meant to, since the Government itself backs up the plantation owners' attempts to secure unwilling labourers.

In 1965, the Army went into some villages in the Department of San Marcos and rounded up peasants at gun point to work on the cotton plantations.[9] The Army was also used in at least two other Departments and although physical force was used, guns apparently were not.[10] In all three cases, the action was taken by the departmental Governors at the request of the Minister of the Interior.[11] These men responded to pressures by the National Cotton Council.

In 1966, when enough migrant workers could not be found to pick the cotton (it is estimated that between three hundred and four hundred thousand are needed to harvest the crop),[12] the Government was roundly condemned by the landowners for scheduling an election that interfered with their labour-seeking campaign.[13]

Since conditions on the cotton plantations are even worse

8. ibid., 15 October 1963.   9. ibid., 21 April 1964.
10. ibid., 15 April 1964.   11. ibid., 23 April 1964.
12. ibid., 10 June 1966.   13. ibid., 16 February 1966.

than those on the coffee *fincas*, obtaining workers for the harvest is not easy. Much of the difficulty can be ascribed to the use of deathly insecticides. The Institute of Social Security announced that there had been five cases of deaths and 151 cases of intoxication reported during the months of July, August and September 1963, all due to insecticide poisoning.[14] Cases such as these are not often reported, so the figures available can be considered to be conservative. The Director of the Social Security Institute maintained that 325 *fincas* had secured authorization for spraying without the necessary legal inspection. He himself had denied authorization to many other owners only to have the permission granted by the Minister of Agriculture.[15] Nowhere is there mention of any landowners being taken to court for the poisonings and deaths of their workers. Nor is there apt to be.

The treatment that the migrant workers receive from the landowners is consistent, if not just. They work for eleven hours a day and are paid sixty centavos, as in Cotzumalguapa.[16] Sixty-three peasants from Cobán working in Tiquisate were not paid at all and managed to escape from the farm and get a ride to Guatemala City. There, the Red Cross found them all sick from not having eaten for several days. They were fed and sent home – nothing happened to the plantation owner.[17] Another thirty peasants were dumped on the highway after having worked on a cotton plantation without pay. Of the thirty, 'twenty-seven were sick with malaria, malnutrition and bronchial infections'. The Red Cross got to them after they had gone forty-eight hours without food. They were fed and sent home. Nothing was done to the plantation owner, but he promised to pay their salaries, owing probably to the fact that news of the incident reached the

14. ibid., 18 September 1963.
15. ibid., 18 September 1963.
16. ibid., 16 August 1965.
17. ibid., 11 October 1965.

papers.[18] How many similar incidents occurred that were never reported in the Press can only be conjectured.

Labour unions had been established on the plantations during the administrations of Arévalo and Arbenz in order to help avoid this kind of abuse. Under Castillo Armas they were broken and suppressed. Then, with the reluctant permission of Ydígoras, they began to take on new life. He apparently wanted, over the objections of the landowners, to build them up as a political force for his own party.

Peralta Azurdia, however, dedicated himself to the persecution of these same unions, seeing them as a communist threat. He imprisoned many of the movement's leaders as a 'preventive measure'. He sent secret police to work among the peasants in order to identify and capture the leaders of these organizations. When the secret police found the field work too difficult, he promulgated Decree 332, which ordered the Army to take over the obligations of the national police on the plantations.[19] Article 5 ordered that whatever aid is needed by the plantation owners or their administrators is to be given; while Article 6 demanded that 'those who get the peasants excited' be reported to the Army. The law is rather open-ended as regards punishment.

A projected law, reminiscent of Ubico, was submitted to Congress by the Minister of the Interior. Fortunately, because of the outcry against it, the law was not passed. It was to have been a law against vagrancy and Article 6 stated:

Any individual detained for what is classified as dangerous vagrancy will be sent to a work camp where he will be obliged to work for a period of not less than six months nor more than six years.[20]

18. ibid., 27 May 1966.   19. ibid., 24 February 1965.
20. ibid., 7 July 1965.

It was meant to apply to anyone between the ages of sixteen and sixty years.

As the situation of the peasants deteriorated, the guerrilla movements obtained more backing in the Escuintla, Zacapa and Izabal areas. Encounters between the Army and the guerrilla forces became more frequent, and the Government had a difficult time determining where the guerrillas were picking up their support. On 8 March 1966 the police moved into Río Hondo, Zacapa, and took prisoner every adult male in the village, over one hundred men:

It is not known where they are ... they were detained by members of the police, and until this time it is not known where they are or why they were detained.[21]

Actually it was very well known why they were detained. The guerrilla movement of Luis Turcios Lima was very active in the area and the Government was desperately trying to find out what peasants and villages were supplying the combatants with food and information.

Turcios Lima had participated with Yon Sosa in the 13 November 1960 uprising and had continued the struggle with him. But as the two of them studied the politics of armed revolution, they had a parting of ways, Yon Sosa following a Trotskyist orientation, and Turcios Lima, under the name of FAR (Armed Forces of Rebellion), a stricter Leninist philosophy. FAR aligned itself with the PGT (Partido Guatemalteco del Trabajo) but subsequently broke that relationship, reunited with Yon Sosa and his MR-13 (13 November Movement), then broke off again. The difficulties seemed to revolve more around the tactics of the revolution than about its objectives, because all three groups maintained that a principal aim of the revolution was to give land to the peasants, as declared by the FAR:

21. *El Gráfico*, 8 March 1966.

The fact is that we fight for a democratic and nationalist programme; we fight to effect an agrarian and anti-imperialist revolution. ... We are after an agrarian revolution, the rapid expropriation of the large *latifundios* by the peasants themselves and by this means to restructure our whole national economy, all our industrial planning. ... The replacement of the large landowner by the peasant is not done by slaps on the back and loving embraces. It is done by force ...[22]

As the battles between the Army and the guerrillas became more frequent, often with the Army coming out on the losing end, the Government became more desperate in trying to gain control over the situation. In Quirigua the military commissioners forcibly entered peasant homes and nine men were reported missing and not consigned to any tribunal.[23] Two days before the peasant round-up in Río Hondo, the Government had also captured twenty-eight other persons, leaders of the PGT, union organizers and guerrilla sympathizers, taking them from their homes. Víctor Manuel Gutiérrez, and Leonardo Castillo Flore, labour organizers under Arbenz, were among them.[24] As the government claimed no knowledge of these captures, the guerrillas of the FAR staged a daring daylight kidnapping of the Secretary of Information of the Government and the Head of the Supreme Court. They followed this up with the capture of the President of Congress, who was also Head of the PID, the political party set up by the military Government to participate in the coming elections. FAR offered to exchange these three men for the twenty-eight persons still presumed to be in the custody of the Government. The Head of the Red Cross, the Head of the National University and the Archbishop of Guatemala City all offered to be intermediaries in the ex-

22. *Prensa Libre*, 26 August 1966.
23. *El Imparcial*, 28 February 1966.
24. *El Gráfico*, 6 March 1966. (Among 'the twenty-eight' were two women; one was Yon Sosa's cousin.)

change but the Government continued to deny knowledge of 'the twenty-eight's' whereabouts.

It became known months later, when the military Government was no longer in power, that 'the twenty-eight' had been murdered by the Government's No. 2 strong-man, Col. Rafael Arriaga Bosque[25] and so no exchange could be made. Upon learning of the execution of their twenty-eight companions and judging it to be politically wise, the FAR released two of their prisoners. The President of Congress, Menéndez de La Riva, had already managed to escape from his captors. The hostilities were becoming more pronounced and the Government did not seem capable of handling the situation.

The United States' Military Mission in the country, as well as other sectors of the AID programme being offered to Peralta Azurdia, were being ignored. For one thing, the Head of Government was trying to put his balance of payments in order and he couldn't accept help that would cost him money. It was a common thing during the last days of Peralta's rule to hear expressions of despair in the corridors and offices of the Cruz Azul Building (AID headquarters) in Guatemala City from the Directors of the Alliance for Progress. Their chagrin was only matched by Peralta's stubbornness in refusing offers of loans for every conceivable (or ill-conceived) project. This also included his unwillingness to allow MAP (US Military Assistance Program) to expand its activities; however, this refusal was apparently due to a military and nationalistic pride, rather than the US price-tag. It was in such an atmosphere that the guerrilla revolutionary bands were able to expand their activities and that the Army found it very difficult to control them. The landed aristocracy and the business sectors of the populace were becoming quite upset with Peralta's refusal to co-operate with the United States. When Senator Wayne Morse, of Oregon, made a

25. ibid., 17 July 1966.

public statement to the effect that the United States would interfere in Guatemala if things didn't get better, Peralta was furious and his Government responded: 'We are not the Dominican Republic. The Guatemalan Government can handle by itself any internal subversives.'[26] It was on the promise of closer co-operation with the United States, especially militarily, that Col. Miguel Angel Ponciano and the MLN (National Liberation Movement, Castillo Armas's party) were building their election campaign.

The United States House of Representatives had not helped the situation six months previously by also making a public statement duly reported in the Guatemalan press:

The US or any other American country has the right of uni-laterial intervention in order to keep communism outside the Western Hemisphere.[27]

The vote had been 312 to 52 in favour of this resolution and although it was not a law, it expressed the sentiments of the Congress and gave the US President 'liberty of action'. Although the resolution seemed directed primarily at the Dominican Republic and was an attempt to justify the military action there, it was seen as a threat by almost every other Latin American country, especially the proud Peralta. It was condemned as a 'stupid attitude' by the Chilean Congress, and four Mexican dailies condemned it as the 'worst threat ever faced by the peoples of Latin America'.[28] The declaration never became known to the majority of the landless peasants of Guatemala, but the landowners breathed a sigh of relief.

A month later, Thomas Mann, Assistant Secretary of State for Interamerican Affairs, declared in the name of the US government that 'the cornerstone of the Interamerican system is non-intervention'. He was answered by ex-President Jacobo

26. ibid., 3 March 1966.   27. ibid., 21 September 1965.
28. ibid.

Arbenz, then broadcasting from Havana, who said he would continue 'to struggle for the liberation of the people of the Americas, oppressed by imperialism'.[29] The next day, the International Development Bank announced, in headline news, that it had more money to lend to Guatemala for development.[30]

This time, however, the United States could not be accused of trying to defend the lands of the United Fruit Company. Ever since the anti-trust case had gone against them in a New Orleans Court on 4 February 1958 the banana company had been trying to unload its lands. The Court had ordered the company to sell thirty per cent of its assets to competitors, since it had been functioning as a monopoly in the US.[31] Lands seemed to be the most vulnerable asset the Company owned, so President Sunderland had stated in April 1960:

The United Fruit Company has decided to sell or rent or nego-tiate, up to a reasonable point, the lands that it owns in Latin America. The Company will buy the production of the new owners or renters. The times are changing in Latin America and consequently we ought to change also. There exists a completely natural and understandable desire on the part of the citizens of the countries in which we operate, to own their own lands and to cultivate their own crops in order to sell them in international markets. We will try to change according to the rhythm of the times and to negotiate with them in a manner they find accept-able.[32]

By early 1964, Guatemala understood what these words meant. Two thousand five hundred workers were fired by the Company as it closed down operations[33] in Tiquisate. The workers' union made a vain attempt to try to buy the lands from the Company, but Ted Holcombe, manager of UFCo. in Guatemala, said that the lands had already been sold to

29. ibid., 13 October 1965. 30. ibid., 14 October 1965.
31. ibid., 5 February 1958. 32. ibid., 24 March 1960.
33. ibid., 4 January 1964.

'twelve former employees of the company'.[34] These 'former employees' of the Company included Holcombe himself, his son and his son-in-law, who were in the process of becoming large cotton-farmers. The workers protested against the sale and threatened to go to Court in the US to demand that the lands be sold to them because they had applied as soon as the offer of sale had become public knowledge.[35] The threat of appealing to a US Court was impossible for them to carry out. The Company refused and the sale went through to the 'twelve former employees of UFCo'.[36]

It was a profitable arrangement: UFCo. now dealt with these former employees, having sold off its lands to 'competitors' as the New Orleans Court had ordered; they no longer looked like the big bad wolf; they no longer had to deal with a solid union, since the workers were split among several owners; most of these owners were native Guatemalans, consequently denying the workers the cry of imperialism that had formerly united them; and the Company could discontinue expensive educational and health services.

But the new deal did not discourage the guerrilla movement from continuing its blasts at the US as the backbone of the oppressive social, economic and political structure of the country; the former UFCo. workers did not feel that the anti-trust decision of the New Orleans Court had been in their favour; nor did the resolution of the House of Representatives convince the politicized segments of Guatemala that the US was seeking the best interests of the people of that Central American nation.

The Peralta Azurdia Government did say that it backed the workers' petition to purchase the UFCo. lands.[37] No one paid much attention to the statement, however. It was recognized that the Government was concentrating on demonstrating its honesty and its anti-communism.

34. ibid., 31 January 1964.   35. ibid., 5 February 1964.
36. ibid., 24 February 1964.   37. ibid.

The Government's suppression of peasant leagues and union activities, as well as its attempts to stamp out the guerrilla movements, were its anti-communist banners. Its honesty was demonstrated by its reclamation of the National Fincas, its withdrawal from other questionable commercial enterprises, and its fulfilment of the promise to be only a transitory Government.

It was this proud banner of *Operación Honestidad* that finally spelled Peralta's political demise. He was determined to prove to the people that he was all that he claimed to be and this included holding to his word that he would 'prepare a favourable political climate that would permit the Guatemalan people a free election of the person who will direct the destiny of our country without pressure of any kind'.[38] He realized that an honest victory at the polls was impossible for himself, and even if it were, he knew that it would not seem so to many of his countrymen. Rather than be accused of the electoral legerdemain that made Ydígoras so hated, he preferred to establish a political party headed by a candidate other than himself, who would perpetuate the firm hand that he had brought to the nation. So the PID (Institutional Democratic Party) was formed and a colleague of Peralta, Col. Juan de Dios Aguilar, was chosen as its candidate.

38. Azurdia, vol. lxxxii, p. 21.

CHAPTER 12

A Momentary
Coerced Unity

Thus society is in a perpetual state of war. Lacking moral and rational resources to organize its life, without coercion, except in the most immediate and intimate social groups, men remain the victims of the individuals, classes and nations by whose force a momentary coerced unity is achieved, and further conflicts are as certainly created.

REINHOLD NIEBUHR

After having promised to turn the country over to democratic rule, Peralta Azurdia led the nation to the polls on 6 March 1966. The chance that the election would terminate the military Government was slim indeed, since two of the three candidates were Army colonels: Col. Juan de Dios Aguilar was the candidate of the Institutional Democratic Party (PID), set up by the military Government to represent its interests; Col. Miguel Angel Ponciano was the candidate of the MLN, the Liberation Party, and ran on the Castillo Armas platform of anti-communism, private property (big business and large land-holdings), increased counter-insurgency warfare and Church rights. Julio César Méndez Montnegro was the civilian candidate for the Revolutionary Party (PR) and ran on a platform of social justice, the mystique of the 1944 Revolution, an anti-military government and sympathy for his dead brother, Mario Méndez Montenegro.

The latter had become the head of the revolutionary elements in the country since the Arbenz overthrow. He had opposed Ydígoras Fuentes for the presidency in 1957 and 1958 and was thought to be making a deal with Arévalo when Peralta overthrew Ydígoras. But Mario Méndez Montenegro caused much confusion among his followers when he gave his blessing to the Right-wing dictatorship of Peralta Azurdia, stating that he 'supported the coup against Ydígoras in order to avoid allowing the country to fall into chaos'.[1] He allowed his party to join Peralta's rubber stamp Congress even while the Christian Democrats refused to participate in this political farce, and he finally seemed to have given himself a political *coup de grâce* as far as the Left was concerned by stating: 'Arevalism is something of the past.'[2]

On 31 October 1965 Mario Méndez Montenegro was found dead by his wife and son, shot to death in his own home. The Government claimed it was suicide and his brother, Julio César Méndez Montenegro, ex-Dean of the University's Law School, maintained that it was murder. The Secretary of Information of the presidency stated:

The Government does not have the slightest interest in interfering in the investigation of this painful incident, which is being carried out by the tribunals of justice. It will not permit, however, that baseless speculations be made that give birth to even more painful situations. The paraffin tests are positive and the bullet corresponds to Mario Méndez Montenegro's own gun.[3]

Julio César Méndez Montenegro maintained that the paraffin tests were negative and that the bullet was not from his dead brother's gun.[4]

But the death of Mario Méndez Montenegro remains in doubt to this day and is listed with the murders of Col. Francisco J. Arana and Col. Carlos Castillo Armas as murky

1. El *Imparcial*, 8 August 1965.   2. ibid.
3. ibid., 2 November 1965.   4. ibid.

political events of primary magnitude in a murky political environment.

The campaign was a bitter one and full of acrimonious and exaggerated charges. The Liberation Party wanted to make some kind of agreement with the Government Party to run only one candidate, Col. Miguel Angel Ponciano, under their dual banner. But the PID turned down the proposition.[5] The Government also refused to allow the DCG, the Christian Democrats, to run their candidate, with the excuse that they had not fulfilled the stipulation of presenting a list of 50,000 bona-fide Party members before the legal deadline.[6] The real reason was probably the fall from grace suffered by the DCG when they had refused to participate in Peralta Azurdia's rubber stamp Congress. When the DCG said that they would tell their adherents to deposit blank ballots to show their lack of support for the elections, the Director of the Electoral Register (the authorizing commission) said that the Party would be sanctioned for attempting 'to obstruct the right of the free exercise of voting'.[7]

The accusations reached a high pitch in early February when the Revolutionary candidate charged the military Government with trying to assassinate him, with having burned the seven small aeroplanes being used by the PR for propaganda purposes, and with imprisoning a number of his bodyguard without benefit of legal charges or court trials.[8] The PID (the Government Party) denied all the accusations and responded that it would take Julio César Méndez Montenegro to Court for his calumnies.[9]

The following day the Government followed up with a broadside of its own, accusing Méndez Montenegro, of 'excessive flights of the imagination or a sneaky spirit' and claiming that his denunciation of attempted assassination was a

5. ibid., 25 January 1966.   6. ibid., 26 January 1966.
7. ibid., 7 February 1966.   8. ibid., 9 February 1966.
9. ibid.

'theatrical statement incessantly repeated in every tone of voice as a part of his political campaign'.[10] It further guaranteed that the electoral process would develop normally 'under the protection of the Armed Forces'.

The PID charged that the PR (Revolutionary Party) was communist-controlled, which in turn prompted a vehement denial by its candidate.[11]

The vice-presidential candidate for the PR was Clemente Marroquín Rojas, chosen not for his political ideology (he was not even a member of the PR) but rather because of his fearlessness in attacking in his own newspaper *La Hora* each and every institution. The choice was a good one and his newspaper was a valuable vehicle for mounting attacks against the Government and the Liberation Party. A typical editorial of his consisted in enumerating the faults and failures of the Peralta Azurdia Government and even questioning the caudillo's masculinity, following it up with abuse for the MLN:

As for the Liberationists: is it heroism to be at the service of the Yankee police, the dictators of the Americas, in order to invade Guatemala with Honduran troops? ... Castillo Armas didn't do anything even though his opposition was scattered, he had high prices for coffee, he was the spoiled brat of the *gringos* and their money. Ydígoras had low coffee prices, the *gringos* didn't like him and he did nothing. Peralta didn't try to do anything. ... Why does the MLN complain about Castro intervening? They invited the *gringos* to intervene. When they win from intervention it is good; if they lose, it is bad.[12]

There is no question about Marroquín Rojas's pen playing a big role in the campaign for Méndez Montenegro, and there is justification for speculating that the PR couldn't have succeeded without him. Nevertheless, there were many occasions when Méndez wondered whether the sharp-tongued Right-

10. ibid., 6 February 1966.   11. ibid., 18 February 1966.
12. ibid., 19 February 1966.

wing newspaperman was more of a liability than an asset.

The MLN and the PR did line up against the PID on one issue: they wanted observers from the OAS to oversee the legitimacy of the elections. Col. Juan de Dios Aguilar, as the hand-picked successor of Peralta Azurdia, however, was confident that the Government machinery would guarantee his election, and publicly stated that outside observers would be an insult to the political maturity of the Guatemalan people.[13]

A few days before the casting of ballots, the issue of religion came up. The Church hierarchy had maintained a prudent silence even when Col. Ponciano had said that all the lands confiscated from the Church seventy-five years earlier should be given back to her. Col. Aguilar apparently felt he did not need the help of the Church, and neither the presidential nor the vice-presidential candidate of the PR was known as *muy católico*, very catholic. When a group of Catholic women paid for an advertisement in the newspapers saying that they were voting for the PR, they were assailed by another group of five hundred women in another advertisement saying that no Catholic could vote for the PR because of its anti-Catholic vice-presidential candidate.[14]

But it was too late, the die had been cast. Julio César Méndez Montenegro closed off his campaign on the night of 5 March with a blast at the Government for the imminent fraud it was about to perpetrate on the country, while Peralta Azurdia assured everyone of his intention to maintain calm throughout the nation during the following day's activities.

6 March came and went. It was followed by days of speculation in the Press as to who had won. Most agreed that the PR seemed to be pulling a majority. The turn-out had not been as large as expected – little more than fifty per cent of the registered voters. This was an even smaller numerical turn-out than for Ydígoras's election in 1958, and just a few

13. ibid., 19 February 1966.   14. ibid., 4 March 1966.

more than for Castillo Armas's plebiscite in 1954. By 10 March the MLN was demanding a new election, alleging fraud, and the PID declared that it had knowledge of 'grave anomalies'.[15] Both charges seemed an admission of defeat even though the results were still not published.

Then the MLN declared that Peralta was to blame for the defeat of the 'anti-communists' since he had split them into the MLN and the PID, while on the other hand uniting the 'communists' into the PR by not letting the Christian Democrats run.[16] Two days later the results were made official, more than a week after the polls had closed. The PR had a plurality of 60,000 votes over the PID, but since it lacked an absolute majority, the election would be thrown into Congress.[17]

During this week, while the results were withheld, there was much movement evident among the candidates. There were rumours that Col. Ponciano had been the object of an attempted assassination and that Méndez was in jail.[18] Talk flowed freely as to what the US Government would do about the elections, and many people even believed that Méndez Montenegro had the Embassy's support. The Liberation Party considered US support as its birthright, and Ponciano had gone to the US during the campaign and had come back declaring that he had obtained more US military aid to defeat the communist guerrillas. Finally, two days after the results were published, the Embassy felt constrained to issue a statement:

The Embassy of the United States has received information to the effect that one of the political parties is not satisfied with the election results, and is trying to get backing from certain elements of the military in order to effect a *coup* against the Government, while claiming that it has the backing of the U.S. Embassy. The

15. ibid., 10 March 1966.   16. ibid., 12 March 1966.
17. Johnson, op. cit., p. 19: PR – 191,000 votes; PID – 136,000 votes; MLN – 103,000 votes.
18. El Imparcial, 11 March 1966.

Embassy categorically denies that it favours or supports any attempt against the government or any effort of any party that would result in the annulment of the elections.[19]

This served as a warning to both the public and the MLN that the Embassy actually did support Julio César Méndez Montenegro and wanted to see him in the presidency. It surprised many, especially the MLN.

But this was not enough. Méndez still needed the Guatemalan Army's backing, or at least the approval of the segment from which Peralta Azurdia drew his support. Peralta was now in a difficult position. He obviously hadn't expected that the PR would win the election, especially after throwing the Government apparatus and treasury behind Col. Juan de Dios Aguilar. However, he had made 'honesty' the watchword of his Government and had put much pride in the clean-up campaign he had carried out. Now that the election results were in and Julio César Méndez Montenegro was the winner, what could he do? He had to go through with his pledge of honest elections and let the PR take over – but not before eliciting promises to guarantee that the orientation of the new Government would be very similar to that of the military Government itself. On 19 March the Secretary of Publicity of the PR said that their attitude towards the army was 'one of respect', and they accused the MLN of printing handbills criticizing the Army and signing the PR's name to them.[20] The following day, Méndez himself said, 'I will respect the organic structure of the Army' – quite a switch from his campaign, when he had said that some Army colonels had to be retired.

But the secondary election by Congress was still a hurdle to be passed. If the election of deputies to Congress was allowed to stand, the PR would have a plurality of four members over a coalition between the MLN and PID and would thus guarantee the election for Méndez Montenegro.[21] So the

19. ibid., 15 March 1966.   20. ibid., 19 March 1966.
21. ibid., 31 March 1966.

MLN proceeded to label a number of PR Congressmen as 'communists' and maintained that their election was illegal under the 'Law of Defence of Democratic Institutions'.[22] The matter was taken to the Supreme Court and a week later the Court handed down its decision: none of the PR Congressmen had been convicted under the law, although some had been arrested by its application, and thus they could not be legally prevented from taking their congressional seats.[23] Since the military Government's 'Constituent Assembly' was still in session, and was to remain so until the new Congress could take over on 5 May, the bloc of MLN deputies and some of the PID members of Congress refused to attend the meeting designed to set up commissions for the transference of powers.[24] The PR deputies maintained that they would take their new seats on 5 May regardless.

Finally, as the inevitable approached, the Constituent Assembly, as its last act of legislative duty, passed a bill granting 'amnesty for all members of the Army, all policemen and all superiors for all the acts they committed in the repression of subversive activities'.[25] All the Congressmen voted for the law, making its passage unanimous and thus healing some of the wounds that had been opened up in the preceding days' debates over congressional seats.

On 10 May 1966 Julio César Méndez Montenegro and Clemente Marroquín Rojas were elected by Congress to be the new President and Vice-President of Guatemala. Congress, immediately before adjourning, appointed a commission to search for the twenty-eight members of the Labour Party who had been captured by the previous Government.

Being elected President of the Republic of Guatemala by the Congress of that country was the end of one series of difficulties for Méndez Montenegro, but the beginning of another,

22. ibid., 13 April 1966.   23. ibid., 19 April 1966.
24. ibid., 22 April 1966.   25. ibid., 28 April 1966.

far more complex. If he ever hoped to rule, it was necesssary for him to line up solid support among the political powers of that country. With only one fifth of the population registered to vote, and only just more than half of those registered participating, the lawyer and ex-Dean of the University Law School had managed to poll only forty per cent of the ballots cast.[26] The popular vote in his favour was numerically less than that received by Juan José Arévalo twenty-two years earlier when the population was just over fifty per cent of what it was in 1966. His popular support, nevertheless, was impressive and surprised everyone, including the candidate himself, but it was not sufficient to give him the small lever of power he needed to bargain with other political groups. Even his control over the PR was very tenuous, since his entrance as its head was more a duty fulfilled to his 'martyred brother', than anything else. He was in a very weak position.

One of the first blocs he courted was that of the Catholic hierarchy. He went to the Archbishop of Guatemala City, Mario Casariego, and begged him for public support. The Archbishop, an astute politician himself who had taken over after the death of Mariano Rossell, was not about to allow the opportunity to strike a blow for God and the Church to slip by. He protested that he could not publicly support the President-Elect because the latter was not a practising Catholic, never having been married in the Church. Méndez replied that he had always wanted such a marriage but had never had the time; he requested that the Archbishop perform the marriage himself in his private chapel. This was done within the week without any public announcement. Very soon afterwards the Bishops were requesting prayers for the new President and his Government from all the faithful.

The United States Government had already shown its support through the Embassy statement. Méndez Montenegro had previously conferred with Ambassador John Gordon

26. ibid., 31 March 1966.

Mein and had promised to seek more US counter-insurgency aid to stop the guerrilla movements as soon as he took office, offsetting in this way the stubborn and proud resistance to such help from the Peralta Azurdia Government.[27]

Statements were also made by the President-Elect that he supported private property – synonym for both big business and big land-holdings – in a meeting with the Chamber of Industry and the AGA (General Association of Agriculturalists).[28] He went so far as to denounce the invasion of lands by peasants as a trick to make things difficult for his Government. He maintained that he had become President legally and that he would not tolerate the 'danger of bringing violence to Guatemalan agriculture by taking advantage of dissatisfaction or by means of unrealizable promises'.[29] It was beginning to look as if his Government was not going to be so very different from that of his predecessor.

But there was only one real power in the country and it was imperative that Méndez cultivate and develop its favour: the military. The Armed Forces had established themselves too firmly to be seriously challenged and they constituted the most significant political power.

When the families of 'the twenty-eight' charged the Peralta Government with murdering their relatives, the now PR-controlled Congress called the case 'very delicate'[30] and later, by a secret vote, unanimously rejected the claim, thus covering up for the Peralta Government's mass murder. 'Even if it were true, the amnesty granted for such acts by the Constituent Assembly covers this case.'[31]

27. That such a deal was made has been denied. The facts seem to indicate otherwise. The authors heard from reliable sources on various occasions, even before Julio César Méndez Montenegro took office, that the price of US backing was his suppression of the guerrilla movements.

28. *El Imparcial*, 27 May 1966.   29. ibid.

30. ibid., 21 May 1966.   31. ibid., 1 June 1966.

When the Army picked up another 125 peasants in Zacapa and no further trace could be found of them, no outcry came from the President-Elect.[32] But when some guerrillas returned the compliment and ambushed an Army patrol, Méndez Montenegro went personally to the Mariscal Zavala Brigade and expressed his condolences for the captain and the ten soldiers killed in the encounter.[33] He told all the assembled military brass that 'the Government and the Army must stand together'.[34]

A few days before Peralta was to turn over the staff of office to his successor, he made a public speech to the Army but directed it to the nation, and specifically to the new President. He told his companions in arms: 'You will be responsible before the nation for what happens to the future of Guatemala.'[35] Méndez Montenegro could not miss the message, and he did not.

On 1 July Méndez took over as the first civilian President in sixteen years (no one was ever sure of the status of General e Ingeniero Miguel Ydígoras Fuentes). He wasted no time in naming Col. Rafael Arriaga Bosque, Peralta's right arm, as his Minister of Defence. US Ambassador Gordon Mein and Peter Costello, AID director for internal security matters, visited the new Minister of the Interior a few days later to offer their help in stabilizing the situation of the country.[36] On 11 July the new President began a trip to visit all the important military bases in the country, accompanied by Col. Arriaga Bosque. The first stop was Zacapa: 'I hope that you will interpret my conduct as a friend of the Army, a friend who recognizes and esteems the true worth of the Armed Forces.'[37]

When the chief of the secret police of the former Government admitted that 'the twenty-eight' had been murdered,

32. ibid., 25 May 1966.   33. ibid., 28 May 1966.
34. ibid.   35. ibid., 25 June 1966.
36. ibid., 6 July 1966.   37. ibid., 11 July 1966.

nothing was said.[38] Then at the Army base in Poptún, Petén: 'The Army can be sure that my attitude is one of respect and esteem.'[39] The following day's papers headline was: 'The Army is united against the threat of subversion.' Arriaga Bosque, in the company of the military high command, stated: 'We only await orders from our Commander-in-Chief, our President.'[40] At the base in Jutiapa, the President declared: 'We hope for and count on the loyalty of the Army of Guatemala and I can assure you that there will be no obstacle in our common road.'[41] When he went to the Retalhuleu air-base and the Quezaltenango western command he said: 'My first duty consists in presenting myself at all the military centres in the Republic, in order to personally present my cordial best wishes and express my personal regards. This duty has been doubly gratifying because of the promises of loyalty that I have received from the Armed Forces.'[42] He even found it propitious to give homes to twelve colonels 'in gratitude for the protection they have given the nation'.[43]

Then Clare H. Timberlake and William L. S. Williams of the US State Department came to Guatemala to accompany Ambassador Mein on a visit to the Minister of the Interior in order to make 'an evaluation of the programmes of internal security conducted with the collaboration of the US Military Assistance Program (MAP) and the US Agency for International Development (AID)'.[44] Although the President had offered amnesty to 'all who had borne arms from 1 November 1960 to 26 July 1966, with the exception of those guilty of the murder of Mario Méndez Montenegro',[45] he was obviously preparing to crush the guerrilla movements in a way that Peralta Azurdia never had been able to do alone. It was undeniable that for his political survival he had to demon-

38. ibid., 16 July 1966.
39. ibid., 18 July 1966.
40. ibid., 19 July 1966.
41. ibid., 25 July 1966.
42. ibid., 1 August 1966.
43. ibid., 22 November 1966.
44. ibid.
45. ibid., 27 July 1966.

strate quickly and decisively that he would not tolerate the actions of the extreme Left.

In order to comprehend the policies of the Méndez Government, it is necessary to understand the basis of his power, or rather, its lack of a true base. He called his administration 'the Third Government of the Revolution' and there is no reason to believe that ideologically he cannot be identified with most of the principles of the Arévalo and the Arbenz Governments. It is worthy of note that he was one of the major participants in the October 1944 Revolution and he periodically makes statements to show that his heart still belongs to the movement. But the forces at work in Guatemala in 1966 were different from those of 1944, and Julio César Méndez Montenegro obviously did not have support such as was given to both Arévalo and Arbenz. This forced him to align himself with all the *status quo* power blocs in the country and to deal with crying social needs only peripherally.

CHAPTER 13

A Piece
of Cake

Let them eat cake.

Attributed to MARIE ANTOINETTE

The agrarian policy of the Third Government of the Revolution was expressed in a three-part programme officially adopted as of 'national urgency' at a Cabinet meeting on 19 August 1966.[1] It included the distribution of the remaining National Fincas to the workers living on them; the restructuring of the existing agrarian zones; and the use of the unexploited Government lands in Izabal, Quiché, Petén, Alta Verapaz and Huehuetenango. Although this was announced as a new plan of agrarian reform, it can hardly be so considered. None of the three aspects of the plan were new. The colonization of the unexploited lands to the North had been seriously planned since 1963 and initial attempts had already been made. The agrarian zones that had been started during the Castillo Armas Government were in grave need of reorganization. They principally needed to have the undue growth of population reduced. More important, neither of these two aspects of the programme represented a real agrarian reform.

The National Fincas had gone through a long history of changing Government policy. This particular proposed dis-

1. El Imparcial, 20 August 1966.

tribution was an authentic attempt at agrarian reform in itself but it now represented such a small extension of land as to be negligible in the national context.

In less than a month after the 'new plan' was announced, the INTA office had received two thousand new requests for land and by 10 October they had twenty thousand requests from the South coast alone, in what the newspapers termed an 'agrarian explosion'.[2] However, most of the peasants either did not hear of the Government's proposed plans or were still intimidated after their experience with the promises broken and the threats fulfilled of the three previous Governments.

The agrarian reform programme had been declared of 'national urgency' and on 22 December 1966, Decree 1653 was urgently approved. It ordered that the National Fincas (the least controversial object of the three-pronged programme), which were still under the control of the Liquidating Commission of the ex-Department of National Fincas, be turned over to INTA to be distributed to the peasants who were working on them. The stated goal of this distribution was to give impulse to the socio-economic development of those families. The land was to be given free of charge to the co-operatives that would be established therein. If INTA determined that a given *finca* could sustain more than the workers already living there, provision was made so that other peasants could receive land.[3]

The free distribution was subject to two provisions: (1) that the lands could not be sold or exchanged within thirty years, and (2) that if within this length of time INTA judged that the lands were not being used for agricultural production or if they were being exploited below a

2. ibid., 10 October 1966.
3. *El Guatemalteco, Diario Oficial*, Tomo CLXXVIII, No. 61, 12 January 1967.

predetermined level, the lands could be taken back from the recipient.

Ninety days were given as the deadline for the transfer of the National Fincas into INTA's jurisdiction. In March 1967, when the deadline was almost up, and nothing had yet been done, a presidential Decree commissioned the Minister of Agriculture to intervene in the transfer of the *fincas*. Those *fincas* that were under Court injunction to determine ownership owing to Ydígoras's hand-outs were exempted until the matter was settled. However, INTA's budget had not been drawn up with the new item of the *fincas'* administration in mind and this constituted a veritable impediment. Article 6 of Decree 1653 was too vague to be applicable and INTA demanded a revision of the legislation.

The law covering co-operatives had already been amended on 10 September 1966 to include the projected establishment of a federation of co-operatives of the distributed National Fincas to be supervised by INTA.

Two more plantations were claimed by the government after a long legal process and this brought the number of National Fincas owned by the State to twenty-six. The Banco Nacional Agrario and INFOP (National Institute for the Development of Production) were in control of a number of *fincas*, approximately seventeen, that they had received as payment for uncollected loans from the Department of National Fincas as well as from beneficiaries of Decree 900 who had been dispossessed and were unable to pay their debts. Both the BNA and INFOP tried to sell some of these at auction in order to avoid being deprived of them. Other Government agencies had *fincas* which were administered to provide operating funds for the agency.

Finally, on 7 June 1967, Decree 1679 was passed amending and clarifying the original Decree 1653 and on the 27th of that month INTA at last received the twenty-six *fincas*, valued at Q10 million plus Q400,000 in the treasury of the Department.[4]

It was announced on 28 June 1968 that Juan Mini was returning to the Government the thirteen *fincas* he had received from Ydígoras. But their number has not officially been added to the total received by INTA.

The first distribution took place on 8 July 1967: 'Cacahuito' in Santa Rosa, 22 *caballerías*, valued at Q115,000, to 203 families. 'Las Cabezas', 4·3 *caballerías*, also in Santa Rosa, was given out in October of the same year to 172 families. The third *finca* to be given out was 'Güiscoyol' in Escuintla on 4 March 1969 to 85 families; however, the proceedings for this distribution had begun many years earlier under the auspices of CONTRAGUA (Confederation of Workers of Guatemala) and under the new legislation they were finally successful in obtaining it.

At the distribution in October, President Méndez Montenegro spoke, 'visibly moved':

The Third Government of the Revolution is for social justice. It is giving land to the landless. We have given out hundreds of titles. The Revolution of 1944 is in full march ahead because it is the one that vindicated the rights of the people who had been trampled on by tyranny.[5]

The 'hundreds of titles' mentioned in his talk was a reference to several minor distributions of lands, most of which were of insignificant extent. He was attempting here the ploy of his three predecessors of lumping all distribution totals together.

The President had not been able to wait for the passages of Law 1679 on the distribution of the National Fincas, because pressures were building up too quickly. Invasions of land by peasants continued and the director of INTA claimed that 'unscrupulous leaders' were advising the people to carry

4. *El Imparcial*, 11 July 1967.   5. ibid., 17 October 1967.

out such invasions.[6] The Head of the Instituto Politécnico (Guatemala's West Point) said: 'The Army will not long tolerate what is going on outside this institution's walls.'[7] Marroquín Rojas, the Vice-President, argued that no peasant leagues should be created 'until the peasants have a cultural level that is indispensable to act with liberty'.[8] Méndez himself then declared, 'Things had better get peaceful fast in the rural area.'[9] A Q216,000 allotment was made to the Minister of the Interior to hire more rural police,[10] even as the Head of the National Police announced that: 'This institution will co-operate with INTA to bring order to the rural zones.... 500 new special police jobs are being created.'[11]

But the new President had another image to protect and he spoke with apparent sincerity:

I speak of liberty that will permit us to resolve the great social, economic and cultural problems of the people of Guatemala. The liberty to die of hunger or to die of misery is not liberty but a fallacy.[12]

However, it did not look as if he would have the time to even face these 'great problems', let alone solve them. The Armed Forces of Rebellion demanded that he do something about 'the twenty-eight',[13] and the Liberation Party demanded an end to FAR's activity.[14] The Vice-President didn't help matters by publicly denouncing three Congressmen of the Government Party for 'agitating the workers on the plantations'.[15] Then the Liberationists decided that they had had enough of the Government's toleration and warned: 'The Government should not consider it strange that the citizenry organize to take justice into their own hands.'[16] It was from

6. ibid., 7 September 1966.
7. ibid., 1 September 1966.
8. ibid., 5 September 1966.
9. ibid., 8 September 1966.
10. ibid., 9 September 1966.
11. ibid., 8 September 1966.
12. ibid., 16 September 1966.
13. ibid., 10 September 1966.
14. ibid., 14 September 1966.
15. ibid., 24 September 1966.
16. ibid., 27 September 1966.

here that the development of the Right-wing terrorist organizations was openly noticeable and Méndez Montenegro had less and less to say about the conduct of his own Government.

By early October the President was desperate, and he promised that his agrarian reform would give lands to 150,000 peasants,[17] while the President of Congress assured the nation that the reform made by the Third Government of the Revolution would be 'based on the Constitution, that is, with respect for private property'.[18] Then, on 11 October, Méndez gave out his first 534 titles in ten different zones for a total of 7,483 hectares (18,484 acres).[19]

Loans for sixteen million dollars from AID were announced[20] as well as a new tax law that would bring in ten million *quetzales* to be used mostly for internal security.[21] Forty members of the Interamerican Defense Pact, under the direction of Vice-Admiral Bernard L. Austin, came to Guatemala to check on the 'security of the hemisphere'.[22]

By early November the MLN had carried out its threat of developing vigilante groups for self defence and was engaged in terrorist activities. Twenty-five of the top members of that Party were jailed for the possession of 'war material',[23] held for almost a month and released in early December.[24]

There were other land distributions, but these were smaller and their purpose was obviously more propagandistic than anything else. At such a distribution in December 1966 to fifty-two peasants in Los Amates, Izabal, a focal point of guerrilla activity, the President begged the peasants to back him and the Army in its struggle against the guerrillas.[25] A week later, Alberto Méndez Martínez, the Secretary General of the PR and oldest son of the deceased Party leader Mario

17. ibid., 10 October 1966.   18. ibid., 21 September 1966.
19. ibid., 11 October 1966.   20. ibid.,
21. ibid., 17 October 1966.   22. ibid., 29 October 1966.
23. ibid., 3 November 1966.   24. ibid., 2 December 1966.
25. ibid., 20 December 1966.

Méndez Montenegro, gave out sixty-four titles for lands in Champerico on the Pacific Coast, stating: 'The guerrillas say that this Government is not revolutionary. With the assignment of these land titles, we give them the lie.'[26]

These references to the guerrillas were backhanded compliments acknowledging the effectiveness of the guerrilla movement and an indication of the cause they were constantly emphasizing to the landless peasants. The Army had been staging numerous demonstrations of support around the country, trucking peasants to and fro in military vehicles, in an obvious orchestration of peasant backing for the Armed Forces and repudiation of guerrilla activities. Even in Río Hondo, where the Army had kidnapped and apparently murdered over a hundred men as guerrilla supporters only eight months before, it was publicized that the people there 'were asking for guns to fight the guerrillas'.[27] Then the Government decided to designate all plantation owners and their administrators as its special police, allowing them to carry guns, make arrests and shoot those who tried to evade justice.[28] The President himself had already survived two attempts by Right-wing factions in the Army to topple his Government, and he could not afford to allow anyone to doubt his loyalties:

The Revolutionary Party has decided to support the Army in those determinations that it takes in order to maintain peace and tranquillity, to strengthen our mutual relationship, in view of the fact that the Army is our guarantee of national sovereignty.[29]

A few days later, on a visit to the Permanent Commission of the Council of Defence of Central America, the President announced that 'popular support for the Army and Govern-

26. ibid., 30 December 1966.   27. ibid., 24 November 1966.
28. ibid., 6 December 1966.   29. ibid., 7 December 1966.

ment is increasing' and that in view of this he would augment its services of internal security, health and education.[30]

On 13 December the Press announced that a Chicago newspaperwoman had talked with the Guatemalan Chief of Police and he had confirmed rumours that there were US Green Berets in the country.[31] The writer, Georgie Anne Geyer, quoting a guerrilla source, set the figure at 1,000. She was the object of a death threat made by a Right-wing terrorist organization for establishing contact with the guerrilla organization. Washington immediately denied the report and said that the US had only four members of its Special Forces in the country and that they were working with the Guatemalan Army's civic action programme.[32] Arriaga Bosque, Minister of Defence, also denied the allegation, as well as the reports that his Army was working hand in glove with the Right-wing terrorist organizations. 'Because,' he said, 'this is against the Constitution.'[33] Meanwhile, the Director of the National Police solicited funds for the creation of 561 more police jobs.[34] The squeeze was obviously increasing on all sides and Méndez acted like a wind-tossed boat on a stormy sea. He continued the lesser distributions and the drum-thumping propaganda: in January 1967 thirty-three titles were given out in Escuintla;[35] in February it was announced that 1,000 families would receive lands within four months in Izabal;[36] in March it was declared that the National Finca 'Las Cabezas' would be given to 200 families as soon as the new law passed Congress;[37] the acknowledgement that a half-million dollar contract had been signed with AID for the development of the areas of Izabal (where Yon Sosa's 13 November Revolutionary Movement was active) and of Zacapa (where the Armed Forces of Rebellion func-

30. ibid., 10 December 1966.   31. ibid., 13 December 1966.
32. ibid.   33. ibid., 12 December 1966.
34. ibid.   35. ibid., 23 January 1967.
36. ibid., 24 February 1967.   37. ibid., 14 March 1967.

tioned) came in April.[38] Finally, in June, Law 1679 was passed, transferring the National Fincas to INTA and it was announced that the Third Government of the Revolution was finally going to begin its land reform.

Méndez Montenegro was thinking principally of Nueva Concepción and La Máquina when he stated that the second basic aim of his agrarian reform would be 'to restructure the agrarian zones' started by Castillo Armas. Shortly before he had taken office, it became public knowledge that the Peralta Azurdia Government had been transferring people out of these zones to the banks of the Pasión River in the Petén jungles. This news item was accompanied by a discouraging description of conditions in the Nueva Concepción zone :

These people have been in a calamitous situation that any Guatemalan can see for himself if he visits the zone; especially in the area of Palo Blanco, where thousands of families live jammed together without lands, without work, in a desperate situation of misery and in the worst possible hygienic conditions.[39]

By December 1966 INTA had finally completed the construction of thirty small bridges, a school and an assembly hall – ten years after the founding of Nueva Concepción.[40] But the task loomed too big for INTA's resources and in September 1967 the President called for a meeting of all the interested national and international organizations in the country to discuss the means of strengthening these zones. The urgency of the matter increased when several individuals were found murdered in Nueva Concepción.[41]

The settlers' principal crop was corn and it was suffering tremendous price depressions because of difficulties in getting the produce to market. Priority in INTA's meagre budget

38. ibid., 7 April 1967. 39. ibid., 14 March 1966.
40. ibid., 21 December 1966. 41. ibid., 8 and 28 September 1967.

was given to the construction of four more bridges, which were finished by the following December. But the basic problem remained: an excessive population influx, nearly 40,000 people instead of the 6,000 planned for at the project's initiation.

Finally, it was announced that the Organization of American States (OAS) and other international institutions were providing a three-million-dollar loan in an attempt to salvage Nueva Concepción.[42] The need became even more obvious when two months later it was revealed that thirteen bodies of murdered individuals had been discovered in the zone in a three-day period.[43] This was typical of news items that were being repeated with frightening persistence throughout the nation.

In September Méndez Montenegro decided to visit the area himself.[44] He was met by 5,000 chanting peasants who carried signs: 'We demand new legislation that conforms to reality' and 'We demand that uncultivated lands be expropriated.' Not all the signs were threatening, however: 'We will defend the constitutional Government' and 'We will defend the Revolutionary Party.' The President responded with one of his impassioned discourses of self-defence:

The efforts generated by my Government are for the people and we are in power thanks to the popular will, especially the will of you, the peasants, who make up the vast majority of our people. ... Despite the enemies of the people and the problems we have, I will finish my term with accomplishments and not with promises. Especially will we progress in the matter of agrarian reform which we have already planned because I am, and I always will be, a sincere friend of the peasants.[45]

His promise to finish his term of office with accomplishments and not just promises seemed to be an answer to the

42. ibid., 21 May 1968. 43. ibid., 29 July 1968.
44. ibid., 20 September 1968. 45. ibid., 20 September 1968.

accusation that his only preoccupation, since reaching the half-way mark of his four-year tenure, was to remain in office and finish his constitutional term. Such a feat would automatically guarantee Méndez his place in Guatemalan history books – he would be only the second man to do so in a hundred years. Nevertheless, it looked as if the accomplishment would have to be made at the expense of real progress: trying to placate all segments of the population, especially the peasants, with meaningless promises. The difficulties continued. When the administrator of a plantation in Escuintla was killed and two others were shot in March 1969, the plantation owners announced that they were forming their own vigilante group. This was followed by four more murders in Nueve Concepción and the protest of the inhabitants of the area that a list of unknown origin had been published containing sixty names of persons marked for execution.[46] The Army and Police did their part by sweeping through the whole project and arresting 'over a hundred people'.[47]

A source of the trouble is discernible in a letter, written by an inhabitant of the Pacific Coast area in which the zone is located, directed to the authorities and published in the Press. The writer charged that the people living in La Máquina and Nueva Concepción were delinquents, since in their majority 'they are persons who fled before the Liberation Movement from the Eastern part of the country to the South [Pacific] coast'.[48] The author of the letter goes on to describe the illegal activity of gun smuggling from Mexico into the agrarian zones, but leaves the impression that its object is simple delinquency. The Government, however, has maintained on many occasions that these zones are fertile fields for guerrilla activities.

La Máquina has not received the same attention as Nueva Concepción, yet its problems seem not much different. It too

46. *Prensa Libre*, 31 March 1969.　　47. ibid.
48. ibid., 28 April 1969.

has a population of nearly 25,000 instead of the original quota of 6,000. The two projects represent one half the total land distributions made in the category of agrarian zones, the heart and soul of the 'agrarian reform' begun by Castillo Armas and continued by all his successors.

In February 1965, eight weeks after the founding of the La Máquina project, a road twenty-seven kilometres long was finally built to facilitate the marketing of the corn production of the zone. But it had not been built by the Government; rather it was the product of the labour of the people themselves.[49] By October 1967 these same inhabitants had managed to build themselves a 'modest dispensary' and had purchased an ambulance in an attempt to provide themselves with much-needed medical care.[50] The Red Cross, finally acquiescing in the pleas of the local populance, took charge of the vehicle and stocked the dispensary with medicines.

The excess population of La Máquina was dealt with by transferring people to the jungles of Petén, much as was done in Nueva Concepción. Two hundred people had already left[51] when in December 1968 ninety families were taken out, but this time they were not given land in any other area. The Secretary General of the regional peasant organization wrote an open letter to the President describing conditions in the zone, requesting the much-needed technical help that was supposed to be the basis of the original programme and denouncing the injustice of the Government authorities in expelling the ninety families.[52]

It is obvious from these two examples that the agrarian zones do indeed need 'restructuring'. But what that restructuring will be remains to be seen, since the Government has yet to admit that the basic flaw in the programme is that there are too few lands for too many people. The three million dollars that are now earmarked for Nueva Concepción may or

49. *El Imparcial*, 5 February 1965.   50. ibid., 11 October 1967.
51. ibid., 27 September 1967.   52. ibid., 24 December 1968.

may not resolve the crises of that particular area. But what of the rest? Will the international organizations continue to foot the bill for other programmes or projects of restructure? Given that the basic premiss or orientation of the agrarian zone is colonization, the expense must be astronomical. One of the problems from the beginning has been that only massive transfusions of money can make the agrarian-zone concept of land reform work. And money is one thing the DGAA and now INTA have never had enough of despite the international helping hand.

Méndez's attempts to pass even modest tax legislation that would enable him to find funds for his programme have met with solid resistance. It has come from the same socio-political structure that has obliged a succession of Governments to turn to colonization in lieu of land reform. This socio-political structure has never permitted a tax legislation that would cut their profits, and so the Government has no resources for dealing with the problem of the land. Internal security is about the only battle-cry that will carry tax reform through Congress,[53] and even then it has been a very inconsequential one, since they take advantage of the United States' propensity to pay for such expenses.

Even though Méndez declared his first attempt at new tax legislation to be necessary for internal security, it was met by AGA and other landowning and business lobbies with the cry: 'The Government wants equality of poverty for all Guatemalans.'[54] In order to get it passed, the President responded with the promise that the tax would only be in effect for one year.[55] The proposed tax law called for an increase in the land taxes raising the rates from a miniscule ·3 per cent on land evaluations made in the early 1930s to a progressive tax that would go up to 2 per cent on properties valued at

53. ibid., 17 October and 9 December 1966.
54. ibid., 25 November 1966.   55. ibid.

Q600,000. 'Opponents denounced the progressive property tax as confiscatory and communistic.'[56]

When the Archbishop of Guatemala blessed fifty-four new radio police-cars in March 1967, he congratulated his countrymen on their efforts for internal security and he said to the police, 'It is important that you take good care of these vehicles since they were purchased with money of the people.'[57] Actually, much of the cost had been borne by the Alliance for Progress,[58] nevertheless, the local contribution had been significant.

In its attempts to rectify its fiscal deficit, the Government admitted in December 1967 that the country was in a 'terrible financial crisis'[59] and followed this up with the statement that Guatemala was sixty-third out of sixty-four countries surveyed as regards the percentage of income taxed.[60] These declarations were the culmination of the régime's struggle to maintain in effect a five-per-cent general sales tax with levies up to twenty per cent on some luxury goods. 'Tax collection machinery was inadequate, but some officials believe businessmen deliberately sabotaged the new measure by exploiting the initial confusion and by price gouging.'[61]

The consequent uproar over the tax resulted in demands for the resignation of the Minister of Finance and shook the Méndez Montenegro Government to its foundations.[62] The President decided the issue was not worth the effort, so he rescinded the tax and the Chamber of Commerce immediately expressed their support of their enlightened President.[63]

In December, when new tax legislation was being discussed for 1969, the association of coffee growers had their 'eight-

56. *New York Times*, 3 December 1966.
57. *El Imparcial*, 14 March 1967.   58. ibid.
59. ibid., 22 December 1967.   60. ibid., 5 January 1968.
61. *New York Times*, 27 January 1968.
62. *El Imparcial*, 6 January 1968.   63. ibid.

year fight for justice'[64] crowned with victory when Congress began to discuss a bill that would eliminate all taxes to be paid on coffee exports.[65] The rationale was that this 'would make the income-tax burden much lighter'.[66] And so the struggle to obtain the same dispensation for the cotton growers was taken up with renewed vigour. By late 1969 its passage looked certain.[67]

It is no wonder then that one of the Government programmes hardest hit by the financial squeeze has been INTA. By September 1967 INTA had to fire 300 employees.[68] Five months later, another 520 technicians and employees were discharged by the Institute,[69] all while Méndez was talking about 'restructuring the agrarian zones'. But the dismissals did not go unnoticed. The peasants in La Máquina protested that they would be left without the schools and roads promised by the new government.[70] Two weeks later, the inhabitants of Nueva Concepción also raised their voices in protest as the inconsistency became apparent.[71] Four Congressmen qualified the firings as the 'beginning of the end of INTA'.[72] The accuracy of their prophecy was seen by February 1969, when thirteen Congressmen appealed to the Minister of Finance to resolve INTA's budgetary problems. Fuentes Pieruccini deftly shifted the blame right back where it belonged, on the legislative body : 'The difficulty resides in the fact that the tax laws of last year were never enacted.'[73]

This fundamental difficulty, which results in the ineffectiveness of any meaningful social legislation, is directly attributable to the lack of Méndez's political base. It cannot be repeated too often that the peasants, even though they con-

64. ibid., 18 December 1968.
65. ibid., 13 December 1968.
66. ibid.
67. Prensa Libre, 16 May 1969.
68. El Imparcial, 12 September 1967.
69. ibid., 2 February 1968.
70. ibid., 8 February 1968.
71. ibid., 21 February 1968.
72. ibid., 2 February 1968.
73. Prensa Libre, February 1969.

stitute seventy-five per cent of the population, do not represent a political power. They never have been allowed either by the succession of Governments or by Right-wing terrorist groups to organize themselves in a meaningful way since the fall of Arbenz. Now their progress and development depend on the non-existent good will, understanding and foresight of the power blocs mentioned earlier, and will remain so until larger numbers of them decide to take into their own hands the control over their destinies now held by the landowners.

Leopoldo Sandoval, INTA's first Director under the Revolutionary Government, did what he could to fulfil his President's promises, even though with scanty funds. One of the aspects of his programme was to continue the clean-up campaign begun by the military Government of revoking titles that had been issued to undeserving beneficiaries. In January 1967 he denounced one of the frauds of the Ydígoras Government. It had given thirty *caballerías* to fifteen people, among them military officers, members of the DGAA (INTA's predecessor), an Ydígoras *aide*, as well as others, who had joined together to form a co-operative called 'Sacred Heart of Jesus'. This co-operative had borrowed Q30,000 from the BNA and had gone into the lumber business. As the land was cleared of forest, it was rented out to peasants.[74] A month later, another five complete agrarian zones were cancelled for 234 *caballerías* (25,693 acres) in Izabal because 'the recipients had not fulfilled the requirements that the law demanded' for the beneficiaries of the programme.[75] Sandoval promised that these lands would be given to 1,000 peasants families 'in the near future'.

Shortly thereafter another 263 lots were cancelled, also in the department of Izabal, 'because their owners were not using them'.[76] When it was revealed almost a year later that

74. *El Imparcial*, 13 January 1967.
75. ibid., 24 February 1967.   76. ibid.

one of these farms had been given to Fuentes Mohr, Minister of Foreign Relations in the Méndez Government, who had also been Ydígoras's Finance Minister, it caused only a slight flap.[77] Fuentes Mohr defended himself by claiming that he had previously notified INTA himself that he did not want the farm. No notice was taken of the fact that the law stipulates that beneficiaries be landless peasants.

These illegal apportionments of land perhaps do not represent a significant percentage of the total distributions, but neither do they represent all the recipients who were not qualified as beneficiaries. Among them can be counted the Bishop of Quezaltenango, the number-two man in the country's Catholic hierarchy. However, it cannot be expected that Méndez's limited political power was sufficient for him to right the wrongs that even Peralta had felt constrained to ignore.

There have also been claims and counterclaims that the same farm has been awarded to several recipients, and that the same individual has received more than one farm. These failures may not always be intentional, but they contribute to the suspicion that the agrarian-zone phase of the land-reform programme has never been as the DGAA or INTA propagandists have painted it. This was even more evident when, in November 1968, there was a meeting of the inhabitants of the South (Pacific) coast zones in an attempt to federate themselves for their own protection.[78] The necessity of the move became obvious a month later when the peasants of three zones all protested that the BNA was forcing them to pay an unjust debt that went back to the days of the Liberation Government. At that time, they had been obliged to mechanize their crops and the contract was given to a company, Agrimec, established precisely for this purpose. Agrimec charged them from Q75 to Q96 each for work that was calculated to be worth Q15, then the company had never

77. ibid., 31 January 1968.   78. ibid., 22 November 1968.

finished the job. The peasants were billed at the same time for homes that had never been built.[79] They insisted that they could not nor would they pay what was being charged them.

So went the second of the three-pronged agrarian effort of the Revolutionary Government's programme. It was not a successful effort, partly because there were no financial resources to strengthen the programme. As Colom Argueta, a recent Director of INTA, admitted in late 1968 when talking to the peasant leaders on the South coast: 'The narrow economic situation of INTA is a reality, but we have plenty of good will. Money without good will is worthless.'[80] He failed to observe how valuable is good will without money.

79. ibid., 12 December 1968.   80. ibid., 11 November 1968.

CHAPTER 14

By Virtue
of Wealth

And when a group of men controls the commonwealth by virtue of their wealth, their birth, or any advantages they happen to possess, they form an oligarchy but they call themselves leading citizens.

CICERO

The third and by far the most important part of the Government's 'new programme of national emergency' was the colonization of the unexploited, State-owned lands in Izabal, Alta Verapaz, Petén, Quiché and Huehuetenango. There are three main colonization projects in this area: Ixcán Grande in Northern Quiché and Huehuetenango; Sebol–Chinajá in Alta Verapaz; and the co-operative colonies of Petén. Since the Government had continually made the differentiation between the colonization and agrarian zone programmes, we treat them here as distinct, even though, as had been noted previously, the agrarian zone approach is also essentially colonization: 'The spirit of the law for the agrarian zones gave the new programme all the characteristics of a colonization rather than a reform.'[1]

In the case of what has been done in the jungles of Petén there is no confusion, because this is clearly labelled colonization by all parties. The Ixcán Grande project has always been designated as colonization although there is not the slightest

1. CIDA, op. cit., p. 47.

difference between it and the plans for Nueva Concepción and La Máquina. It could easily be referred to as an agrarian zone. The major project in Alta Verapaz is alternatively de-nominated 'the Agrarian Zone of Fray Bartolomé de las Casas' and 'the colonization project of Sebol–Chinajá'. We have chosen to include it as colonization because it represents an even smaller public investment of money on communal facilities than those executed in Nueva Concepción or La Máquina, even though the original plans drawn up by the military Government foresaw a cost of Q64 million. This leaves the major portion of the task of settlement to the in-dividuals concerned and is obviously colonization rather than even rhetorical reform.

The Ixcán Grande project was initiated by the Maryknoll Fathers[2] in January 1966 in Northern Huehuetenango and Quiché, in an area that was being colonized spontaneously by Indians from the Western *altiplano*. By March 1967 INTA claimed that it had located 170 *caballerías* (18,666 acres) of State lands that could be used for the settlement of 240 families and that they would localize more lands so as to expand the project to include 2,000 families.[3] By May 1968, 135 families had received their lots of twenty *manzanas* (thirty-four acres) each[4] but at the time of writing none have received their legal titles. There were arguments over whether the State really owned these lands because many conflicting claims are still being made by *latifundistas* of Huehuetenango, as well as those resulting from a few confusing grants which were made earlier in the century to the people's militias from Malacatancito and Chiantla for defending Guatemala's borders against the Mexicans,[5] but which they had never claimed. Many of the original settlers have also left because of the arbitrary conditions established by the first priest-director, one of which was that the recipient had to be a

2. See p. 189.
3. *El Imparcial*, 28 March 1967.
4. ibid., 11 May 1968.
5. ibid., 4 May 1964.

practising Catholic. He has since been replaced by another priest, much more understanding of the Indian culture and needs, who has received renewed promises from INTA for further extensions of colonizable lands. INTA has given no aid other than technical help for the localization and measurement of the lands as well as sundry promises to push a road into the area. Meanwhile, the official interest in developing the area is attracting more and more attention from the *latifundistas* and consequently their claims of ownership to lands in the zone are becoming more concrete, more determined and more expansive.

The Sebol–Chinajá project does not seem to find itself in any better situation than the Maryknoll project in Huehuetenango. Much of the difficulty, as has been noted, is the veritable impossibility of controlling the influx of land-hungry people once it becomes public knowledge that the Government is going to distribute lands in a given area. Leopoldo Sandoval, Director of INTA, felt obliged to give a stern warning that anyone settling in the Sebol–Chinajá area without INTA authorization would never be considered a suitable subject for a land grant. By May 1967 Col. Oliverio Casasola, director of all the projects in Petén, was accusing INTA of a 'four-year paralysis in the land programme of Sebol'.[6] Only 530 farms had been given out in the area and already by July 1967 more than 7,000 people were living on them.[7] The total project calls for a settlement of 6,000 families in the area, and roads are being built to facilitate the colonization. By September 1967 INTA had spent a quarter of a million dollars on the main road[8] and with its completion the perennial disputes over land ownership began.

As has been noted, uncultivated lands held by the Government usually means one of two things in Guatemala: either the lands themselves are physically worthless or they are

6. ibid., 24 May 1967.   7. ibid., 17 July 1967.
8. ibid., 11 September 1967.

completely inaccessible. The road to Sebol–Chinajá, which is planned to go into Petén, has made accessible many of these lands and so the historical pattern of land tenure has begun to take over. On 26 November 1968 a meeting was held in Cobán with the Director of INTA, the Governor of Alta Verapaz (an Army colonel like all other twenty-two departmental governors), the head of the military zone and the Mayors of the Department. The meeting was called to deal with a 'serious problem': people from outside the Department, thirty in number, had filed claims for 409 *caballerías* (44,798 acres) which Indian settlers had occupied for years in the Sebol–Raxuha area.[9] The peasants had been given the choice of vacating the lands or working for the new owners as *colonos*. The accusation was being made that the outsiders had obtained the titles surreptitiously with 'the aid of the authorities' and by using 'the law of suppletory title'. These were the same lands that INTA thought were available for their colonization projects.

Regardless of these projects, when one speaks these days of colonization in Guatemala, one automatically thinks of Petén – not to disparage the efforts being made in Ixcán Grande or Sebol–Chinajá by INTA with its parsimonious budget, but rather because Petén represents such a huge and unexploited area. In addition, the Government seems to be able to provide a fair amount of money for FYDEP.

FYDEP means *Fomento y Desarrollo Económico de El Petén*, or Institute for Economic Progress and Development of the Petén. The area represents one third of the national territory and practically everything that goes on there falls under the direction and control of FYDEP, giving its Director far more power than the Petén Governor. Col. Oliverio Casasola, the FYDEP Director until August 1969, had managed to survive the change of Government, as did many other military men.

9. ibid., 26 November 1968.

Ingeniero Leopoldo Sandoval, Head of INTA, insisted that his Department be given the job of colonizing the Petén region and that FYDEP limit itself to building roads, bridges, schools and hospitals.[10] He was only echoing the opinion of a 1965 UN study that had stated:

There are two organisms that have jurisdiction for colonization, FYDEP and INTA. Both are planning colonization programs with totally different criteria ... it is not possible to think of structuring a national program of colonization when there are two institutions working with different criteria and motivations.[11]

The United Nations Commission opted for INTA to handle the whole programme because of its experience in the field.

The Council of State went to Petén in February 1967 to see for itself what FYDEP was doing, and were told of Col. Romeo Samayoa's success in colonizing the banks of the Pasión and Usumacinta Rivers. They were not shown the colonies, going only to Sayaxché, and part of the reason was the terrible state the colonies were in. About nine co-operatives existed at this time, having been literally dumped at various points along the river with no means of communication with the outside world, no living quarters, very little food and less medicine. Sickness and hunger plagued all the co-operatives except that of Cabricán,[12] and people began leaving as fast as new colonizers were coming in. FYDEP's desire for rapid and haphazard colonization was creating more problems than solutions.

The Council of State returned to Guatemala City very pleased with what they had not seen, stating that the banks of the rivers 'possessed one of the areas most suitable for colonization since the fertility of the banks of the Pasión

10. ibid., 12 December 1966.

11. OIT, op. cit., p. 105.

12. Cabricán enjoyed the benefit of money provided by the Maryknoll Fathers and the Defense Department's permission to use the abandoned training-base of the Cuban invaders at San Juan Acul.

River could not be better'.[13] This was just one year after the AID technicians had told the Cabricán co-operative that the land along the rivers was useless for agriculture. The FAO study revealed the same information.

In March FYDEP publicly admitted to the Mayors of Petén just what their criteria for colonization were: Mexico was making a study in preparation to building a dam on the lower Usumacinta River which would flood these Petén lands, therefore it was necessary to place people along the banks of the rivers immediately in order to thwart the Mexican plan. The urgency of the situation demanded prompt colonization, the Mayors were told. They had been upset by the type of people being brought in to colonize.[14] At the end of March Méndez Montenegro visited Mexico and it was reported that he was going to sign an agreement with that country for the construction of the Usumacinta dam.[15] The President denied this report and declared that he would not compromise the lands of the Usumacinta basin.[16]

In May, FYDEP announced that Caritas (Program of US Catholic Bishops) was aiding it to feed 536 persons in three co-operatives along the Usumacinta: Cabricán, San Bernardino and Felicidad.[17] The latter had experienced a number of infant deaths, other families had abandoned the project and discontent was general and open owing to the lack of food and the bad administration by the co-operative's inexperienced president.

The internal fight over FYDEP's control continued. Some members in Congress wanted to remove Col. Casasola for running the enterprise as if Petén were his private empire,[18] others wanted the Department transferred from the Ministry of Defence to the Ministry of Agriculture; and Leopoldo Sandoval wanted the colonization, at least, under INTA. In

13. *El Imparcial*, 22 February 1967.   14. ibid., 17 March 1967.
15. ibid., 21 March 1967.   16. ibid., 22 March 1967.
17. ibid., 11 April 1967.   18. ibid., 18 April 1967.

May the Council of State returned to Petén to look over the situation and it reported, still without having visited the colonies, that the colonization should be in the hands of FYDEP. INTA should 'help but not interfere'.[19] At the end of May 1967 eighty-seven heads of families went to form two more co-operatives on the Pasión River under FYDEP'S auspices.[20]

Col. Casasola, now concerned about the possibility of INTA taking over the colonization of Petén, appealed to the public through the newspapers:

Now the hour for giving out lands in Petén has arrived, the prized colonization. There cannot be an agrarian reform in the Petén because you cannot reform what does not exist. If FYDEP turns over its banner to some other entity, hundreds of thousands of Guatemalans, attracted by the false siren of reform, will leave their lands in other areas of the country to hurl themselves into a massive migration, disordered and anarchical, with no possibility of progress.[21]

He went on to state that FYDEP was doing a good job of colonization and was thereby preventing Mexico from flooding the 'best lands that Petén has in this region'. He told of his plans to establish sixty-three co-operatives along the rivers in this area with over 15,700 people, with each family possessing one *caballería*. He maintained that eleven of the sixty-three were already functioning. 'FYDEP is going to colonize the banks of the Usumacinta River as fast as it can, establishing an army of farmers that will be an obstacle to the Mexican plans.'[22] These colonization plans were not aimed at solving the agrarian problems of the peasant masses.

In July the President himself went to Petén to see the FYDEP colonization programme. He was able to visit only two co-operatives, Cabricán and Felicidad, the two oldest in the area.[23] He gave a speech in the former, promising the

19. ibid., 16 May 1967.   20. ibid., 24 May 1967.
21. ibid.   22. ibid.   23. ibid., 14 July 1967.

peasants titles to their cleared lands when the Indian leader of the co-operative voiced his fear that some day the lands would be stolen from them if they had no titles. In Felicidad he heard the same complaints as well as one about an onerous debt on the shoulders of the co-operative, placed there by 'La Fundación del Centavo', run by an American businessman. He promised to see what he could do. Both co-operatives were the best in the area and he was not shown the miserable living conditions of the others.

In September ninety-one colonizers left for Petén to join the co-operatives Buena Fé, Canaán and Sinaí on the Pasión and Usumacinta Rivers. They were from the floating population of the Agrarian Zones of Nueva Concepción and La Máquina, having been preceded by 600 other colonizers from these same zones who had worked there as peons for other owners.[24]

In October FYDEP announced that it was firing 150 workers 'because of the Q100,000 cut in its budget that was being used for the internal security of the country'.[25] This same month, Col. Casasola in an interview talked about Petén, saying:

Poptún has shown that planned colonization does not attract true colonizers and it is absurd to attempt to place men on lands not their own when subsidies and State paternalism intrude. Fifty thousand peasants will be the tolerable maximum after a very slow process of careful selection. Decades will pass before Petén will be able to absorb 150,000 inhabitants.[26]

He blamed the American anthropologist, Sylvanus Morley, for the excessive estimates that were being made as to the maximum number of inhabitants that Petén could support. He stated that 'it is a false idea that Petén once housed from six to twenty-six million Maya'.[27]

24. ibid., 27 September 1967.   25. ibid., 31 October 1967.
26. ibid., 18 November 1967.   27. ibid.

In April 1968 FYDEP announced that it had trained thirty teachers for twenty-two co-operatives who were going to teach 321 peasants to read and write.[28] This would put the number of colonizers in the Usumacinta Basin at that time at approximately 1,600 people. In June 1968, 250 families who were in Guatemala City, preparing to go to Petén, were refused transportation by Col. Casasola and thus he managed to bring the trickle of immigrants to a halt. That same month Casasola announced that the saw mill built by FYDEP near Sayaxché would be sold with lumber rights for 470,000 hectares for Q40 million, with the explanation that

Petén is an economic experiment, not a political one. The Government must give out the lands to capitalist enterprises so that the lands are developed and populated progressively. Therefore, it is necessary that Congress pass the law they now have in their hands so that this dangerous and anomalous situation of provisional land-settling can be terminated. It is like giving out clouds.[29]

When the saw mill 'Rosario' was inaugurated a week later, he stated that 'Petén has to stimulate great capitalist enterprises.'[30]

The 'dangerous and anomalous situation of provisional land-settling' referred to by the Director of FYDEP represented an interesting situation. There exist few legal titles of direct ownership to the lands in the Petén region and most of these go back to colonial days. None of the successive Governments, up until the Government of Peralta Azurdia, had ever bothered to officially inscribe this huge territory as national land. This was probably due to the fact that no one was ever sure what the country owned there, and, besides, myriad problems revolved around the boundaries with both Mexico and Belice (British Honduras). Without roads in the

28. ibid., 5 April 1968.   29. ibid., 1 June 1968.
30. ibid., 8 June 1968.

area, everyone tended to forget Petén until it was time to draw a map. This led to the 'anomalous situation' that contemporaneous Governments were not the 'owners' of Petén and therefore could not grant legal titles in the area. Peralta had begun the process of rectifying the situation when he published Internal Resolution 57 on 4 November 1964: 'All natural or juridical persons are prohibited from taking possession of uncultivated lands in Petén. These will be under the jurisdiction of FYDEP until the regulations for such a purpose are adopted.' Decree 266, also passed by Peralta, gave FYDEP the powers already delegated to INTA by Decree 1551 for other areas of the country, that is, 'to survey and register all uncultivated lands in Petén'.[31] Finally, the military Government also promulgated Law 354, which granted FYDEP the power to colonize, especially the Usumacinta Basin. But none of this legislation authorized the distribution of land titles.[32]

Many lawyers maintained that all that had ever been needed was a presidential decree permitting FYDEP to distribute ownership rights. Others believed that only Congress could pass the law that would make such distributions legal. The dispute seemed to be more political and social than legal. Peralta would certainly not have had any difficulty in passing such a law through his 'Asamblea Constituyente', a rubber-stamp Congress. In August 1969, three years after Méndez Montenegro had taken over the government, his Congress finally passed such a law.

The underlying problem has been the wealth that is at stake. It is speculated that fabulous treasures exist in the Petén, contained in the recently discovered oil and ore deposits. The precious lumber content of its forests has been recognized for decades. Now that roads are finally being

31. OIT, op. cit., p. 35.

32. El *Guatemalteco, Diario Oficial*, Tomo CLXXIII, No. 85, 11 June 1965.

pushed through the area, dreams of agricultural and cattle production multiply geometrically. Today, there are concrete reasons for the Government to give out legal land-titles, and Congress has activated itself to meet such needs. It only remains to be seen who gets how much.

Meanwhile, FYDEP continued to give out provisional contracts of settlement that Casasola compared to 'giving out clouds'.

Some of the biggest landowners in the country have thereby got their foot in the door; Ralda, Berger, Costello are already operating in Petén but FYDEP refuses to say how large are the extensions of their lands. Also there are a number of US businessmen who have obtained 22·5 *caballería* (2,471 acres) farms in the Santa Ana area. Their lands are situated along the roads that FYDEP is constructing in that zone. The amount of land given to the president's nephew, son of his dead brother and General Secretary of the PR, is not known. But a huge area is reserved for him and 'other relatives' along the main road from Flores, capital of Petén, to the Belice Border.

There are of course the 1,600 Maya and mestizo peasants on the relatively inaccessible lands along the banks of the Usumacinta and Pasión Rivers. Nature, we are told by AID technicians, will probably turn these lands into swamps within five years; if, that is, the Mexican Government does not do the job first. Nevertheless, it is doubtful that any more peasants will be allowed to settle lands in the area unless it is for similar reasons and on land of the same calibre. Casasola explains this in his book, *Grandezas y Miserias del Petén* (Greatness and Misery of Petén):

Let us speak clearly. It is not a question of settling Petén at any price and thus contaminating from its birth an organism that must remain imperatively healthy in order to communicate its health to the whole country. An example: the illiteracy rate in Petén had been one of the lowest in Guatemala and Central

America, but in the last few years it has gone up 22 per cent. The cause? The Kekchí Maya immigrations to the municipality of San Luis, due to the economic and agricultural failure of Alta Verapaz. ... We would also clarify that of the 2,849 immigrants to Petén, 1,908 were Indians and 941 non-Indians, coefficient of regression, since no matter how much sympathy we may have for the Indian problem, they are not the human contingent that Petén needs to progress.[33]

In November 1968 Méndez Montenegro named a commission to study the situation and to draw up a law that would govern the distribution of land titles in Petén.[34] The commission decided that ten *caballerías* (1,098 acres) should be the limit given to any one individual and that no one should be given even that amount if he already owned land valued at more than Q20,000 as a private individual, or over Q50,000 as a juridical person. After much discussion, particularly after observing that FYDEP had already given out many farms far surpassing that limit, it was decided that such restrictions would be too constricting and that extensions of 1,000 hectares could be given out. It was also decided that it was not relevant how much land the beneficiary already possessed, thus assuring that *latifundistas* would be eligible. The only limitation would be that no one person could receive more than one lot of 1,000 hectares in Petén. This was approved unanimously by the commission[35] and an audience was sought with the President to explain the new changes and to obtain his backing in pushing the law through Congress. A few days later, the Christian Democratic Party sent a telegram to the President asking him to reject the commission's projected law in view of the fact that it was obviously designed to continue a state of *latifundismo*.[36]

33. Casasola, Oliverio, *Grandezas y Miserias del Petén*. Guatemala: Indiana Ltd, 1968, pp. 44–6.

34. *Prensa Libre*, 29 April 1969.

35. ibid., 22 May 1969. 36. ibid., 27 May 1969.

The Mayan peoples of Guatemala may not be the 'human contingent that Petén needs to progress', according to Casasola, but if we can judge from the nature of the law that was finally passed on 21 August 1969 after weeks of acrimonious debate, it can be foreseen that as the *latifundistas* take possession of the lands, and their need for cheap hand-labour develops, the 'coefficient of regression' will climb as the landless and illiterate peasants are brought in to perform their historical tasks.

Brief but valiant attempts were made to incorporate a note of 'social sensibility' into the new law that was meant to regulate the distribution of idle lands that comprise almost one third of Guatemala's national territory. Congressman Lionel López Rivera of the PID Party proved to be an unexpected opponent of the law:

The proposed law does not benefit the peasants of Guatemala in any way, nor is it aimed at developing Petén. There is no trace of social sensibility in it since there is not one single article of the law that is going to benefit the poor peasants. The agrarian development of Petén is not even contemplated by the law since the thousands of *caballerías* of land there will be occupied by huge businesses, and for this reason I repeat that the law lacks social sensibility.[37]

The charge was met with outraged cries of wounded pride by the Congressmen of the Revolutionary Party, whose members had composed the commission that drew up the law. They could not afford to allow the accusation of a lack of 'social sensibility' to go unchallenged. Congressman Antonio Morales Baños of the Revolutionary Party took up the standard and sarcastically declared: 'I suppose the only thing this Congress needs now is another Father Bartolomé de las Casas to defend the Indians.'[38] The reference was to the celebrated priest who almost singlehandedly fought the colonial Government and the Spanish Crown in his attempts to pro-

37. *Prensa Libre*, 7 August 1969.   38. ibid.

cure humane treatment for the Indians at the hands of the *conquistadores*. The blast was continued by a confrère of Morales Baños, Congressman Pedro Díaz Marroquín:

Let us be practical when it comes to legislating and not proceed with absurd sentimentality that is prejudicial for making laws. If we wish to look for the solution to the problem of the thousands of poor peasants, then let us reform the agrarian law and there we will find the solution.[39]

The criticism was correct, of course, since colonization could not replace agrarian reform. But the blast was made, not from a profound desire to protect the Indians' rights or to alleviate their needs, but rather to block even this feeble attempt to give them some future in the Petén under the laws of the nation.

The debate continued for weeks as the argument raged back and forth, but all attempts to amend the law were beaten back by the wholesale departures of numerous Congressmen that deprived the legislative assembly of the necessary quorum and rendered further debate devoid of any legality. When it was suggested that the land titles be given out by the FYDEP office in the Petén to ensure that the beneficiaries would have had to make at least one trip to that Department, Congressman Morales Baños, with his usual dry sense of humour, stated that: 'According to my criterion, there is no necessity to sign the contracts for the acquisition of lands on some tree trunk in Petén.' So the office for land distribution would remain in Guatemala City, and be of no assistance to those who had already migrated into the area from the Western *altiplano* and from Alta Verapaz.

Finally, tired and disgusted after weeks of haggling, Congress passed the bill on 21 August 1969 in what the newspapers described as 'a marathon'.[40] Four and a half hours of uninterrupted reading produced the desired result: confirma-

39. ibid.   40. ibid., 22 August 1969.

tion. Only one article provoked any discussion and that was the one limiting the distributions to Guatemalans by birth. This seemed to exclude some of the US citizens and other foreigners who had already received large extensions of land from FYDEP in the Petén, but the article stood. It would not be difficult for such people to form some kind of holding company with willing Guatemalans to avoid this precept of the law.

Strangely enough, nothing was heard from the outspoken Col. Oliverio Casasola during the weeks of prolonged debate. Perhaps his position had been publicized so often before that no clarification was needed. The mystery was compounded when a week after the new law's passage, Col. Casasola resigned as Director of FYDEP, a job he had held with distinction since his appointment by Ydígoras Fuentes. The announcement of his resignation was accompanied by the parallel announcement of a shift in INTA. Its Director, Licenciado Colom Argueta, was named head of the nation's registry of real estate, an extremely important job in view of the implications of the new law. Colom Argueta was replaced as head of INTA by Col. Elías Ayala Herrera.

Some light may have been thrown on these developments by a letter that appeared in the Press two weeks after the new appointments, written by a consultant of Petén's Catholic Bishop and an old opponent of Casasola's, Francisco Sagastume Ortíz, an outspoken critic of FYDEP's neglect of the needs of the peasants:

Now that the electoral campaign is beginning to heat up, Casasola has resigned, knowing that the electoral strategy of the Government requires that it have all key posts in the hands of members of its own party (PR) so that it may exercise coercion in its favour on Government employees, notwithstanding constitutional precepts to the contrary. Casasola never did this nor would he ever allow such a thing, and this in part accounts for his resignation.[41]

41. ibid., 18 September 1969.

The author of this letter, reading the handwriting on the wall as contained in the new law, goes on to give a few words of advice to the retired Colonel:

Casasola has retired precisely at the moment when the law for the distribution of lands in Petén goes into effect. He should be very happy for this, because now history will not be able to condemn him for giving these lands to the new and old *latifundistas*, both Guatemalan and foreign, who, with their greed, take the opportunity to work, and thereby dignify themselves, away from the great majority of Guatemalans who will have to continue as their eternal servants, condemned to die of hunger in the greatest misery, crowned with ignorance and sickness.[42]

Is it any wonder then that a full year earlier, at about the same time that Méndez Montenegro was naming his comission to draw up this law, at a meeting held in Guatemala of all the agrarian reform executives of the Central American countries, agrarian reform in the area was admitted to be 'a myth'. The Director of the Interamerican Institute of Agricultural Sciences of the OAS, Enrique Torres Llosa, stated:

It seems to me that the common denominator of this meeting has been the frank and sincere admission that, in spite of the efforts made by the different organizations that you direct, action for the true transformation of agrarian structures is not and has not been an object of your activities. ... The definition and realization of an authentic policy of integral agrarian reform can no longer be put off.[43]

The director of INTA, Colom Argueta, agreed and added:

The importance to the government of braking the accelerated demographic increase is well known. ... What was an apparently good solution in years past is no longer so. We have two Americas separated by a huge abyss: on one side, the America of deliberations, meetings, resolutions and agreements, but with-

42. ibid.   43. *El Imparcial*, 11 September 1968.

out concrete accomplishments; and on the other side, the America of the disinherited, the great America.[44]

He went on to add, almost as an afterthought, that seventy per cent of the Guatemalan population lived on less than $100 a year.

Nor was the Petén legislation meant to do anything about this situation. Integral or even partial agrarian reform continues to be deferred and Guatemala remains an integral part of the 'America of the disinherited'. This conclusion is no harsher than the facts themselves, as can be seen once we are able to separate them from the soothing rhetoric of governmental agencies and the political propaganda of Méndez Montenegro and his heir-apparent, Mario Fuentes Pieruccini. A common ploy is to announce a number of distributions months in advance, juggling the numbers of beneficiaries, the members of their families and the titles to be distributed. It works thus: on 26 June 1969 Colom Argueta announced that INTA was to give out 402 land titles, without stating where the land was nor its extent;[45] at a Press conference two weeks later, on 11 July, INTA announced that it would give out land titles to 5,000 peasants during the month in progress; the article revealed that the 5,000 peasants consisted of 917 heads of families and the rest were their dependents; among the 917 titles, 402 would go to beneficiaries in Ocós, San Marcos; also mentioned were thirty-two titles in Champerico as well as other listings; almost three weeks later, 29 July, INTA again proclaimed that it would give out thirty-two titles in Champerico on the following Saturday; on 6 August a big ceremony was held to which the Press was invited for the distribution of thirty-two titles in Champerico; on 13 August the newspapers carried a picture of the Vice-President of INTA giving a land title to a peasant, one of nineteen titles, to the 'microplots' in El Coco, Jutiapa; this same distribution was one of those mentioned in the 11 July Press conference; finally, on

44. ibid.   45. *Prensa Libre*, 26 June 1969.

26 August, another big ceremony was held with much Press coverage at which the 402 titles in Ocós, San Marcos, were given out by the Minister of Labour 'on behalf of President Méndez Montenegro'; no more of these titles were given out during the remainder of the year even though only 453 titles of the 917 promised in July had been distributed. The extent of the land distributed was not noted in any of these cases, though those in Champerico and Jutiapa were called 'microplots'.

Approximately 2,150 land titles had been distributed in the three categories of agrarian zones, communities and 'microplots', with more than one half of these classified as microfarms or *minifundios*. Some of those not classified as such, the community distributions, for example, have extents that place them also in the category of *minifundios*.

By 31 December 1969, 530 provisional titles had been given out in the Fray Bartolomé de las Casas project. INTA had another 600 titles ready to distribute if the legal complications of the land claims to 409 *caballerías* (45,560 acres) made by 'thirty outsiders' could be cleared up. In Ixcán Grande, 125 families had land and no titles and the same situation existed for 321 families taken into Petén by FYDEP. Thus, the grand total of families aided by the Méndez Montenegro 'agrarian reform programme' up till 31 December 1969 was 3,739 families, many of whom were not even given provisional titles. It is generous to estimate the number of families to whom the President may give land by the time he finishes his tenure on 1 July 1970 (if indeed he lasts that long) at 5,000. Still, the annual increase of peasant families living on subsistence agriculture or less averages 20,000 a year.[46] And so we have the 'Third Government of the Revolution' receiving the dubious distinction of awarding lands of insufficient acreage to 5,000 out of the 80,000 landless families that have proliferated during its four-year régime.

46. CIDA, op. cit., p. 200.

CHAPTER 15

The Road
to Hell

The road to hell is paved with good intentions.

Author unknown

When compared with the three men who preceded him in the President's chair, Julio César Méndez Montenegro can be characterized as a man with a developed social conscience. That he has not translated this conscience into a realistic programme of social development cannot be blamed on the President alone, since, as we have noted, he does not have the political power necessary to do so. Nevertheless, during his régime the same negative occurrences aimed against the peasants have continued as they did during those of his three predecessors. And though far fewer in number and fury, Méndez's outspoken protestations have been limited to a lame defence of his Government's activities in the face of Guatemala's enormous social ills. The peasants continue to live in the tenuous situation of never knowing when they will be expelled from lands on which they have lived for years but to which someone else repeatedly acquires the 'legal' title.

On 21 January 1967 sixty families in Jacaltenango, Huehuetenango, complained that they were being expelled from communal lands by the Mayor so that he could share these lands with two other large landowners. The peasants declared that they didn't have the money needed to hire lawyers to defend their claims.[1]

Two months later, another anguished cry rose from the throats of a group of peasants. It is worth repeating in full for it tells succinctly the story of the ever recurring dynamic of Guatemalan rural life :

We demand that the President of the Republic, who himself is a revolutionary and has said that his Government will support the peasants, intervene immediately in order to bring to an end our anguish of forty-two years duration by giving us titles to our own lands which we purchased as members of our community of Monjas, Jalapa. In 1923 we bought fifty-four *caballerías* for 40 thousand pesos for 623 peasant families from Lawyer Antonio Godoy, General David Barrientos and Engineer Benedicto Cárcamo, who had obtained them from President Orellana. The lands were measured then and in 1943 they were measured again, but we were never given titles. Now we are collaborating with the Institute of Community Development and still nothing. We suffer from this insecurity.[2]

On 16 May 1967 the Indians of Cahaboncito in Alta Vera-paz claimed that Oscar Lemus had stolen land that they had owned for over a hundred years, the burial place of their ancestors. They stated that he had done so by means of a fraudulent bill of sale.[3]

Three hundred peasant families in Santiago, Sacatepéquez denounced their Mayor in January 1968 for underhand dealings in his attempts to give the lands on which they had lived to his political friends.[4] By June of the same year, an even bigger problem had arisen : 'Several hundred families abandoned without lands or roof in Taxisco.'[5] Two days later, on 20 June, the Red Cross reported that it was feeding the 1,700 people in Candelaria, Taxisco, where they were with-

1. *El Imparcial*, 21 January 1967.   2. ibid., 9 March 1967.
3. ibid., 16 May 1967.   4. ibid., 2 January 1968.
5. ibid., 18 June 1968.

out lands and 'living exposed to the elements'.[6] INTA sent a commission to resolve the conflicting claims between what was said to be two peasant groups of 15 and 392 families respectively and published the following information:

The problem is not new; it began in 1954 when the peasants were violently expelled from the lands of the *finca* Chiquihuitán in Taxisco, where they had been settled by the previous Government. From among the expelled families, many dispersed and fled while others took refuge in the area between the Pacific Ocean and the Chiquimulilla Canal.... There are now fifteen families there on state lands employing 115 families as *colonos*. We are going to divide that land equally among all.[7]

By the end of August it became clearer who was behind these difficulties, when Manuel Ralda Ochoa demanded that INTA expel the 'hundreds of peasant families' from his *finca* Chiquihuitán in Taxisco.[8] Ralda Ochoa is the largest cattle-rancher in the country, was a member of the three-man commission named by Ydígoras to dispose of the National Fincas and had already obtained huge holdings from Col. Oliverio Casasola in Petén. His view of the problem was different: 'INTA says that this *finca* was expropriated in 1953. But this is not true. It was invaded and then everything was straightened out later under Castillo Armas.'[9] INTA responded two days later saying that when the peasants were expelled in 1954, the owner, who later sold out to Ralda, also laid claim illegally to State lands near by and it was these State lands that INTA was going to give to the *campesinos*.[10] A year afterwards, in late 1969, the peasants still did not have title to the lands in Taxisco, nor is it likely that they will ever get them, though INTA put up an unusually spirited defence of the peasants. Ralda's own final public word in the affair was to show how important the land was to him: 'I have 20,000

6. ibid., 20 June 1968.   7. ibid., 12 July 1968.
8. ibid., 31 August 1968.   9. ibid., 7 September 1968.
10. ibid., 9 September 1968.

workers on the *finca* Chiquihuitán and a weekly payroll of Q40,000. It produces 2,500 calves annually.' [11] He goes on to denounce the trouble as the work of agitators and does not even refer to his public admission of paying his workers an illegal salary averaging twenty-eight cents a day.

In the meantime, slight notice is taken of the fact that the Mayor, the municipal secretary and the municipal authority in charge of measuring lands in San Juan Ixcoy, Huehuetenango, have murdered an Indian and his wife because of a land dispute. There is speculation about the Mayor's immunity from prosecution.[12] At the writing of this book, neither man has been charged with the crime.

On 27 November 1968, 300 Indian families were put off their lands in Palín and their coffee was confiscated as indemnization. The action was taken by the municipal authorities, who belonged to the Revolutionary Party. The people had been given the lands by Arbenz and had lived there 'since 1954'.[13] In February 1969, some of these same Mayans held a news conference, a novel event in the history of Guatemala's fourth estate, to which two reporters went: 'Some were barefoot; some spoke Spanish with difficulty. But all of them knew with precision what they wanted to say ... that the Press publicize the truth about their situation: the abuse of authority and the open robbery of which they are victims.' [14]

The day following the expulsions in Palín, sixteen families were put off the *finca* Acapalón in Champerico.[15] The news item noted that this was the second group thrown off this particular *finca*. And in December INTA itself began getting into the swing of things by ejecting ninety families from La Máquina, an action which was denounced by the regional peasant organization. Three months later, the *Prensa Libre*

11. ibid., 16 September 1968.   12. ibid., 31 July 1968.
13. ibid., 27 November 1968.   14. *Prensa Libre*, 26 February 1969.
15. *El Imparcial*, 28 November 1968.

published a letter from Silvino Sánchez, representing forty families from Acasaguastlán, El Progreso, who had lost 'their land, corn, fruit trees and coffee' to INTA in 1964. They had been appealing to INTA since that time to give the lands back and grant them their rightful titles.[16]

By May 1969 INTA was situating 400 families in Los Angeles and Sehilá and another 250 families in Río Negro, all in the Department of Izabal. 'All of these people had been expelled for diverse reasons from lands that they had been cultivating.'[17] There is no mention of their receiving titles for their new lands. Izabal is the area in which Yon Sosa and his guerrilla movement have been having such success in educating the people to the dynamics of the Guatemalan land-tenure pattern.

A good example of the process can be seen in the story of the small village of 'La Esperanza' in Izabal, where two hundred families had cleared a section of the jungle for themselves. In mid-1963, the military commissioner of the area told them that they had to move out since the land was owned by a wealthy family by the name of Padilla. When the peasants refused, soldiers were brought in, the homes of the former were burned and tractors used to plough up their crops. They complained to the Governor of Izabal but he did nothing about the case since 'he and the Padilla brothers used to drink together; the orders of investigation were filed away while our small children died of hunger because we then had to live in the jungle like animals'.[18] Finally, these same people were able to clear another section of the jungle for themselves, but again the Padilla brothers moved off, backed up by another newly acquired title. 'It seems like those evil men had decided not to let us live and we were losing all hope when we met the guerrillas and they told us that they would kill the Padillas and give us back our land.'[19]

16. *Prensa Libre*, March 1969.   17. ibid., 10 May 1969.
18. CIDOC, *Dossier No. 21*, p. 4/104.   19. ibid.

In the early part of 1964, the Padilla brothers were killed in an ambush near Quiriguá Viejo. The Army immediately sent out a patrol looking for the guerrillas and the lieutenant-colonel in charge was killed in another ambush. The military was furious and arrested the ten most outstanding peasant leaders in the area, including the peasant leader of the Christian Democrats, throwing them all in jail where they remained until Peralta Azurdia turned the Government over to Méndez Montenegro. The wife of one of the arrested men said:

A few nights ago the guerrillas came to see me. They told me that the government was after them for defending the poor and that the only solution left was for everyone to join them in order to defeat the soldiers and put in a government of the working people.[20]

Another situation in the same area may provide the setting for a similar dynamic. We refer to the small town of Chichipate on Lake Izabal, where the population grew from zero in 1950 to 346 inhabitants in 1964. All these migrants were Kekchí Indians from Alta Verapaz who moved to Chichipate in an attempt to obtain land to sustain themselves. 'The greatest sense of disappointment has come, though, from the fact that private absentee owners suddenly appeared after the Chichipateños had cleared the land.'[21] When the absentee owners established their claim, they sold the lands to the International Nickel Company and an adjacent *finca*. The Company allowed the settlers to remain where they were but insisted that no more be allowed into the area so as not to interfere with their extensive mining operations. The owner of the Yuscarán *finca* was also more generous than is usually the

20. ibid., p. 4/105.
21. Carter, William E., *New Lands and Old Traditions*. University of Florida Press: 1969, p. 3.

case, for he 'entered into an agreement whereby Chichipateños living on his property would work for him at their discretion, in return for which they could make milpa on Chichipate land and would receive cash payment of 50¢ per man-day of labor'.[22] Such an arrangement was very generous in view of the common practice in Izabal of obliging the *colonos* to 'give two weeks of free labor per month during the periods of planting and harvest. Another [custom] is to require him to clear and cultivate approximately 60% as much for the landowner as he clears and cultivates for himself.' [23] Perhaps this favourable treatment was indirect recognition of the guerrilla activity that existed in the area. But expulsions in other areas did and do continue.

On 6 June 1969 'a group of military police came into Montufar, Jutiapa, interrupting the tranquillity of the neighbours with several bursts from their machine-guns, followed up with insults and threats while ordering six peasant families to abandon their homes under threat of death'.[24] The aforegoing accusation was made by Emilio Gómez Galicia in the name of the other families and he produced documents from INTA demonstrating their legal ownership of the lands from which they had been expelled. The Secretary of Public Relations of INTA immediately protested that the accusation was false, since the agrarian authorities in the region had informed the Institution that Gómez Galicia possessed 'large extensions of land' and that he was *persona non grata* in the area.[25] On the 24th of the same month a suit was brought against INTA by Gómez Galicia in the name of 'nine families' that had lived on the lands since 1905, stating that they had first tried to get their titles legitimized by DGAA and then by INTA, having been successful with the latter Institution.[26] No more is heard of the incident.

22. ibid., p. 5.
24. *Prensa Libre*, 12 June 1969.
26. ibid., 25 June 1969.

23. ibid., p. 4.
25. ibid., 13 June 1969.

The following month another problem came up in the same area, Jutiapa, which again landed INTA in the Courts. This time the Government was on the side of the peasants, though not for long. The owner of the *finca* 'Armenia', Francisco de Jesús Valenzuela Reyes, had thirteen families expelled from his lands on 16 April 1969. INTA subsequently intervened and returned the dispossessed *campesinos* to the lands, and this action resulted in the suit.[27] INTA won the day by maintaining that it had already cancelled its former resolution in favour of the peasants even before the suit was filed.[28]

Toward the end of July 1969 seventeen peasant families who had been expelled from national lands in Sebol–Raxuha, Alta Verapaz, were allowed to settle in the Agrarian Zone Fray Bartolomé de las Casas 'until their juridical situation is resolved'.[29] INTA threatened legal action against those responsible for the expulsions, 'who, in this case, have violated the law of suppletory title'.[30] The threat was never carried out.

In September of the same year, 1969, a delegation representing 1,000 people who were being expelled from their homes in Zones 5 and 8 of Guatemala City protested to the Vice-Minister of the Interior that they had lived on their lands for thirty years and were now being put off by two lawyers who had taken over the lands from a German company.[31]

At the end of this same month, another group of fifty men tried to construct 'cardboard houses' in the ravine 'El Tuerto' in Zone 1 of the Capital but were driven off by the people who lived there.[32] The former had lived in other ravines around the City but their homes had been washed away by the rain and 'El Tuerto' looked drier and safer to them. The

27. ibid., 12 June 1969.   28. ibid., 30 July 1969.
29. ibid., 23 July 1969.   30. ibid.
31. ibid., 4 September 1969.   32. ibid., 29 September 1969.

occupants, no better off than the 'invaders', refused to share their refuge with the newcomers.

On 8 October 1969 a family with fifteen members had to abandon its home in Chiquemula because the military commissioner in the area claimed that the land belonged to him, and he threatened them with death if they did not pack up and leave. He had already shot and wounded one nineteen-year-old-son.[33]

Two Maya inhabitants of Itzapa, Chimaltenango – Cornelio Tahul and Victor Xiquinajay – protested on 23 October 1969 that INTA was expelling them and 211 other peasant families from the lands to which they had title.[34] INTA defended itself by maintaining that the lands had been given to these families in 1956 by the Government of Castillo Armas for each lot of which they were to pay Q422. Since the money had never been paid, INTA claimed they were executing their right to expel the peasants and turn over the land to other families.[35]

It must be noted that these accounts are taken from Guatemala's most conservative Press, *El Imparcial* and *Prensa Libre*. If they are slanted at all, it is on the side of the Government and landowners. These newspapers report no more than a small percentage of such incidents that occur throughout the country. Their news stories are supplied mostly by part-time reporters living in the major centres of population, seldom venturing into the countryside.

A look at other fields of social concern reinforces the picture already painted and shows, if nothing else, at least a consistency in governmental policy. As was true when the military was openly in control of the Government, so is it still true today that the cotton plantations remain the most blatant offences to human dignity.

On 8 December 1966 the Organization of University

33. *Prensa Libre*, 8 October 1969.
34. ibid., 23 October 1969.   35. ibid., 25 October 1969.

Students (AEU) asked the Méndez Government to set up a special commission to work with Ministers of Labour and Public Health to investigate the cotton plantations and sanction those cotton growers responsible for the sickness and death of their workers.[36] The plantation owners often do not provide the education or equipment needed by the peasant for protection against insecticides. When the sub-director of the Social Security Institute of the Government in 1967 complained publicly that the cotton-growers were not abiding by the legal recommendations for insecticides, a campaign of vilification was mounted against him in the newspapers by the National Cotton Council that resulted in his losing his job.[37]

Often a plantation owner will order his field sprayed and will not pull the workers out while the operation is effected.[38] The result of this is sickness or death for the workers. In late 1967, in one thirty-day period, over a hundred cases of insecticide intoxication were reported, 'many of whom died'.[39] One of the authors has heard spray pilots talk about how they would swoop down and spray an unsuspecting group of labourers in the field, to be met by the protest of a few hurled sticks, stones or even hats. There is no recorded punishment either for them or for the plantation owners.[40]

Once in a while some of these conditions will come to the notice of the Minister of Labour or the Institute of Social Security and a well-publicized trip will be made to one or another part of the country, and after a 'heart to heart talk' with a few plantation owners the official comes back with the encouraging news that the landowners will see that something is done to eliminate the problem.[41]

In November 1968 the National Cotton Council thanked the Institute of Social Security and the Minister of Agricul-

36. *El Imparcial*, 8 December 1966. 37. ibid., 9 January 1967.
38. ibid., 5 and 17 October 1967. 39. ibid., 11 November 1967.
40. ibid., 17 October 1967. 41. ibid., 19 January 1967.

ture for their help in the campaign against poisoning. They congratulated those cotton growers who had had no cases of intoxication and requested those who did have to try 'twice' as hard in the future to avoid them.[42] The campaign consisted of flying over the plantations and dropping leaflets on the illiterate peasants explaining that they should not drink, eat or smoke, unless they first wash with soap and water; that they should bathe and have a change of clothes after being sprayed themselves; and not to enter the plantations for forty-eight hours after the spraying. The fact that few plantations have adequate washing or bathing facilities for the workers, that most peasants do not have a change of working clothes, and that it is not their decision when to enter the fields, does not seem to have occurred to the National Cotton Council.

Only two days before this campaign began, it was headline news that workers from El Salvador were being 'smuggled' across the border with the help of immigration authorities, having been promised 'fabulous salaries'. When they finished picking the crop, they were made to sign onerous contracts or were released without wages and threatened exposure for illegal entry if they complained.[43] This has never been a difficult operation for the landowners to effect as long as the authorities co-operate, since El Salvador's land problems are even worse than those of Guatemala. In 1969 the insecticide intoxications continued, still with no evidence of any legal sanctions against those responsible.[44]

On 9 October 1969 the Press contained a little-observed notice tucked away on an inner page: '4,000 people affected by the *grippe*. An average of five to six people a day are dying from the *grippe* on the *finca* Oná, in El Quetzal, San Marcos ... the attempts that have been made to combat the sickness have been useless, since the *grippe* has been propagated enor-

42. ibid., 21 November 1968.   43. ibid., 19 November 1968.
44. ibid., 27 October and 4 November 1969.

mously and many workers and their families are sick.' [45] No mention is made of the living conditions that would allow the sickness to spread so devastatingly.

The relationship existing between the large land-holdings on one hand and the need for landless peasants to work them on the other, continued to manifest itself under Méndez Montenegro. This balanced equation between *latifundismo* and *minifundismo* can be maintained as long as the peasants are not allowed to organize in unions. Arévalo and Arbenz both saw a strong labour movement as the principal protection for the rights of those agricultural workers who would remain working the lands of others as employees. Since the labour movement was purportedly a centre of communist agitation, it was a main target of Castillo Armas's wrath. Ydígoras kept up the pressure, although he did encourage the organization of openly 'Ydigorista' unions. Peralta Azurdia imitated the Castillo Armas attitude in this field, and proclaimed a law making it a crime to get a peasant 'excited', thus effectively outlawing any union activity. The Third Government of the Revolution that had 'come to power by the will of the people, the peasant people', as it constantly reminded everyone, had to show itself a friend of organized labour. So it was that under Méndez Montenegro the number of labour syndicates and rural co-operative increased impressively. The President made it a point to appear at most of the important national meetings of the labour movement and reiterate his support for the working man. On 1 May 1969, International Labour Day, such a meeting was held. Méndez attended and spoke. He was followed by a labour leader who roundly criticized the Army for interfering in politics.[46] A few days later, the Army issued a hot denial of the charge and the President had to do some fast back-pedalling to demonstate that the speaker had represented only his personal point of view.

45. ibid., 9 October 1969.   46. *Prensa Libre*, 2 May 1969.

Méndez's inability to give the labour movement the strength that it needs to work effectively is only consistent with every other aspect of the President's attempts to make effective his deals for social change. He cannot give what he himself does not have : political power.

The labour movement has always been considered a haven for communists and Marxist-oriented agitators and as such it is the recognized target of anti-communist activities. There is no question that communists and so-called fellow-travellers have been instrumental in both the development and, at times, as under Arbenz, the control of large segments of the movement, but this has not been true since the advent of the Liberation régime. Since that time the Christian labour movement has increased its activity. Nevertheless the battle-cry for the control and suppression of the movement since the Liberation has been in the name of freedom and democracy as interpreted by the anti-communist landowners.

Méndez Montenegro has had a problem relating to this situation because he cannot withstand the charge of being soft on communism. The landowners, the Army, the Church and the United States Government are the principal institutions that keep him in power, and all consider a vaguely defined communism as their chief enemy. The labour movement suffers as a result.

Walter Widmann's feud with the union in his sugar plantation is an example. Widmann, a prominent Catholic layman,[47] owns Concepción, one of the largest sugar plantations in the country. Under the Ydígoras régime, he tried to destroy the union, alleging communism, by firing hundreds of families on several occasions. The union appealed to the Labour Court for protection and in fact did manage to have labour inspectors come to the plantation and demand that the

47. He is a lay member of Opus Dei, a conservative Catholic association. He used to pay $500 to a minor official during Arbenz's Government to obtain entrance visas for Maryknoll missionaries.

fired workers be restored. Then, with the help of Col. Pedro Cardona, the administrator who was the local military commissioner as well, a second union was sponsored by the employer and the workers were forced to join.[48] In order to gain government support, it was publicized that this second union was 'Ydigorista' while the first one was communist. The law specifies that only one union can be legalized on a plantation and there is chronological preference. The Ministry of Labour supported the first union and insisted that the fired labourers be rehired.

But in February 1963 three peasant leaders were jailed as communists. The union secretary protested that it was a false accusation.[49] When Peralta became President there was no longer any political lever in an 'Ydigorista' union, so the plantation was forced to rehire the men. They continued, nevertheless, to be persecuted [50] and turned over to the police. When Méndez came to the presidency, the peasant labour federation of that zone raised its head and in August 1966 threatened a strike.[51] They were blocked from organizing it and as a result Col. P. Cardona, the administrator, was assassinated the following week. Later the Armed Forces of Rebellion attempted the assassination of Widmann himself but were unsuccessful. On 11 September 1967 Pedro Fajardo Ajín, the Secretary General of the workers' union, was kidnapped and murdered, along with two other union members. It was never discovered who did the killing. After that a military guard was based permanently on the plantation, and even the clergy were prevented from talking to the workers.[52]

Neither the landowners nor the peasants are resting easily. The problem of land tenure is the basic factor stimulating

48. El *Imparcial*, 12 January 1963.   49. ibid., 4 March 1963.
50. ibid., 26 June 1963.   51. ibid., 12 August 1966.
52. Recounted to the authors from the personal experience of a fellow Maryknoller.

the militancy of both groups, but rights are violated on the two sides, confusing the issues. It is impossible to unravel the murders from the executions, the personal vendettas from self-defence. Calculations of the number killed from July 1966 to June 1968 oscillated from 2,000 to 4,500.[53] The papers carry daily the pictures of those who have disappeared and the descriptions of unidentified and mutilated bodies found here and there. The Right-wing terrorist groups function in the City as well as in the rural zones, paid by the wealthy and actively assisted by the Army and police. It is hard to distinguish organized guerrilla activity from isolated peasant action in the countryside. This is what the Méndez Government has had to face. Late in September 1966 the plantation owners demanded that the Government step up policing activities in the country districts and the Chief of Police promised squads of patrolmen to protect all threatened landowners.[54] By December of the same year the owners and administrators of plantations were commissioned as members of the National Police.[55] In February 1967, 20,000 tons of sugar cane were burned on fifteen different *fincas*.[56] Other fires were followed by the landowners' insistent demand for further protection.[57]

The Government requested that the workers' right to organize be respected but the landowners usually replied with violence. In August the Government sponsored a campaign to teach the peasants to read and write. One hundred landowners co-operated by allowing teachers on to their plantations and granting them facilities for the activities. It was requested of all of them at this time that they allow union organizing to be carried out among their workers.[58]

53. *Washington Post*, 16 June 1968; and CIDOC Dossier 21, Centro Intercultural de Documentación: Cuernavaca, Mexico, 1968, p. 512.
54. *El Imparcial*, 20 September 1966.
55. ibid., 6 December 1966.   56. ibid., 27 February 1967.
57. ibid., 3 April 1967.   58. ibid., 12 August 1967.

The following month the Secretary General of the workers' union on Concepción and two of his assistants were murdered.[59] Five weeks later, Méndez attended a meeting of 2,000 delegates to the Guatemalan Workers Confederation (CONTRAGUA) and assured his listeners that his Government was with them.[60] A month later the under-secretary of peasant affairs for the Christian Democrats in Izabal was jailed.[61] He had already spent two years in jail under Peralta Azurdia for his 'communism'. Archbishop Casariego didn't help matters for the Government when on 14 December 1967 he requested that it produce the 273 people who had been arrested and never consigned to any tribunal.[62] The police and the Minister of the Interior maintained that they knew nothing of the whereabouts of the individuals named on the list.

But peasants continued to disappear. In March 1968 the two leaders of the labour union in the plantation Cerro Redondo, Santa Rosa, were abducted, never to be seen again.[63] By the end of the same month, lists were published naming twenty-five leaders of Central worker organizations who had been marked for execution by Right-wing terrorist organizations.[64] The same day 15,000 tons of sugar cane burned on the largest plantation in the country, El Salto, in Escuintla. Another 41,000 tons went up on three other plantations in the same area.[65] In July nine peasants were kidnapped and murdered in Chiquimula.[66] In September, when 300 coffee harvesters protested against the intolerable conditions on a plantation in Quezaltenango, the police were called in and arrested the ten leaders.[67]

The Government Party itself was the target of anti-com-

59. ibid., 11 September 1967.
61. ibid., 25 November 1967.
63. ibid., 4 March 1968.
65. ibid.
67. ibid., 5 and 9 October 1968.

60. ibid., 16 November 1967.
62. ibid., 14 December 1967.
64. ibid., 27 March 1968.
66. ibid., 20 July 1968.

munist activities. Two Congressmen, three regional party heads and a number of other notable members of the Revolutionary Party, all active in the labour movement, were assassinated.

On 12 October 1969 the Secretary General of the Confederation of Workers of Guatemala, Hugo Vásquez Barrientos, was shot and wounded by unknown assailants in Utiapa. Two days later, Reinero Zan Hurtarte, a Director of the Confederation of Syndicates (Unions) of Guatemala, was also shot, but this effort was more successful and the labour leader died as a result of his wounds. He had been threatened many times before his execution.[68] The newspapers reported a few days later that the leaders of the labour movement had been 'threatened by masked men with machine-guns not to insist that the assassination of Zan Hurtarte be cleared up'.[69] The dead man was a leader of the Revolutionary Party in the area of Escuintla and it is interesting to note that the Government's interest in clarifying the crime was not sufficient by itself but had to be prodded by the insistence of the labour movement.

It is impossible to ascertain the number of murders, killings, assassinations and executions that have occurred while Méndez Montenegro has been President. In an editorial written in April 1967, the Director of *Prensa Libre* calculated that the country was averaging over a hundred political murders a month at that time.[70] His figures were based on the number of deaths reported, an elusive criterion at best.

The situation progressively worsened during 1967 and the first months of 1968. But the incident that sent reverberations throughout the country was the kidnapping of the Archbishop, Mario Casariego, in March, in broad daylight, a block and a half from the presidential palace. For a city armed to the teeth, and under martial law, with two submachine-gun-

68. ibid., 15 October 1969.   69. ibid., 17 October 1969.
70. *Prensa Libre*, 5 April 1967.

toting soldiers on every corner, and pairs of police radio cars patrolling every street with two or three bullet-proofed officers pointing guns out of the windows, such a derring-do was clearly impossible without official police and Army connivance. These connections had been known publicly for more than a year and it was impossible to deny them any longer. The Government swiftly relieved three top men of their posts: Col. Arriaga Bosque, the Minister of Defence; Sosa Avila, the head of the National Police; and Col. Carlos Arana, commander of the Zacapa Army base. The police also managed to murder Raúl Lorenzana, Right-wing terrorist leader and scapegoat, after he had been taken into custody. An unofficial truce seemed to have been called.

The respite was not long-lasting and it flared up again when the police captured Camilo Sánchez, the FAR's second-in-command. The FAR's reprisal was swift: the attempted kidnapping of the US Ambassador, John Gordon Mein. When the Ambassador broke from his captors and began to run, they panicked and shot him. The Government's response was predictable: they murdered Camilo Sánchez in jail. These were mutual signals to intensify the conflict.

A year later, Col. Carlos Arana Osorio, the fired military commander, was back in Guatemala to campaign for the presidential elections of 1970; and Sosa Avila was back in good grace to occupy the post of Minister of the Interior, promising to reaffirm public order and emphatically denying any previous liaison with clandestine terrorist organizations.[71] The following months were bloody and Méndez Montenegro's political longevity did nothing to ameliorate the situation of Guatemala's landless and long-suffering masses.

71. ibid., 20 June 1969.

CHAPTER 16

Opportunity
for Glory

It is this influential nucleus of aggressive, ambitious professional
military leaders who are the root of American evolving militarism.
... Civilians can scarcely understand or even believe that many
ambitious military professionals truly yearn for wars and the opportunity for glory and distinction afforded only in combat.... Most
military people know very little about Communism.... Defeating
'aggression' is a gigantic combat-area competition rather than a
crusade to save the world from Communism.

GENERAL DAVID M. SCHOUP
Former Commandant, U.S. Marine Corps

There is only one door to progress and development in
Guatemala : an integral agrarian reform. No dictatorial totalitarianism can be more oppressive than is hunger and
ignorance and those who would talk of freedom and rights
in such a context know not whereof they speak. It was for
this reason that the Alliance for Progress Charter stipulated
certain conditions for Latin American countries to receive
continued US aid, primary among them : an integral agrarian
reform and a reform of tax structures (both closely related).
Guatemala has so far been unwilling to effect either of these
reforms and it is doubtful that she will do so in the near
future for reasons that we would underline here.

The problem rests basically on the mentality of the landowners themselves. Their religio-cultural heritage does not
permit them to admit that there exists a problem, let alone

take effective measures to deal with it. Catholicism, especially Spanish Catholicism, is imbued with a spirit of resignation that preaches 'everyone in his place' and that one's life condition is the result of God's Will. It is not that the landowners are exceptionally religious people, but rather that Catholicism appears to give them, on a religious level, the justification they need for the dehumanizing socio-economic system that is Guatemala's. 'Thou shalt not covet thy neighbour's goods' is effectively used by the landowners and the wealthy in addressing themselves to the destitute to keep them from becoming dissatisfied with their lot. Thus it was that the Archbishop of Guatemala City could say to the poverty-stricken people of La Limonada, one of Guatemala City's cardboard and tin *barrios*:

You, the humble ones of this colony, are the most cherished by me; I was poor like you; you live in shacks like that of Bethlehem that housed the Infant God, but you are happy because where there is poverty, there is happiness.[1]

La Limonada is one of the numerous colonies that have sprung up around Guatemala City in the ravines that encircle it. They are called the 'Crown of Thorns' and house the tens of thousands of landless peasants who have left the countryside and have come to the City hoping for work, for a livelihood. Often they have to turn to crime or mendicity to stay alive, and just as often they fail at this also.

When, in early 1968, *Time* magazine published a letter from the authors referring to the misery of Guatemala's masses, AGA demanded equal space and offered this rebuttal:

No human being has to be a priest to be on the side of the poor, and Guatemala, under no circumstances, is the most impoverished nation in the world, nor are we indifferent to wanting to improve the conditions of our poor. The program 'Against Poverty' of President Johnson shows that many fellow citizens

1. El *Imparcial*, 24 February 1967.

of Thomas Melville live in greater necessity and poverty than many Guatemalans. We have here more than 417,344 owners of plantations and lands, and if each one of these represents a family of five members, it signifies that more than half of our people own their own lands.[2]

Thus AGA, representative of the landowners' mentality, consoles itself that Guatemala is not the poorest country in the world, and that some US citizens are worse off than some Guatemalan citizens, both facts that cannot be denied. But the cynicism of this defence can be seen in the claim that more than half of all Guatemalans are property owners, while there is no mention made of the extent of these holdings, nor whether they are sufficient for supporting a family. No recognition is made that only 7·3 per cent of these holdings are legally registered, this lack facilitating extemporaneous expulsions and thefts. Therefore, when the newspapers report a lack of corn in Huehuetenango on the Western *altiplano*, with its corresponding hunger,[3] as they did in August 1967, no relation is made to Guatemala's land-tenure pattern. So too in Chiquimula, on the Eastern *altiplano*, it was observed the same month that the 'peasants want to give away their children in order to save them from hunger'[4] and the problem can be attributed to the Will of God. Every year, as more corn has to be imported, and then rice, the basic cause of the problem is still ignored. For the first time in its history, Guatemala imported black beans in 1967,[5] thus winding up with a shortage of all three of the peasants' basic staples.

When someone describes the extent of the problem, he is promptly labelled a communist and an agitator and becomes open game for Right-wing terrorists or for the Government itself. Ydígoras refused to allow the publication of a study that attributed 50,000 infant deaths a year to malnutrition, as a

2. *Prensa Libre*, 20 February 1968.
3. *El Imparcial*, 8 August 1967.
4. ibid, 28 August 1967.   5. ibid., 11 November 1967.

'communist document'.[6] When Dr Moisés Behar, Head of the United Nations' INCAP (Institute for Nutrition of Central America and Panama), made a declaration on the nutritional state of Guatemalans, he did so in Washington and not in Guatemala City: 'The pre-Columbian Maya ate better than the people today.'[7]

The question that presents itself then is, how can a problem be solved that is not recognized as a problem by the very ones causing it? The answer, of course, is obvious: the solution to a given problem is effected by those who struggle under its weight. One must not wait for those who have intentionally created the problem in the first place, to suddenly repent and solve it.

In a democracy, the agrarian problem could be solved by electing a President and a Congress who recognize the injustice of the existing situation and have the power to do something about it. But Guatemala bears only the façade of democracy, and therefore it is not difficult for 2·1 per cent of the population, the wealthy landowners, to control and manipulate their fellow citizens who own insufficient lands and suffer from the consequent poverty. Even when a person such as Julio César Méndez Montenegro, who is progress-orientated, is successful in reaching the presidency, his ability to effect change is sharply limited. Méndez was forced to operate under the restrictions imposed by a Constitution drawn up by the military Government that preceded him, even though this Constitution was declared illegitimate by the Fourth Juridical Congress of Guatemala, since is was 'not a product of the popular will'.[8]

Even before taking office, his presidential power was curtailed by having to accept the guide-lines laid down by the military as the *sine qua non* conditions for averting a *coup*. Once in office, his puppet-status was demonstrated during his

6. ibid., 6 January 1964.   7. ibid., 27 June 1968.
8. ibid., 21 September 1966:

visits to all the main military bases in the country, where he publicly acknowledged his respect for the Army and his willingness to uphold the Armed Forces' 'duty and right to safeguard the Constitution'.

It is no secret in Guatemala that the Army and the police (under military control) hold the sole political power of that country today. The uneasy, but mutually beneficial, alliance that exists between the Armed Forces and the landed oligarchy enables the 2·1 per cent to rule over, or overrule, the rest of the population. With few but happy exceptions the officer corps is made up of aspiring members of the middle class who would like to take their place among the upper class before or after their retirement from the military establishment. It is in their best interest to co-operate with the people who can facilitate that process.

The uneasiness of the power alliance comes from the civilians' inability to judge the extent of influence a given officer wields within the Armed Forces. The alliances and counter-alliances make the military far from the monolithic structure that some outsiders seem to think it is. Thus it was indispensable for Méndez Montenegro to visit each commander throughout the country and proclaim his respect for each one of them personally and not confine himself to talking to his Minister of Defence. The President's condition of dependency on the military was obvious to the public who observed him making his visits around the country, a ·45 calibre pistol strapped to his hip, while the Minister of Defence, Col. Arriaga Bosque, was just two steps behind, watching everyone Méndez spoke to. The macabre joke was made, not without subsequent evidence of truth, that the ·45 pistol was carried by Méndez Montenegro more to protect himself from Arriaga Bosque and his friends than from any wild-eyed assassin.

But the alliances within the Armed Forces, based on what is commonly called *personalismo* (personal relationships

rather than ideological ones), can be used by a clever politician to his advantage. Méndez Montenegro, while certainly
not a clever politician, was able to take advantage of a political
blunder and, counting on the competing loyalties within the
military establishment, to rid himself of its apparently
strongest block and his biggest threat.

This blunder was the kidnapping of Archbishop Mario
Casariego in March 1969, which was seen by the Guatemalan
people as obvious collusion between the Right-wing terrorists
and the Army. The Government had immediately accused the
Left-wing guerrillas but this was popularly viewed as a
smoke screen. It was not hard to guess who was responsible,
it was only a question of their motivation.

Mario Monteforte Toledo[9] says that there were three
reasons for the kidnapping of the Archbishop: Casariego did
not align himself with the Liberation Party and the privileges
of the wealthy, as did his predecessor, Archbishop Rossell;
Casariego had not lent himself to the anti-communist campaign, nor to condemning guerrillas as if they were the only
ones responsible for the deplorable national conditions (as a
matter of fact, he had imprudently embarrassed the Government by publicly petitioning it to turn over to the proper
tribunals 273 people who had been arrested and had disappeared while in police custody);[10] and, most important, the
kidnapping would produce an outpouring of public revulsion
and thus the citizens, expressing their lack of confidence in
Méndez Montenegro, could have publicly demanded a military *coup* that would then have been easily executed.[11]

The plan back-fired for several reasons. Church authorities
remained calm and asked the country to do likewise. Archbishop Casariego is not a popular man in Guatemala, and

9. Monteforte Toledo was the President of Congress in the Government of Juan José Arévalo.

10. El *Imparcial*, 14 December 1967.

11. CIDOC, *Document* 68/61: Cuernavaca, Mexico, 1968.

even among the clergy the kidnapping was greeted with more amusement than outrage.

The Right-wing terrorist–military collusion was confirmed after a few days when it was discovered that the Archbishop had been held prisoner in the home of the former Secretary of Information of the Castillo Armas Government, Dr Carlos Cifuentes Díaz. Furthermore, any doubts that may have lingered were dissipated when the Minister of Defence refused to heed Méndez Montenegro's request to cut short his visit to the United States and return home. Arriaga Bosque was visiting the Pentagon and other US military installations[12] where Guatemalans were training, making public statements denying his relationship to Right-wing extremist groups.[13] He prolonged his visit five days beyond Casariego's kidnapping and in effect told the President that he would return only when the Army requested it, and not as Minister of Defence, but as head of a new military Government.

Méndez moved fast. Congress censured the Vice-President, Marroquín Rojas, a staunch backer of Arriaga Bosque and a vociferous defender of Right-wing terrorism, for his editorials justifying the kidnapping. Then Méndez sought and obtained promises of support from various quarters, said to be the Air Force, the Mariscal Zavala Brigade in the Capital, and the US Embassy. Finally he called in three men who were most often linked to the Right-wing extremists: Col. Rafael Arriaga Bosque, as Minister of Defence, was responsible for the indiscriminate arrests and executions perpetrated by the Army; Col. Carlos Arana Osorio made efficient use of terrorist bands against purported guerrilla sympathizers in the Zacapa area; Col. Manuel Sosa Avila was accountable for the hundreds of arrested citizens who could not be located in any police detention centre.

12. ibid, 13 March 1968.
13. *Washington Post*, 15 March 1968.

From the day he was sworn into office, the President had found these three men to be his most powerful opponents on the Right and the watchdogs of his administration. When the Liberation Party issued a repeated call to the country to join the 'national crusade in order to demonstrate to the Castroite subversives that the Government, the people and the Army, have joined to form a single combat force',[14] the true meaning was only vaguely hidden:

In view of the Government's indolence in confronting with decision the challenge of the armed rebels, and in view of the lenience of the Courts in judging them, diverse sections of the citizenry, reacting justifiably to the growing Leftist offensive, have spontaneously organized themselves, have adopted a posture of self-defence, and have begun to respond to the enemy with the same arms and the same tactics.[15]

It had been openly commented on by both the radio and the Press that the Army and police forces were involved in the Right-wing terrorist activities sponsored by various anti-communist groups. The relationship could hardly be hidden, why else the law of amnesty passed as the final act of Peralta's Congress 'for all members of the Army, all policemen and their superiors, for those acts committed in the repression of subversive activities'?[16] Arriaga Bosque himself came close to admitting the relationship in December 1966, when he stated that he was 'grateful to the public for their help in fighting communism' but added that he could not make deals with these secret organizations since this was 'prohibited by the Constitution'.[17] The kidnapping of Archbishop Casariego, however, was just one act, although the most blatant, in a whole series of subversive and murderous Right-wing activities that could not have been accomplished without the co-operation of military and police authorities.

14. El *Gráfico*, 16 May 1967.　　15. ibid.
16. El *Imparcial*, 28 April 1966.　　17. ibid., 12 December 1966.

The President told the trio that he was removing them from their posts, but he offered them compensations that may yet prove to be his downfall : Arriaga Bosque would go as Consul to Miami and Arana Osorio as Ambassador to Nicaragua. Both places are centres for Latin American intrigue and plots, the temporary homes for political exiles from many nations. Arriaga Bosque made a last effort to save himself, appealing to the Armed Forces to 'remain united in their fight against communism'.[18] The ploy did not work and no one rallied to his side. Méndez Montenegro, in an attempt to salvage some of the tarnished image of the military, explained the changes as 'democratic removals' that occur regularly within the Armed Forces.[19] No one was deceived.

The seeming ascendancy of the President over the military was short-lived. By November Col. Arana Osorio, speaking from Nicaragua, was announcing that he was the Liberation Party's candidate for the presidency in the 1970 elections.[20] He had been in Nicaragua only eight months, but this was sufficient time to make some necessary alliances. By coincidence, the same day as Arana's announcement, Méndez Montenegro visited the CONDECA headquarters (Central American Defence Command) and was quoted as saying: 'Central Americanism is not just a platitude, but a reality.'[21]

CONDECA had ostensibly been established to facilitate co-operative military training exercises and to co-ordinate an appropriate military response in case of a foreign invasion. Its efforts were more concerned with internal security, however, and it was acknowledged that the participating governments would aid one another where the pacification of the citizens of one or other nation was more than the respective government could handle. Guatemala's Minister of Defence,

18. ibid., 29 March 1968.
19. ibid, 9 April 1968.
20. ibid., 29 November 1968.
21. ibid.

Col. Chinchilla Aguilar,[22] when he was named President of CONDECA in July 1968, stated:

CONDECA embraces not only actions that are purely military for the defence of democratic institutions of our countries, the maintenance of our territorial integrity, independence and liberty, but it also involves the maintenance of an environment of peace and security that will permit the respective governments and inhabitants to begin [sic] the development of economic, social and cultural programmes.[23]

CONDECA, then, is really an international police force meant to be used to keep the citizens of Central America in line – not that such a force would actually be deployed physically, except in case of extraordinary need, but rather because the psychological advantage gained by such a threat is real and should not be underestimated. Individuals or groups who are political fugitives from the internal security forces of their own country know that they will be pursued across neighbouring borders with no ensuing international incident. They also realize that if they are captured in a neighbouring country, their fate is no more likely to be determined by legal considerations than if they were back home. Thus it is that the international alliances established among the individual military commanders of Central America (also based on *personalismo*) are certainly secondary to the domestic alliances, yet do play an important role in determining the political standing of a particular officer in his native country.

It is only in the light of these military alliances, especially with the Armed Forces of the Somoza family, that Arana's

22. Many considered that Col. Chinchilla Aguilar, previously Minister of Education, was being groomed as the next PR candidate for the presidency, and the one favoured by the US Embassy. He succeeded Arriaga, but later fell from grace within the counter coup.

23. *El Imparcial*, 1 July 1968.

ambassadorship to Nicaragua and his subsequent political comeback can be understood. Méndez Montenegro's statement, on the day Arana's candidacy was announced, contained a bitter core of truth for the President: 'Central Americanism is not just a platitude, but a reality.'

Arriaga Bosque went to Miami. Aviateca, the Guatemalan national airline, has two flights a week to Miami, flown by Air Force pilots. It is a good place to be if one has to be out of the country and wants to maintain close contacts. Hundreds of thousands of Cuban exiles float around Miami, dreaming of going back to their fatherland some day, ready and willing to co-operate with anyone who might facilitate the undertaking. Many of them were trained for the Bay of Pigs invasion in Guatemala and are friends and acquaintances of Arriaga Bosque. Many others have invested in Guatemala what they were able to get out of Cuba. General Wessin y Wessin was there too, an old anti-communist fighter from the Dominican Republic, exiled from his country on much the same basis as Arriaga, preparing to go back as the presidential candidate of his country's Right-wing forces. Roberto Alejos, owner of the Helvetia plantation, training ground for the Cuban invasion troops, and hand-picked successor of Ydígoras for the presidency, also spends much time in Miami as principal stock-holder of one of its main banks. Then too, there is the Honorable Chuck Hall, Mayor of that city, who periodically flies to Guatemala to take care of business interests and to strengthen his political connections.[24] It is in this light that Arriaga Bosque's appointment as Guatemalan Consul in Miami must be seen.

Such a view of the situation in that resort city also lends perspective to the visit of the top brass of CONDECA to Miami in March 1969.[25] Present were Gen. Doroteo Reyes Santa Cruz, who replaced Chinchilla Aguilar as Minister of

24. *Prensa Libre*, 25 and 30 June 1969.
25. ibid., 13 March 1969.

Defence in Guatemala; Col. Florencio Iraheta of Salvador; Col. Samuel Cárcamo from Nicaragua; and Col. José de la Cruz Hernández of Honduras. Ostensibly the reunion was for the purpose of pinning a medal on Col. Enrique Peralta Azurdia, former military dictator in Guatemala, for 'his extraordinary and relevant contribution to the common defence and military solidarity of Central America'.[26] It would have been more proper that Col. Peralta Azurdia receive his medal in Guatemala or in some other Central American city, except perhaps that some of the participants in the meetings in Miami were not Central Americans, and their presence in Central America would have made foreign involvement even more obvious than by having CONDECA travel to the United States.

Be that as it may, two months after the meeting Colonel Arana Osorio was conducting his political campaign in Guatemala with the self-confidence of a man already elected. Roberto Alejos had withdrawn his candidacy for PID in favour of Arana Osorio in order to form an 'alliance of all the anti-communist and patriotic sectors of the nation'. Arana lashed out at the Revolutionary Party and blamed them for dragging their feet on suppression of the guerrillas, generously excluding the President from his attacks.[27] Daily his pronouncements on sundry subjects were repeated in full detail in the Press. One day he was condemning the new immorality of motion pictures and the next he was announcing that the MLN (Party of National Liberation) and the PID (Independent Democratic Party) would co-sponsor the bill in Congress for the exoneration of export duties on coffee.

The real measure of Arana's new power was demonstrated on 11 June 1969. The Liberation candidate visited the President, accompanied by many of his high-level backers. After an hour alone with Méndez Montenegro (his retinue waited in the foyer), the Colonel told reporters: 'We exchanged im-

26. ibid.   27. ibid., 12 May 1969.

pressions in order to find a formula that would permit the coming elections to take place in a climate of peace and tranquillity.'[28]

The next day it became clear in what the climate consisted. The Liberation Party sent a declaration to the newspapers:

The MLN views with sorrow the increase of negative forces which, aided by the little efficacy or total lack of it on the part of the authorities charged with maintaining order and security, frightens the citizenry preparing for the 1970 elections. If these groups continue in this destructive and discouraging work, the citizenry itself will have to take into its own hands the means of self-protection and then Guatemala will enter the worst of anarchies.[29]

The Liberation Party's accusations of lack of efficacy in suppressing the guerrillas and Left-wing terrorists were aimed at the Minister of the Interior, Mansilla Pinto. It was he whom Arana was referring to in his first attack on the Government and it was he whom the Colonel had demanded be replaced in his meeting with the President on 11 June. There was immediate rumours throughout the Capital that Mansilla Pinto was out and that none other than Col. Manuel Sosa Avila was back in power, not as Head of the National Police, but now as Minister of the Interior.

Mansilla Pinto had been a target of the Right-wing extremists since his appointment. The Mano Blanca, one of the many Right-wing terrorist organizations, but one whose connections with the police department were particularly strong, published a flier stating:

Is not President Méndez Montenegro responsible for what happens when his Minister of the Interior is shown to have obvious sympathies for communism and is completely incapable of fulfilling his obligations? Licenciado Mansilla Pinto is undermining the stability of the government with his incompetence and it is absurd to think that the Revolutionary Party is not aware

28. ibid, 12 June 1969.   29. ibid., 13 June 1969.

of the dissatisfaction and lack of tranquillity that is noticeable among the people.[30]

The publication went on to state what it believed to be the proper attitude of the Minister of the Interior or any other Government official:

> The question that the MANO poses is this: On which side is the Revolutionary Party? A third position will not help to solve the problem. Either one aids the communists or one is against them. This bloody situation, this war unto death, will only terminate when one of the two bands in this struggle triumphs completely over the other.[31]

When, only three days after Arana's visit, the private secretary of the President announced the appointment of Col. Sosa Avila as the new Minister of the Interior, he qualified the change of Ministers as a 'routine appointment in a democratic system',[32] reminiscent of the very words used a year before when Sosa Avila and his two companions had first been fired.

The new Minister took office promising to do all in his power to establish law and order. He denied any connections with Right-wing terrorist groups, but not everyone believed him. The University Students Association protested against the appointment.[33] And up in Miami, Cuban exiles were openly jubilant about what they referred to as 'our first *coup*'.

This, then, is the democracy of Guatemala: the sovereignty, the liberty and the freedom of Guatemala are the sovereignty, the liberty and the freedom of the Guatemalan Army and oligarchy. Whoever is on top in the Armed Forces is also on top in the country. Is it correct to talk about the military being the guardian of the country's constitutionality when it has thrown out two constitutions in the last

30. CIDOC, *Dossier* 21: Cuernavaca, Mexico, 1968, p. 4/283.
31. ibid.   32. *Prensa Libre*, 16 June 1969.
33. ibid, 17 June 1969.

fifteen years and rewritten them to suit its purposes and those of the landowners? If Arana or some other military alliance does not overthrow Méndez Montenegro in the last year of his administration, it is only because they feel that they can lend an air of legitimacy to what they do by going through the motions of an election.

It is no wonder that Méndez Montenegro feels that it will be quite a feat for him to finish his term. This he should be able to accomplish if he does what he is told. So far he has not done anything serious enough to anger either the Army or the landowners. If, in the meantime, competing interests in the military can work out a balance or a compromise, Méndez Montenegro may yet have his place in history.

Any interested observer, sympathetic to the plight of the Guatemalan peasants, cannot avoid wondering what will be the resolution of this centuries-old conflict of values and needs. The landowners have virtually all the economic power, all the political power and all the physical power (represented by the Armed Forces and the police) that is needed to control the peasants' lives. They also have a high degree of intellectual, cultural and spiritual control over the *campesinos*, which is maintained by denying them an adequate educational system, by constantly insisting that the Maya recognize his 'natural inferiority', and by cynically using the teachings of the Catholic Church to justify poverty, misery and injustice.

There are indications, however, that the vice-like grip is finally being loosened, ever so slowly, ever so painfully, aided in large part by the educational process provided by transistor radios, the awareness of politics created by the insurgency and counter-insurgency efforts, and the awakening social conscience of some members in the Church and the community at large.

For their part, the peasants are learning that they have certain 'inalienable' rights that actually have been alienated, and that these rights are possessed only by the man who struggles to obtain and retain them.

John F. Kennedy, in announcing the establishment of the Alliance for Progress, stated : 'Those who make peaceful revolution impossible make violent revolution inevitable.' It is obvious that the large landowners, who have resisted integral development in the structure of Guatemala for over four centuries, are not going to change now unless someone obliges them to do so. It is also obvious that the long-suffering peasants, who have borne the burden of the day's heat these many years, can no longer afford to accept the quiescence of ages past, as demographic pressures race in tandem with their new-found sense of awareness. Yet it is the policy of the Guatemalan governing élite to attempt to control these pressures and to divert this consciousness. Just as in the days of Castillo Armas, he who favours meaningful land reform is branded a communist sympathizer and is ostracized; and he who would dare to work for land reform is believed to bear the mark of Satan himself on his soul and often does bear the marks of the Devil's self-proclaimed avenging adversaries on his flesh. The landowners, in a word, make peaceful revolution impossible.

The military support of the oligarchic structure supplied by the Guatemalan Air Force, Army and police is, by itself, insufficient to oppose and control the rising cries for justice that shatter the calm rural atmosphere. This was clearly demonstrated under Peralta Azurdia when the guerrilla bands were able to operate almost with impunity in the Zacapa and Izabal areas. They conducted literacy classes for children and adults, held public meetings to discuss the ills of Guatemalan society and the method of obtaining the political power necessary to cure them. They would also challenge the local soccer teams to games that were often attended by hundreds of people. Most important, they settled land disputes in favour of the peasants. These accomplishments often meant staying in one locale for two or three days at a time – a very effective demonstration of confidence in the peasants and disrespect for the national Government and its security forces.

The Army is perhaps Central America's best, as is also its Air Force, the former made up of 8,000–12,000 troops and the latter composed of 500 men. The figures on the police force are hard to discover because of the twilight zone within which many of them operate. Press reports acknowledge the creation of 1,500 new police positions in 1967 and another 2,000 in 1968. From these figures it is possible to estimate that the police department has at least as much personnel as the Army. These totals do not seem excessive in a nation of $4\frac{1}{2}$ million people, but it must be remembered that their primary and almost exclusive duty is internal security and not national sovereignty. Yet their numbers have not been sufficient in the past and they will become less so with every passing year. A remedy, however, has been provided for this deficiency, paradoxically by the very Government that insists that basic changes be made in the power structure of the nation: the United States of America. And the US President who foresaw the inevitability of violent revolution where peaceful revolution is rendered impossible, himself initiated the programme called 'counter-insurgency' that not only makes peaceful revolution virtually impossible but assures an ever increasing level of violence in any attempted revolution or even reform.

The programme is based on the following premises: all insurgents are communists or communist-dupes; all communists or communist-dupes are our enemies; all our enemies must be defeated because they constitute a threat to our national sovereignty. All three parts of this equation would be severely questioned by academicians, yet they are the premisses on which the US foreign policy is built. Such a foreign policy spells at least moral decay for the United States and death and destruction for many in Latin America. That such is the United States foreign policy cannot be seriously challenged. Walt Rostow, an economist and close adviser of President Johnson, in a gross simplification of the war in Vietnam, preferred to interpret the conflict in purely military terms and ignore the peasant struggle for land. In addressing the Army's Special Warfare School at Fort Bragg, in reference to the war in Vietnam he told his listeners: 'Communist guerrillas are gaining for the very simple reason known as guns, bombs, fighters.'[34] Some would have us believe that the lessons learned in Vietnam preclude such thinking today. Not so, if we are to believe General William Westmoreland in his speech to the Eighth Conference of American Armies in Río de Janeiro on 25 September 1968, as he makes the same simplistic analysis of Latin America:

I was pleased to accept this invitation because as military men, I believe that we, perhaps more than any other profession in the public service, recognize the immediate threat to the countries and people we serve that is posed by the sort of thing which is taking place today in Southeast Asia. We know that South Vietnam is a communist laboratory. We know that if agression under the guise of 'national liberation' succeeds there, it is ready to be marketed.[35]

Then the General proceeded to tell his listeners that 'agression under the guise of national liberation' will not only fail in Vietnam but will also fail in Latin America because the lessons of Vietnam will be marketed in Latin America, not by the guerrillas, but by the United States and the Latin American Armies.[36] The speech, of course, was consistent

34. Bienen, Henry, *Violence and Social Change*. University of Chicago Press: Adlai Stevenson Institute of International Affairs, 1968, p. 58.

35. Text available from the Pentagon's Office of Information.

36. ibid.

with what was and is the United States policy in Guatemala. In November 1967, when the US Ambassador, John Gordon Mein, presented the Guatemalan Armed Forces with new armoured vehicles, grenade launchers, training and radio equipment and several HU-1B jet powered helicopters, he publicly stated:

These articles, especially the helicopters, are not easy to obtain at this time since they are being utilized by our forces in defence of the cause of liberty in other parts of the world. But liberty must be defended wherever it is threatened and that liberty is now being threatened in Guatemala.[37]

We may think that Ambassador Mein's notion of liberty is different from that of Guatemala's governing élite, just as we tell ourselves that Ambassador Banker's concept of freedom is different from that of Generals Thieu and Ky of Vietnam. But not all Guatemalans believe this. So it should not have come as such a shocking surprise when Guatemalan rebels interpreted Ambassador Mein as they interpret their own officials when the latter talk of liberty, justice and democracy. They ask: whose liberty? whose justice? and whose democracy? and hear the answer booming in their daily lives. When Ambassador Mein was assassinated in August 1968 by Left-wing guerrillas, the US Press characterized the killing as a 'foul, cowardly act'.[38]

The result of such a policy, including the thousands of deaths over the past four years, is to drastically distort the internal dynamics of Guatemalan society. These dynamics operate on a psychological level but their effects are very much social and physical. Thus it is that the landed oligarchy, assured of unlimited US support to suppress 'communist guerrillas', makes no concessions to the just claims of the insurgents, other than a socially insignificant military–civic

37. *El Imparcial*, 10 November 1967.
38. *Washington Post*, Editorial, 30 August 1968.

action programme aimed only at giving immediate and short range satisfaction to felt needs and thus temporarily removing insurgency incentives. It also means that the desperate social conditions which would ordinarily push a society towards insurgency and which would serve as a bell-wether, are dampened and bottled up by the threat of overwhelming foreign intervention, producing a pressure-cooker effect instead. Arbenz's resignation might exemplify this dynamic. The third result has perhaps the most devastating implications for both Guatemala and the United States: the insurgent who realizes that he faces not only his own oppressive government, but also that of the United States, is obliged to make alliances that he might otherwise prefer to avoid. Castro's Cuba is an oft-cited example of a country backing into Moscow's lap because of the US Government's indiscriminate labelling of all insurgents, socialists and Marxists as the professed enemies of the United States who must be fought to the death.

The United States Embassy in Guatemala periodically denies the charges of taking sides in internal conflicts. It obviously is not telling the truth. In 1969 the Embassy maintained that only thirty-four members of the Special Forces were working in Guatemala. What this means is that on the day the announcement was made, there were at least thirty-four Special Forces Troops in Guatemala whom the Embassy was willing to acknowledge publicly. The claim demands no more belief than Henry Cabot Lodge's statement in 1954: 'the situation does not involve aggression but is a result of Guatemalans against Guatemalans',[39] or the repeated denials of complicity in the training of Cuban rebels at Retalhuleu.

Guatemalans have other indications also: a Green Beret from Ohio, by the name of Hornberger, just returned from Vietnam in early 1966, made a mysterious trip to Washington in August of that same year and then left for Guatemala

39. U.S. Department of State, op. cit., p. 14.

the following month, telling his family that he was off to hunt communists. Without, it seemed, any prior knowledge of the country, he evidently knew just where to go and what to look for. His body was finally recovered from guerrilla territory in January 1967.[40] His apparent mission was the assassination of the guerrilla leader Luis Turcios, but whoever entrusted this mission to him was never identified.

Major Bernie Westfall perished in September 1967 in the crash of a Guatemalan Air Force jet that he was piloting alone. The official notices stated that the US airman was 'testing' the aeroplane.[41] That statement may have been true, but it is also true that it was a common and public topic of conversation at Guatemala's La Aurora air base that the Major often 'tested' Guatemalan aircraft in strafing and bombing runs against guerrilla encampments in the North-eastern territory.

When Col. John Webber and Lt. Com. Ernest Munro were assassinated in January 1968 and two US military advisers were wounded in the same attack, Col. Manuel Sosa Avila, Head of the National Police, claimed that 'the plot was hatched at last year's meeting of OLAS, hosted by Castro in Havana'.[42] Another 'informed source' was quoted as saying that FAR had slain the Americans 'to get into the limelight again and put pressure on Castro to extend more help'.[43] This is the usual tack taken by the Guatemalan Government, and one that is guaranteed to get a reflex response from the US Ambassador. Ignored was FAR's own reason for the killings: 'The US military mission is helping the Guatemalan government in pursuing the guerrillas.'[44] Col. Webber had gone to Guatemala as military attaché to the Embassy as soon as Méndez Montenegro had taken over, and he immediately

40. El Imparcial, 2 January 1967.
41. ibid., 26 September 1967.
42. UPI Dispatch, Theodore A. Ediger, 19 January 1968.
43. ibid.   44. ibid.

expanded the counter-insurgency forces, obtaining from the US more jeeps, arms, helicopters, communications equipment and advisers. He made no secret of the fact that it was his idea and at his instigation that the technique of counter-terror had been implemented by the Guatemalan Army in the Zacapa and Izabal areas. When the advisability of arming civilian collaborators and paying them to kill communists and 'potential guerrillas' was questioned, Webber had justified the tactic by saying: 'That's the way this country is. The communists are using everything they have, including terror. And it must be met.' [45]

In November 1967 there was quite a squabble going on between US Army helicopter pilots and the Guatemalan Air Force. The Americans were being used by Guatemala's Geodetic Survey under contract to AID to map all the jungle areas of Petén and surrounding regions, and the Guatemalan pilots felt that they should be given the job. All the US pilots were veterans of Vietnam and one of them confided to the authors: 'If anything ever happens in this country, we'll know the terrain better than the Guatemalans.' The training, money and arms used by the rebels are always attributed to Castro, yet the two outstanding leaders of the guerrilla movements, Yon Sosa and Luis Turcios, were trained at Fort Gulick and Fort Bragg respectively. The money obtained from local kidnappings seems adequate for rebel purposes and it would be a dangerous tactic, unnecessarily executed, if Moscow and Havana were additional sources of finances. The arms captured from rebel bands are consistently of US manufacture, indicating that they are either captured from or given by the Government forces to the rebels. Both rebel bands have broken with and denounced the Communist Party (PGT) and Moscow has declared its disfavour of them.

From 27–31 May 1968 the Southern Command Forces of the United States stationed in Panama conducted joint mili-

45. *Time Magazine*, 26 January 1968, p. 23.

tary operations with the Nicaraguan and Guatemalan Armies in the Department of Izabal, Yon Sosa's base of operations. The 'training exercises', as they were so euphemistically called, were fittingly and officially designated as 'Operation Hawk'.[46] No one in the area failed to get the message.

The United States Embassy claims that every visit of Gen. Robert Porter Jr, or his successor, Gen. George Mather, from US Southern Command, is 'routine'.[47] They also state that all the Guatemalan officials trained in Fort Gulick,[48] all the special police hired with Alliance for Progress funds (3,500 in 1967 and 1968), and the 'model police programmes' developed by AID consultant Peter Costello and implemented with AID money,[49] are no more than what is done by 'similar US missions in various Latin American countries'.[50] The Guatemalan Desk of the State Department states that it gave $1·7 million in military assistance and $500,000 to the police in the fiscal year 1967 and that the US military assistance group is composed of 'about 30 men'.[51] All this may very well be true, or it just may mean that the Department of Defense and the CIA do not inform the State Department of everything they do, because these facts and figures do not explain everything that occurs in Guatemala with a US label on it. Or, too, it may mean that the special missions of men like Hornberger, Westfall and Webber are considered within the concept of ordinary military assistance. But then how are we to explain the counter-insurgency base in Mariscos, Izabal,[52] or the unmarked C47 filled with US paratroopers forced down

46. *El Imparcial*, 1 June 1968.

47. *El Imparcial*, 22 February and 10 November 1967; 1 June and 6 November 1968; *Prensa Libre*, 25 February 1969.

48. *Prensa Libre*, 10 April 1969.

49. *La Hora*, 13 December 1967; *Prensa Libre*, 3 March 1969.

50. UPI dispatch, Theodore Ediger, 19 January 1968.

51. Letter from Guy A. Wiggins, Guatemalan Desk, State Department, quoted in *Tsunami*: Catholic University, March 1969.

52. *El Imparcial*, 17 May 1962.

at La Aurora,[53] or the presence of the Green Berets confirmed by the police chief,[54] or the participants in 'Operation Hawk',[55] or the 'special group of Huey instructors that visited Guatemala recently'[56] and trained Guatemalan pilots? How does the US Government calculate the value of the three HU-1Bs 'given' in 1967 or the C47s 'donated' by Mein's successor, Ambassador Nathaniel Davis in June 1969? Is any account made of the five million dollars worth of arms left behind on Roberto Alejos's plantation after the CIA-trained Cuban rebels left?[57]

All these questions may seem like gnat-picking, but a very important concept is involved. The Guatemalan citizen who understands what is going on, be he of Leftist or Rightist political orientation, believes that even if the figures admitted by the State Department actually represented the truth, it would only be because such quantities and qualities are sufficient at this time for its purposes. Given the US policy towards Guatemala (and the rest of Latin America for that matter), most inhabitants of that country recognize that all the assistance that their Government needs to maintain 'stability' (read 'the *status quo*'), both in men and arms, will be forthcoming from the United States.

And there is no reason for them to think otherwise, now that Richard M. Nixon is in the White House. His political career has been built on the championing of Right-wing causes, and it is erroneous to think that his fears of communism in Latin America will be any more sophisticated than his knowledge or appreciation of the dynamics of Vietnamese society (cf. his speech on the history of the Vietnam War, 3 November 1969, on National Television). The first foreign visitor welcomed to the White House after his inauguration was Galo Plaza, Secretary General of the OAS, former Presi-

53. ibid., 14 January 1963.   54. ibid., 13 December 1966.
55. ibid., 1 June 1968.   56. *Prensa Libre*, 26 June 1969.
57. El *Imparcial*, 2 April 1963.

dent of Ecuador and ardent defender of United Fruit operations in Latin America.[58]

After months of silence as regards his new Latin America policy, indicated by the ill-advised and tumultuous Rockefeller 'fact-finding mission', President Nixon broke his silence on 31 October 1969. The tone of his remarks indicate that his 'new' policy is not so different from the old :

> I would be less than honest if I did not express my concern over examples of liberty compromised, of justice denied, of rights infringed. Nevertheless, we recognize that enormous, sometimes explosive, forces for change are operating in Latin America. These create instabilities and bring changes in governments. On the diplomatic level, we must deal realistically with governments in the inter-American system as they are. We have, of course, a preference for democratic procedures, and we hope that each government will help its people to move forward toward a better, a fuller and a freer life.[59]

What Mr Nixon is in effect saying is that the United States Government is not averse to dealing with dictatorships even though it would 'prefer' democratic procedures. To be sure that such a frank and public blessing of Latin American dictatorships not be misunderstood as an unqualified blessing to all dictatorships, the President immediately indicated that he excluded Cuba from his remarks; that Castro's Government was one government in the inter-American system that would not be 'dealt with realistically as it is' :

> In this connection, however, I would stress one other point. We cannot have a peaceful community of nations if one nation sponsors armed subversion in another's territory.[60]

58. See his book : Plaza Lasso, Galo and Stacey May, *The United Fruit Company in Latin America*. Washington : National Planning Association, 1958.

59. *Washington Post*, 1 November 1969.

60. ibid.

It is doubtful that Mr Nixon was referring to the US intervention in Guatemala in 1954, or in Cuba in 1961 (both prepared while he was Vice-President) or in the Dominican Republic in 1965. None of these can be called 'subversion' since
the interference was so massive. He was rather referring to
the few Cubans in guerrilla activities in Venezuela and
Bolivia. So it is that the US Government continues to accept
the 'examples of liberty compromised, of justice denied, of
rights infringed', just so long as it is done in the name of a
minority that exploits the majority. If the dictatorship is on
the Left, a dictatorship in the name of the impoverished
majority, the US will not tolerate it, because such a government would oppose the exploitative enterprises of US business interests.

The President's speech came a few days before the official
release of the Rockefeller Report, and was obviously based on
Rockefeller's conclusions. Those parts of Nixon's speech
already cited seem to portend the implementation of the
recommendations for military aid to Latin American nations:

1. Creation of a multi-national Western Hemisphere Security
Council.

2. Increase in U.S. military training grants.

3. Provision of jeeps, helicopters, communications equipment
and small arms for internal security support.

4. Removal of congressional curbs to permit more sales of U.S.
military equipment, which otherwise will be purchased from
other sources East or West.[61]

Rockefeller used the same rationale as that used for depriv-
ing the Vietnamese of their right of self-determination:
'Forces of anarchy, terror and subversion are loose in the
Americas. The subversive capabilities of these Communist
forces are increasing.'[62] When the Governor of New York
was asked by a reporter whether he was not offering a
prescription for new Vietnams in Latin America, Rockefeller

61. *Washington Post*, 9 November 1969.   62. ibid.

said that he found the analogy 'utterly irrelevant'.[63] The Report, entitled 'Quality of life in the Americas', demonstrates, however, that the reporter's analogy *is* relevant, as it gives more insight into Nixon's statement to the effect that the US will not tolerate 'export of revolution which is intervention'.[64] Since it is impossible to be part of a revolutionary movement these days without some involved person having read Marx and been influenced by him, all revolutions are 'exports' and 'interventions'. This is the rationale for propping up the Latin military, even though they be anti-democratic. For as Rockefeller believes, 'few Latin countries have the sufficiently advanced economic and social systems required to support a consistently democratic system'.[65] So if the US has to support anti-democratic governments, like that of Thieu and Ky in Vietnam, it is preferable for it to be in favour of the small minority that will look out for US interests such as United Fruit, Grace and Esso, rather than those governments of the Left that will use their national resources for the benefit of all their own peoples. As a further palliative, trade concessions will also be granted which are intended to increase the GNPs of Latin nations, but not their distribution.

And what of the Maya and his poverty-stricken *ladino* cousin, who now eat worse than their pre-Columbian ancestors? What are they to think of their Government and that of the United States? They must believe that insurgency is a useless gesture unless they are ready to 'create two, three, or more Vietnams'. And who is to say that they will not?

And for those of us here in the United States who understand the inhumanity of explosiveness of the Guatemalan peasants' situation, and that of so many of his brothers in other Latin nations, what are we to do about all this? If we love our country and recognize the brotherhood of all men, we are faced with a single course: to dismantle the blind and selfish military–industrial complex of the United States. We must do this in the knowledge that our Latin brothers will thereby be able to overthrow their oppressive national oligarchies, which only spell ignorance, poverty, disease and despair for generations to come. And this they will be able to do with less bloodshed, less hatred, less destruction and less death.

Man–Land Relationships

THE 1964 CENSUS AND CIDA REPORT

That we might get the statistical viewpoint of the national situation of Guatemala, we offer a detailed picture of the man–land relationship as it was painted by the 1964 census and the CIDA Report of 1965. Some of the data may be questionable to those who seek preciseness in such a survey, owing to the untrained pollsters, the unwillingness of the rural populace to supply all the information requested, as well as the lack of scientific criteria for establishing some of the categories. Nevertheless, it is a picture that even in general lines indicates a need for readjustment of the man–land relationship on the part of any Government that would face the socio-economic reality that is Guatemala.

GEOGRAPHICAL DIVISIONS: SIX

Guatemala's total land area is 108,889 sq. km[1] of which approximately one half is mountainous, the 'Cordillera de los Andes', which forms the highlands that extend from the Mexican border on the West, through the Central regions, to the Salvadorean and Honduran borders on the South and East. This splits the country into a number of distinct geographical entities with a variety of climatic conditions, elevations and land fertility that makes Guatemala eminently agricultural, with the capacity to produce almost any crop at some time or another during the yearly cycle. For the purpose of our study, we would limit these divisions to the

1. The statistics given here are from: 'Guatemala: Dirección General de Estadística, *Censo de Población de 1964*', published in 1966.

six named by the CIDA in their excellent work,[2] and enumerate them here (see Maps 1 and 2):

(a) West–Central highlands – from 1,500 to 3,000 metres above sea level; very broken terrain with mostly moderate temperatures that dip below freezing during December and January in the higher elevations; a markedly dry period from November to May, while the rest of the year constitutes the rainy season (winter depends on rain, not temperature); the people are largely of Mayan stock, and *minifundismo* (the holding of tiny farms) predominates; there is much deforestation and erosion; the main crops are corn, wheat and black beans.

(b) Eastern highlands – mostly below 2,000 metres' elevation; the terrain is also very broken, but much drier than the Western highlands; there is less fragmentation of land-holdings, but the lands are even less productive; mostly poor *ladino* population; the main crops are fruits, tomatoes and grass for cattle grazing; needs irrigation.

(c) The Pacific slopes – from 200 to 2,000 metres' elevation; very humid; here lie the best soils in the country and it is the most important area in the national economy; its main products are coffee (in the higher lands), fruits and pasture. Large land-holdings predominate.

(d) The Pacific plains – a band of fertile lands 20 to 40 kilometres wide extending practically at sea level from the coast to the foothills of the 'Cordillera', in an unbroken stretch along the Pacific Ocean; the climate is tropical with much rain, except along the immediate coast. Almost exclusively large holdings with crops of cotton, sugar, bananas, fruits, rubber and cattle pasture.

(e) The Northern slopes – much like the Pacific slopes, but wider and less fertile; perhaps less broken also but there are few roads and poor communications; good coffee country, especially in Alta Verapaz, above 600 metres; the 'Zona Reina' of Northern Huehuetenango and Quiché holds much promise once roads open up the area.

(f) Low lands of the North – consists mostly of the Department of Petén, as well as parts of Alta Verapaz and Izabal; comprises

2. Comité Interamericano de Desarrollo Agrícola, op. cit.

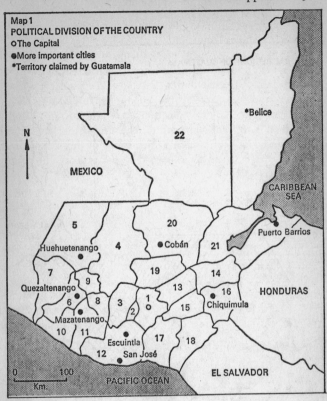

Map 1
POLITICAL DIVISION OF THE COUNTRY
o The Capital
● More important cities
* Territory claimed by Guatemala

DEPARTMENTS

Central:

1. Guatemala City
2. Sacatepéquez

West:

3. Chimaltenango
4. El Quiché
5. Huehuetenango
6. Quezaltenango
7. San Marcos
8. Sololá
9. Totonicapán

South:

10. Retalhuleu
11. Suchitepéquez
12. Escuintla

East:

13. El Progreso
14. Zacapa
15. Jalapa
16. Chiquimulilla
17. Santa Rosa
18. Jutiapa

North Central:

19. Baja Verapaz
20. Alta Verapaz

North:

21. Izabal
22. El Petén

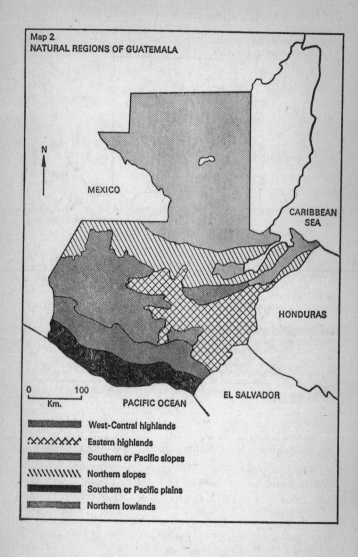

Map 2
NATURAL REGIONS OF GUATEMALA

N

MEXICO

CARIBBEAN
SEA

HONDURAS

0   100
Km.

PACIFIC OCEAN   EL SALVADOR

West-Central highlands
Eastern highlands
Southern or Pacific slopes
Northern slopes
Southern or Pacific plains
Northern lowlands

one third of the country's total area, and holds less than one per cent of the population; its terrain is largely unbroken, under 200 metres high and with a tropical climate. The tropical rains have made this a jungle forest on washed lands of low fertility; few roads; crops are chicle, pepper and fine lumbers.

POPULATION: RACE

In 1964 there were 4,284,473 people in Guatemala,[1] of which 43·3 per cent were listed as indigenous. The authors believe the actual percentage to be much higher than this, owing to the criteria (language, clothing, customs) that are used in judging. This reflects a tendency on the part of the Government to depress the relationship of Maya to *ladinos*. The difference is cultural, not racial, facilitating 'crossovers'.[3] Since census figures are drawn up on a Departmental basis (political divisions) and not according to the geographical divisions we have offered, the location of the population is given accordingly but can be easily related, by using Maps 1 and 2 in conjunction, to the terrains described previously.

Two-and-a-half per cent of the population live in the Departments of Petén and Izabal (mostly the Northern lowlands); 11·3 per cent live in the Departments of Retalhuleu, Suchitepéquez and Escuintla (fertile Southern plains) and the vast majority, 86·2 per cent, live in the other Departments, comprising mainly the two highland areas.

POPULATION: LOCATION

The population is largely rural, 75·1 per cent; a percentage that is decreasing very slowly, so that even by 1980, it is calculated that 68 per cent will still be rural – a figure that means that there

3. From 1950 (when the indigenous population was registered at 55·6 per cent) to 1964, the *ladinos* have increased at the prolific annual rate of 4·4 per cent while the Indians increased at the unlikely rate of 1·4 per cent. The two average the national population increase rate of 3·1 per cent.

will be a far greater number of small farmers than exist today. An artificial distinction between rural and urban is calculated as follows: rural areas are considered villages of 2,000 people or less (1,500 if the village has running water) and anything above this figure is considered urban population. It is interesting to note that of the urban population, about ten per cent live in the capital city, while the second largest city, Quezaltenango, does not even reach ten per cent of the population of the capital itself. This concentration of sophisticated urbanites and trained professionals in Guatemala City has adverse effects on the development of the rural areas. The population explosion in Guatemala City is due largely to the migration of landless peasants looking for work.

The percentage of illiteracy is 72 per cent; 41 per cent of the urban population is without education, while twice that figure, or 82 per cent of the rural population, is illiterate. A literate person is often one who can merely sign his name, so the percentage of functional illiterates is actually higher (see Chart 2).

CHART 2

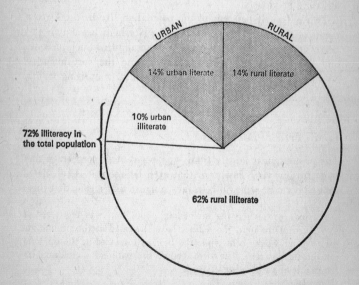

URBAN   RURAL

14% urban literate   14% rural literate

10% urban illiterate

72% illiteracy in the total population

62% rural illiterate

POPULATION: MAN—LAND RELATIONSHIP

There is an absolute scarcity of land in the *altiplano* (see Map 3) where the lands are poorest, necessitating an intensive use that results in more and more deforestation and more and more erosion. This can be seen from the figures on the population density for the five most populated Departments. Guatemala is highest with 366 inhabitants per km.^{2} (due mainly to the capital itself; Sacatepéquez has 170 per km.^{2}; Quezaltenango, 136 per km.^{2}; Totonicapán, 134 per km.^{2}; and Sololá, 102 per km.^{2} All are located in the *altiplano*.[4]

The implications of all these figures and percentages, a few of which we underline here, are obvious. Guatemala is an under-developed nation whose primary resources are its people and its land. The people are largely uneducated, existing on the worst lands in the country: mountain lands. The majority of these people are Maya, a race and culture that is viewed as inferior, and whose destiny, according to the ruling *ladinos* and whites, is to serve for ever.

LAND OWNERSHIP: TYPE OF HOLDINGS

A further implication of these figures, and one that is related to the whole process of development, concerns ownership. We must break these figures down even further, and determine who owns what and where, and how he is using it. For this purpose, we will also use the classifications of the CIDA work, which are the five following categories of land holdings: microfarms, sub-family farms, family farms, medium multi-family farms and large multi-family farms.[5]

The first two of these are commonly called *minifundios* while the latter two are referred to as *latifundios*. The micro-farms have less than one *manzana* (1·7 acres) and the large multi-family farms are larger than 1,280 *manzanas* (2,176 acres).[6] The *minifundios*, then, are farms that are too small to sustain an average family,

4. Guatemala: *Censo de Población de 1964*, p. 14.
5. CIDA, op. cit., p. 19. 6. ibid.

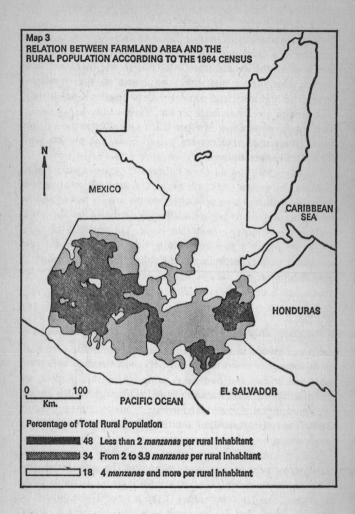

Map 3
RELATION BETWEEN FARMLAND AREA AND THE
RURAL POPULATION ACCORDING TO THE 1964 CENSUS

N

MEXICO

CARIBBEAN
SEA

HONDURAS

0   100
Km.   PACIFIC OCEAN   EL SALVADOR

Percentage of Total Rural Population

48 Less than 2 *manzanas* per rural inhabitant

34 From 2 to 3.9 *manzanas* per rural inhabitant

18 4 *manzanas* and more per rural inhabitant

and the head of the house must seek outside work to make ends meet. We use this CIDA definition because subsistence means more than warding off starvation: it includes the means to pay for simple medical needs, a roof over one's head and a shirt on one's back. The average family of five in the highlands needs approximately one quintal (100 lb.) of corn a week, or 52 quintals a year, since its diet is almost exclusively made up of this cereal. The average highland yield is a quintal to a *cuerda* (approximately 625 square metres), which means that 52 *cuerdas* or 5·5 acres are needed just to supply a family's corn needs and nothing more. The CIDA classification of micro-farms and sub-family farms as having less than 10 *manzanas* (17 acres) seems amply justified.

It can be seen from Chart 3 that the *minifundistas* take advantage of 80–95 per cent of their available lands, that is, practically all of them. The big landowners, on the other hand, only utilize a small part of theirs. We can also observe (Chart 4) that the *minifundios* (micro- and sub-family farms) represent 88·4 per cent of the total farms and together possess 14·3 per cent of the land area. The *latifundios* (medium and large multi-family farms) represent 2·1 per cent of the total number of farms and together possess 72·2 per cent of the lands. The picture that these figures represents is not even as stark as the reality itself, if we take into consideration that all cultivated land is classified as 'utilized' where much of it, in the highlands, should be classified as 'unusable', because the peasants there are forced to use lands that the large landowners would never touch. There are many stories of Indians who have fallen out of their cornfields and been killed, and though this may seem like an exaggeration, a trip down the Pan-American highway through the Department of Huehuetenango will convince one of the danger of working the fields high up the mountain sides. Often the inclination exceeds sixty degrees, better for skiing (although there is no snow) than for planting. If figures were available for the utilization of usable land only, many of the peasants would get percentages of 100 plus. In many areas, small-patch farming is common up to the very peaks of steep rocky mountains. The colourful Indian peasant with only a hoe, a *machete* and a small patch on a mountain side can expect no future betterment in this world (see Chart 6).

CHART 3 *Land Area according to size of Holdings and Use*[7] (in hectares)

Size of Farm	Total Area	Utilized	Not Used	Unusable
Micro	28,575	27,125	—	1,450
Sub-family	504,556	400,503	74,010	30,043
Family	500,830	250,498	205,647	44,685
Medium Multi-family	1,167,532	574,996	502,701	89,835
Large Multi-family	1,519,339	433,239	922,175	163,925
TOTALS	3,720,832	1,686,361	1,704,533	329,938

CHART 4 *Use of Land: Percentages*[8]

Size of Farms	Total Area	Utilized	Not Used	Unusable
Micro	100	94·9	—	5·1
Sub-family	100	79·4	14·7	5·9
Family	100	50·0	41·1	8·9
Medium Multi-family	100	49·2	43·1	7·7
Large Multi-family	100	28·5	60·7	10·8
TOTALS	100	45·3	45·8	8·9

CHART 5 *Number of Farms, Area and Percentages according to Size of Holdings*[9]

Size of Farms	Number	Percentage	Area	Percentage	Average Size
Micro	74,270	21·3	28,575	0·8	0·4 hec.
Sub-family	233,800	67·1	504,556	13·5	2·2 hec.
Family	33,040	9·5	500,830	13·5	15·2 hec.
Medium Multi-family	7,060	2·0	1,167,532	31·4	165·4 hec.
Large Multi-family	520	0·1	1,519,339	40·8	2,921·9 hec.
TOTALS	348,690	100·0	3,720,832	100·0	

(These totals were based largely on figures from the 1950 Census since the 1964 Census was not available when the report was written. If anything, the situation is worse today than that indicated by the 1950 Census or the 1965 CIDA report.)

7. CIDA, op. cit., p. 19.   8. ibid., p. 20.   9. ibid., p. 58.

CHART 6

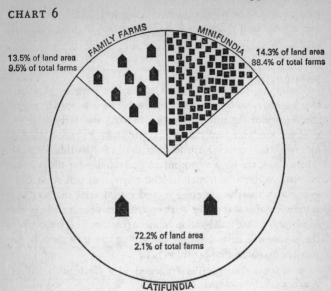

FAMILY FARMS

13.5% of land area
9.5% of total farms

MINIFUNDIA

14.3% of land area
88.4% of total farms

72.2% of land area
2.1% of total farms

LATIFUNDIA

Such an inequitable distribution of the land in regard to the population has many historical causes, as we have shown. One additional cause is the healthy climatic conditions of the mountains that give the sickness-prone and weak physical condition of the peasant added protection against disease. But this, of course, is not sufficient explanation for his remaining in the highlands, while unused lands abound on the South coastal plains, and the Northern jungle areas, as well as on the Pacific and Northern slopes. He stays there largely because the governing class wants him there. It is hard to conjecture how much longer he can afford to remain there, for, all other considerations aside, the population is growing at the alarming rate of over three per cent per year, about 100,000 net increase annually. According to these rates, the Guatemalan population will increase sixteen times in the next hundred years.

Charles Wagley, an anthropologist who has studied Guatemala, said that the present agriculture problem is having too many sons, which means that there is not enough land for each under the present land-system and within the finite boundaries of each municipality. 'The solution,' he says, 'lies in either contraception, infanticide, land reform or a return to the old communal land system.'[10]

POPULATION DENSITY

It is necessary to consider that in the Western mountain region, the density of the rural population in 1964 was forty-three persons per km.^{2}, a figure that will reach seventy persons per km.^{2} by 1980, thus creating tremendous pressures. In this *altiplano*, where there are no government lands available for distribution, an even greater atomization in land cultivation will occur. Since even today there is not enough land for minimal subsistence, it is indispensable that either work opportunities be created or, more importantly, that immigration be made possible. This is something the people will have to do for themselves and they must be prepared to overcome the opposition to it.

10. Wagley, Charles, 'The Economics of a Guatemalan Village', *American Anthropologist*: 1941, p. 81.

Abbreviations

AEU	Association of University Students
AGA	General Association of Agriculturalists (large landowners)
AID	Agency for International Development
CIDA	Interamerican Committee of Agricultural Development (sponsored by the UN, the OAS and others)
CGTG	General Confederation of Labour Unions
CNCG	National Confederation of Guatemalan Peasants
DAN	National Agrarian Department
DGAA	Department of Agrarian Affairs
FAO	Food and Agriculture Organization
FAR	Armed Forces of Rebellion (guerrilla forces)
FYDEP	Institute for Economic Progress and Development of the Petén
INCAP	Nutritional Institute for Central America and Panama
INFOP	National Institute for the Development of Production
INRA	National Institute of Agrarian Reform
INTA	National Institute for Agrarian Transformation
IRCA	International Railroads of Central America
MLN	National Liberation Movement (Party and Government of Castillo Armas)
MR–13	13 November Movement (guerrilla forces)
OAS	Organization of American States
PGT	Guatemalan Labour Party (communist party)
PR	Revolutionary Party
PID	Institutional Democratic Party
Q	Quetzal (national currency equivalent to the Dollar)
UFCo.	United Fruit Company

Spanish Terms

Acuerdo	Agreement; used for governmental declarations that do not have the matter or force of law
Arrendamiento forzoso	Forced rental
Campesino	Peasant
Colonos	Tenant farmers who pay for the use of land with labour
Ejido	Communal landholding
Especie	Goods or produce
Fiesta	Feastday or holiday usually celebrated like a fair
Finca	Plantation
Finquero	Plantation owner
Jornalero	Day labourer, usually a migrant worker
Ladino	A non-Indian, of mixed blood and Western culture
Latifundio	Extensive land-holding
Latifundista	Owner of a large land-holding
Macho	Masculine
Minifundio	Less than a subsistence land-holding
Minifundista	Owner of a minifundio
Patrón	Landlord
Sindicato	Labour union
Zona agrícola	Agrarian zone for colonization

Measurements

1 caballería =	64·4	manzanas
	109·8	acres
1 manzana =	16	cuerdas
	·7	hectares
	1·7	acres
1 hectare =	0·022	caballerías
	1·43	manzanas
	2·47	acres
1 acre =	9·4	cuerdas

More about Penguins
and Pelicans

Penguinews, which appears every month, contains
details of all the new books issued by Penguins as they
are published. From time to time it is supplemented by
Penguins in Print, which is a complete list of all books
published by Penguins which are in print. (There are
well over three thousand of these.)

A specimen copy of *Penguinews* will be sent to you free
on request, and you can become a subscriber for the
price of the postage. For a year's issues (including the
complete lists) please send 30p if you live in the United
Kingdom, or 60p if you live elsewhere. Just write to
Dept EP, Penguin Books Ltd, Harmondsworth,
Middlesex, enclosing a cheque or postal order, and your
name will be added to the mailing list.

Some other books published by Penguins are described
on the following pages.

Note: *Penguinews* and *Penguins in Print* are not
available in the U.S.A. or Canada

Aid as Imperialism

Teresa Hayter

It is an indication of the explosive nature of the contents of this remarkable book that the World Bank tried to discourage its publication, although Miss Hayter was commissioned to make the study by the Overseas Development Institute.

Three of the principal monetary agencies involved in Western aid programmes are the World Bank, A.I.D. and I.M.F. All three are bound very largely by conventional economic wisdom and their priorities are quite different from the human priorities which could be embodied in an aid programme.

They are concerned with short-term solvency and financial stability, no matter if this means severe cut-backs in domestic spending. Poor countries need to feed their hungry and provide the basis for further developments. These two sets of aims, as this study of the World Bank at work in Latin America demonstrates, are contradictory.

Political Leaders of Latin America

Richard Bourne

Latin American politics are of increasing importance in world affairs. This volume contains portraits of six political leaders of the region: individually they stress the diversity that lies between caudillo and Communist; together they may be taken to typify the face of Latin American government and the special problems confronting it.

Che Guevara   The Argentinian revolutionary who conquered in Cuba and died in Bolivia

Eduardo Frei   The President of Chile and the first Christian-Democratic president in Latin America

Alfredo Stroessner   The Army dictator of Paraguay

Juscelino Kub tschek   The President of Brazil from 1956 to 1960 and founder of Brasilia

Carlos Lacerda   who has helped to overthrow three Brazilian presidents

Evita Perón   The glamorous wife of the Argentinian dictator who combined military and labour supporters in a powerful nationalist movement

The Greening of America

Charles Reich

'There is a revolution under way. It is not like the revolutions of the past. It has originated with the individual and with culture, and if it succeeds, it will change the political structure only as its final act. It will not require violence to succeed, and it cannot be successfully resisted by violence ...'

Thus Charles Reich in this extraordinary book which raced to the top of the American non-fiction best seller lists and which (accordingly to the *Sunday Times*) 'has unleashed a debate that reminds some in its impetuosity and effervescence of the one that followed Rachel Carson's *Silent Spring*, and others of the *Kinsey Report*.'

Optimistic, lucid and wide-ranging (across economics, history, law, sociology, psychology and philosophy), *The Greening of America* shows not only how the corporate state has usurped all values but how the young generation – in their creativity, their rediscovery of community and freedom – has set in train a movement that may transform America ... and even the world.

'Enormously interesting. . . . It will affect political thinking and behaviour. . . . I am greatly impressed with his central idea ...' J. K. Galbraith.

NOT FOR SALE IN THE U.S.A. OR CANADA